Biblical Separation

---

*THE
STRUGGLE
FOR A
PURE
CHURCH*

Biblical Separation

THE STRUGGLE FOR A PURE CHURCH

Ernest Pickering

REGULAR BAPTIST PRESS
1300 North Meacham Road
Schaumburg, Illinois 60173-4888

Library of Congress Cataloging in Publication Data

Pickering, Ernest D.
    Biblical separation.

    Bibliography
    Includes index.
    1. Dissenters, Religious.   I. Title
BX4817.P47   262   78-26840
ISBN 0-87227-069-6

BIBLICAL SEPARATION: THE STRUGGLE FOR A PURE CHURCH
© 1979
Regular Baptist Press
Schaumburg, Illinois
Printed in U.S.A.

Second printing   1979
Third printing   1982
Fourth printing   1983
Fifth printing   1988
Sixth printing   1990

Acknowledgments

The following persons read all or portions of the manuscript and made valuable suggestions to the author:

Dr. Wayne Knife
Dr. Rembert Carter
Dr. John Master
Dr. John Millheim
Dr. Reginald Matthews

Contents

Contents

Preface

When the Lord Jesus Christ returned to Heaven, He instituted upon this earth conclaves of His people—churches. They constitute the "called-out ones," Heaven's representatives on earth. Each congregation is to reflect the holy character of the One Who is its Head. But the prince of darkness, Satan, has other plans. He has sought from the beginning to hinder the witness of the churches by contaminating them with unholy doctrine and unholy people. At a very early date the efforts of the Devil were evident in the professing church. Corruption, sacramentarianism and formalism set in, replacing the spiritual vitality that characterized the apostolic age. From that time until the present, many of God's people, living in different ages and under varying circumstances, have sought to maintain the purity of doctrine and practice that is set forth in Christ's standard for His churches—the New Testament.

This is the story of a struggle. The struggle will not end until the Head of the Church returns. Those who struggle have been and are imperfect human beings; hence they never have and never will produce the perfect church. Those who struggle have personal quirks, human biases and manifest weaknesses. Yet they press on to perpetuate on earth congregations of believers that are pleasing to the Lord and are pure testimonies of His saving grace. This book does not defend the notion that all separatists are worthy of emulation, nor does it maintain the position that all nonseparatists are completely devoid of spiritual insight. People who truly love Christ and have been a blessing to the church at large can be found in both camps. We seek in these pages to pursue, illustrate and defend what we believe to be a scriptural principle, that of separation from evil.

For centuries the struggle has gone on. It was seen in the Donatist controversy, the witness of obscure groups in the Middle Ages seeking to battle deep-seated error, the sufferings and testimony of the Anabaptists, the convictions of the separatist Puritans, and the continuing battles of separatists of the last two centuries. While there are among separatists, as among other believers of whatever stripe, those who are self-seeking, petty and spiteful, the separatist testimony as a whole does not spring from such personal weaknesses but rather from a sincere desire on the part of large numbers of believers to obey the Word of God and honor the Savior. Particularly since the height of the fundamentalist-modernist controversy in the early twentieth century, a rather substantial separatist movement has emerged in the United States, as well as to a lesser extent in many other places of the world.

A new generation of separatists has arisen. These have had no personal involvement in the controversies which produced the contemporary separatist movement. Modernism (religious liberalism) is only a term to them. They have not engaged in hand-to-hand combat with the enemy, and, moreover, live in a day when such combat is decried by many who urge Christians to forget their differences and press on to more constructive things. It is all too possible for separatists to become complacent, to be enamored with the current call to peace with its accompanying plea for a cessation of hostilities, and to lose gradually the sensitivity to error and the will to stand against it. Hopefully, the material in this book will be both a warning against such complacency and an encouragement to stand true for God.

The separatist position, to some, represents merely human reaction to certain circumstances. They do not see nor understand the theological and Biblical principles involved. Separatism, they say, has its roots in the perversity of overzealous persons who have unrealistic aims. If this be true, then separatism is a dishonor to God. If, however, as I believe, separatism rests upon clear scriptural mandates, then it has justification for its existence.

The totality of Biblical separation includes the concept of personal separation. This volume, however, deals only with what is commonly called ecclesiastical separation, the principle of separation as applied to the nature and associations of the visible churches. Biblical separation is the implementation of that scriptural teaching which demands repudiation of any conscious or continuing fellowship with those who deny the doctrines of the historic Christian faith, especially as such fellowship finds expression in organized ecclesiastical structures, and which results in the establishment and nurture of local congregations of believers which are free from contaminating alliances.

Ernest Pickering

10

The Early Conflict:
Donatism vs. Catholicism

1

NO SOONER had Christ established His Church on earth than Satan set out to corrupt it. He raised up false ministers (2 Cor. 11:13) to preach a false gospel (Gal. 1:6-9) and thus produce false disciples (Matt. 13:25). Such activity immediately raises some very important questions: What are the marks of the true church of Christ? To what extent is sound doctrine necessary to a true church? When has an ecclesiastical body departed from the faith? If such departure is evident, what should be done by those who seek to preserve the truth?

The impression is sometimes received that such questions, and the inevitable conflicts which surround their debate, are confined to the so-called "fundamentalist-modernist controversy" of the twentieth century, and that "separatism" (renunciation of fellowship with apostates) is largely a contemporary phenomenon spawned by over-zealous fundamentalists. Nothing could be farther from the truth. Conflicts over the purity of the church have rocked the church down through the centuries. Every age has had those who were concerned about the church's departure from scriptural truth, and who have sought to perpetuate by one means or another churches of sound witness to the saving gospel of Christ.

By at least the second century, movements developed within the organized church protesting its impurity and doctrinal drift.

Forerunners of the Donatists

Shortly after the middle of the second century a man in Phrygia named Montanus proclaimed him-

Montanists.

self as a prophet. He and his followers began emphasizing a pure church and the immediate power of the Holy Spirit. They gave special attention to the second coming of Christ. As in so many movements, various forms and levels of fanaticism were found, particularly as it appeared in Asia Minor. Not all of its emphasis, however, can be dismissed as this.

Tertullian was the chief scholarly representative of Montanism as it appeared in the western church. His writings reflect a deep concern for a more spiritual church. He and his followers called themselves the "pneumatics" as contrasted to the "psychical" (carnal) church. Each believer was a priest before God and had the right of direct dealing with God.

Tertullian actually began to manifest Montanist tendencies in his latter writings (e.g., "On Monogamy," "On the Apparel of Women" and "On Fasting"). These discussions do not center around ecclesiology but rather a rigorous view of the Christian life which was characteristic of the Montanists.

As far as Montanus himself is concerned, we have little to go on except for reports of his enemies. Farrar declares that his basic orthodoxy and that of his followers was not questioned, but that the movement went astray in adopting the view that God was giving prophetic messages, and that prophecy was impossible without somnambulism and trance. Fanaticism set in with the acceptance of this view and was apparently the downfall of this movement. "It is beginning to be widely recognized that in many of its aspects Montanism was an honest and earnest effort to restore the discipline and practices of primitive Christianity."[1] Their concerns soon led to the formation of separate Montanist churches in the east. However, in the western church they continued longer within the framework of Catholicism, though finally a separation did take place.

Novatians. One of the early periods of suffering for Christians was known as the Decian persecutions (249-250). During this time a goodly number of professing Christians apostasized and did not stand true to their convictions. At the conclusion of the persecutions, there was debate among the churches as to whether these "lapsed" persons should be welcomed back into the fellowship of the churches or not. The Roman bishop Novatian, along with others, took a strict view and declared that those who had denied the Lord should not be reinstated into church fellowship. Basically, he and his followers were contending for a stricter view of the requirements for church membership than was generally accepted in his day. Already a looser and more accommodating approach to church membership was popular. Novatian stood opposed to such accommodation.

As a result of the contentions of Novatian, a separatist body was formed which continued for centuries. The movement "came to be a separatist church group parallel with the orthodox [Catholic] church."[2] Schaff well describes their position when he writes, "The Novatianists considered themselves the only pure communion, and unchurched all churches which defiled themselves by readmitting the lapsed, or any other gross offender."[3] One has referred to Novatian as the "antipope" of the "Puritan party" within the church.[4]

Cyprian's answer to the Novatians.

Cyprian was bishop of Carthage around 250 A.D. Following the Decian persecutions and the problems just mentioned, Cyprian wrote one of his best-known works, *The Unity of the Catholic Church*. While some disagree, it is probable that it was written against the Novatians. Certainly the sentiments expressed were contrary to Novatianism. In the book Cyprian set forth a very strong view of the church which was developed by others later on into the official Catholic view. He emphasized that the unity of the church was in its hierarchy. "The authority of the bishops forms a unity, of which each holds his part in its totality."[5] He argued strongly against any schism in the church.

> The spouse of Christ cannot be defiled, she is inviolate and chaste. . . . Whoever breaks with the Church and enters on an adulterous union, cuts himself off from the promises made to the Church, and he who has turned his back on the Church of Christ shall not come to the rewards of Christ; he is an alien, a worldling, an enemy. You cannot have God for your Father, if you have not the Church for your mother. . . . Whoever breaks the

peace and harmony of Christ acts against Christ; whoever gathers elsewhere than in the Church, scatters the Church of Christ.[6]

Cyprian used a plea for unity against separatists. He said:

God is one, and Christ is one, and His Church is one; one in the faith, and one the people cemented together by harmony into the strong unity of a body. . . . Nothing that is separated from the parent stock can ever live or breathe apart; all hope of salvation is lost.[7]

He also accused separatists of lack of love. Speaking of Christ, he wrote, "Unity and love together He taught with the weight of His authority. . . . But what unity is maintained, what love practiced, or even imagined, by one who, mad with the frenzy of discord, splits the Church. . . ."[8]

The Historical Setting of the Donatist Struggle

The ideals of the Montanists and the Novatians were not entirely lost; they continued to find lodging in the hearts of others in the ensuing centuries. Early in the fourth century a conflict within the African church was reminiscent of that which spawned Novatianism. In the so-called Diocletian persecutions under the hand of mighty Rome, numbers of professing believers had renounced their faith. Some felt strongly that believers who had renounced their faith should not be received into church fellowship. Some church bishops and members of their flocks had succumbed to government edicts in order to maintain their personal safety. They had not stood courageously for the faith; thus they were suspect in the eyes of those who desired a more uncompromising testimony.

The matter came to a head (from an ecclesiastical standpoint) with the consecration of Caecilian as bishop of Carthage in 312 A.D. His consecration to this office was opposed by numbers of bishops and other leaders because one of his "consecrators" was guilty of traditio, that is, the surrender or betrayal of the Scriptures during the aforesaid times of persecution. They felt, therefore, that Caecilian was "tainted," not fit to hold a position of leadership. The point of debate, of course, was merely reflective of some deeper, underlying issues. What is a true church? To what extent should the purity of the church be sought and protected? The established church tended to be less strict in its demands. The opposition party which first formed under a bishop named Majorinus (312 A.D.) and was later led by his successor, Donatus, was committed to the concept that church purity was extremely important.

The separatist body which began to form grew rapidly. Its adherents were known as Donatists after the bishop who became its chief spokesman. Donatist churches multiplied in North Africa. They became a considerable force in the third and fourth centuries. They operated independently of the established church and became the first large and important separatist body. Neander sees a similarity between Donatism and Novatianism. "This schism may be compared in many respects with that of Novatian in the preceding period. In this, too, we see the conflict, for example, of Separatism with Catholicism. . . ."[9]

The Importance of the Struggle

Some see primarily social and political forces behind the rise of Donatism.[10] While such forces were undoubtedly in play, far more was involved in the struggles of the Donatists. Frend, who authored a definitive work on the subject, put it this way:

> From an early stage there emerge two completely different interpretations of Christianity. On the one hand, there is the orthodox Catholic Church, prepared to compromise with the evils of this world for the sake of unity and peaceful progress. . . . On the other hand, there is the Church of the Holy Spirit, of enthusiasm, of open hostility to the world, individualistic and intolerant.[11]

If this assessment is correct, then the Donatist controversy is of intense interest to all students of church history. It is rightly said that the "permanent interest of Donatism is in the theological issues involved. . . ."[12]

The Donatists were biblicists; that is, they had a high view of Scripture (though, unhappily, not without errors spawned by ancient Catholicism). "Martyrdom and devotion to the Word of God in the Bible was the heart of Donatism."[13] The established church, while seeking to employ scriptural defense where possible, did not hesitate in its defense against the Donatists to call upon tradition and "the established order of things" as a valid argument for maintaining the status quo. They were "accommodationists" for the sake of peace. On the other hand, the Donatists were purists. "One of the most striking features of African Christianity in the third century was its uncompromising hostility to the institution of the Roman Empire. . . . The sharpest of contrasts was drawn between the Church and the pagan world."[14]

It was in the conflict with Donatism that important and lasting theological concepts were hammered out which have affected the church for the remaining centuries. It was on the anvil of this battle that the foundations of the Roman Catholic Church were laid.

> Donatism represents an attempt . . . to resist the process of secularization by which the Church was gradually transformed from a community of holy persons into an institution of mixed character, offering to secure salvation for its members by means of grace over which it had control. . . . It was met by the defenders of Catholicism with a new emphasis on the objective character of the sacraments, and upon the holiness of the Church apart from the holiness or otherwise of its members and clergy. It was in the controversy with the Donatists, therefore, that the Catholic doctrine of the Church was completely developed.[15]

The Particular Issues

Here, as we shall see is true with many other movements, it is difficult to obtain from available sources the whole picture. Many have noted that it is not easy to draw up a complete account of the entire controversy due to the fact that "none of the original sources has survived and all later documents are products of the opposing party."[16] Sufficient evidence has been found, however, to enable us to discern some of the major issues.

Generally speaking, separatist bodies through the centuries have contended for a high view of the meaning of church membership. Newman states, "The fundamental question discussed in the debate . . . concerned the holiness of the Church as conditioned by the moral state of its members."[17] The Catholic Church contended then (through Augustine) and still does to this day that the church's holiness exists whether or not its members are holy. The Donatists, on the other hand, believed that "every church which tolerated unworthy members in its bosom was itself polluted by the communion with them" and it thus "ceased to be a true Christian church. . . ."[18] They were not only concerned about local congregational purity, but also that this not be compromised by impure fellowships; thus they refused to fellowship with the existing Catholic churches.

The necessity of stricter requirements for church membership.

We find among the Donatists a view of the apostasy of the church which continued through the Dark Ages among separatist bodies. The professing church had fallen into apostasy, had repudiated vital Christian doctrine and was thus under God's judgment. They believed that the church had fallen in the days of Constantine and that it was their duty to reconstitute the church, to begin again to establish it on earth.[19]

The fact and extent of apostasy in the established church.

The Donatists were strong in their denunciations of the established Catholic Church. "In the great imperial church, embracing the people in a mass, they saw a secularized Babylon. . . ."[20] The Donatist bishops, in their preaching, spoke of the corruption of the church, and they generally assigned the cause of that corruption to the confusion between the church and state.

The heart of the Donatist controversy centered around whether or not a church could be a true church if its ministers and people were not living godly lives. The Donatists argued that the validity of the sacraments depended upon the worthiness of those who administered them. Since the established

The necessity of godly ministers.

Catholic Church tolerated, yes, approved, unworthy ministers, the sacraments administered in that church were not valid and acceptable. The Scriptures, said they, demand that those who serve the Lord and lead His people be holy. To what extent the Donatists understood clearly the doctrine of justification by faith is debatable. Unfortunately, we have practically nothing from their own hand to tell us what they believed. From evidence at hand, however, we believe the following analysis to be accurate:

> This demand for purity on the part of those holding ecclesiastical office was the central concern of the Donatists. For a church which tolerates deniers and traitors in its midst cannot possibly be the true church of Jesus Christ; hence it cannot possess the true sacraments. The validity of the sacraments and of every ecclesiastical act therefore not only depends upon the worthiness of the servants who administer them, but also is destroyed if they are administered in a church which does not excommunicate clerics suspected of having denied the faith.[21]

The Catholic party, led by Augustine, declared that the holiness of the church was intrinsic and did not reside in its ministers or members.

The Donatist View of the Church

It is in the area of ecclesiology, the doctrine of the church, that the Donatist controversy centered. What did they believe about the church?

The true church is to be a fellowship of the saints.

The Donatists believed that people should have a personal relationship to the Lord in order to be members of a church. Their protest was the first of a long series to be given against the notion that the church is inclusive of all who make some sort of profession and live within a certain geographical area.

The true church is to be separate from false churches.

It is at this point that special note should be taken. The Donatists dealt with an issue that is still with us today. If a visible church has departed from the faith, should Christians remain within it? The

Donatists said no. Separatist bodies who have followed them have given the same answer. Von Mosheim faults them for their view, but in so doing, he gives us an excellent summary of the truth for which they contended.

> That the Donatists were sound in doctrine, their adversaries admit; nor were their lives censurable, if we except the enormities of the *Circumcelliones* which were detested by the greatest part of the Donatists. Their fault was, that they regarded the African church as having fallen from the rank and privileges of a true church, and as being destitute of the gifts of the Holy Spirit, in consequence of its adherence to Caecelian.... And all other churches also which united the communed with that of Africa, they looked upon as defiled and polluted; and believed themselves alone, on account of the sanctity of their bishops, merited the name of the true, pure, and holy church; and, in consequence of these opinions, they avoided all communion with other churches in order to escape defilement.[22]

Separatist bodies have tended to hold to the separation of the church and state. The very nature of the separatist position would tend to guarantee this since it champions a free and a pure church. This doctrine was not embraced by the Reformers, and, insofar as they were separatists from Rome, the premise just stated would not hold. But the Reformers were not thoroughgoing and consistent separatists. Their sworn enemies, the Anabaptists, saw the issue much more clearly.

The true church is to be separate from the state.

The Donatists believed that the union between church and state which had been effected under Constantine, the Roman emperor, was detrimental to the spiritual well-being of the church. Their aim, in contrast to that of the Catholics, was

> ... To bring out again from the dead mass of simply baptized Christians, the pure Church of the regenerate; to substitute, in a word, the Christian communion for an ecclesiastical corporation.... The Donatists saw that the unity and freedom of the Church were imperilled by its union with the State, and they declared against the State-Church doctrine....[23]

The significance of Donatism for separatists is simply this. The Donatists championed a church which was pure, a church which was intolerant of those elements which would contaminate it. A chief emphasis of the Donatists was upon the holiness of the church. While some writers (such as Neander) repeatedly accuse them of "separatist pride," it was the genuine concern of the Donatists to pattern the church after the apostolic model. As is true of everyone else who has had this goal, they fell short of its accomplishment. Their aims, however, were admirable. In their controversy with Augustine, one of the major differences between separatists and inclusivists became clear. Separatists give *priority* to the holiness of the church; inclusivists, such as Augustine, give *priority* to the unity of the church. This is not to say that either is completely unconcerned about the other attribute, but the emphasis which they give governs the attitude toward the church as a whole and its relationships. Philip Schaff, noted historian, gives a fine analysis of the essence of the controversy between the Catholics and the Donatists which serves to highlight current lines of conflict between separatists and nonseparatists.

> The Donatist controversy was a conflict between separatism and catholicism; between ecclesiastical purism and ecclesiastical eclecticism; between the idea of the church as an exclusive community of regenerate saints and the idea of the church as the general Christendom of state and people. . . .

> The Donatists, like Tertullian in his Montanistic writings, started from an ideal and spiritualistic conception of the church as a fellowship of the saints. . . .

> In opposition to this subjective and spiritualistic theory of the church, Augustine, as champion of the Catholics, developed. . . .[24]

Augustine's Attack upon Donatism

With Donatism on the rise and their numbers multiplying, the established Catholic Church needed someone of ability to take up the cudgels against them. A very capable man was found: Augustine, bishop of Hippo. His name has gone down in the annals of church history as one of the great Church Fathers. Theological concepts which he propounded are still the basis of some contemporary theological systems. He is admired for the great truths which he championed, many of which would be accepted by orthodox Christians today. But, in fairness, we must also recall (albeit painfully) the serious errors that originated with him as well. We thank God for all spiritual truth, for that comes from the Holy Scriptures. We repudiate errors because they are not of God and are not found in His Word.

Augustine wrote at some length in various treatises against the Donatists and their teachings. Many of the arguments he employed against the separatists of his day are still being used by anti-separatists today. What were some of them?

Augustine rejected the purist concept of the church held by the Donatists. He argued that the true church possessed episcopal succession, and that severance from the visible Catholic Church meant severance from the true church. In writing of the Donatists, he said, "Let them have a bitter sorrow for their former detestable wrong-doing, as Peter had for his cowardly lie, and let them come to the true Church, that is, their Catholic mother. . . ."[25] The Catholic Church alone possessed the marks of a true church, he said. Thus he laid the foundation for the apologetic that was later used effectively by the defenders of the Roman Catholic system. In response to the argument that the Donatists were living more godly lives than many of the run-of-the-mill professors of that day, he replied:

His defense of the holy Catholic Church as the true church.

> Whoever, therefore, shall be separated from this Catholic Church by this single sin of being severed from the unity of Christ, no matter how estimable a life he may imagine he is living, shall not have life, but the anger of God rests upon him.[26]

While Augustine uses some Scripture in seeking to refute the Donatists, his argument for the nature of the church is built more upon a plea for "apostolical tradition, church usage, custom, testimony, and authority." The perpetuation of the status quo and rev-erence for tradition and established order have often been characteristic of the opponents of separatist movements. Frend has well described the significance of the conflict between the Donatists and Augustine at this point:

> . . . Two contradictory interpretations of the Christian message took root. The germs of Catholicism and Dissent, the authority of an institution as against the authority of the Bible or personal inspiration, existed from the earliest moments of the Christian Church.[27]

The same problem has recurred over and over again through the centuries. Nonseparatists tend to protect the existing order, find excuses for it and argue for its purification and continuation even as it progressively grows worse. Separatists, on the other hand, desire the establishment of new and fresh witnesses to God's Word.

His appeal for unity and love.

Augustine, like many after him, viewed the separatist Donatists as "the bad guys." They were the "troublers of Israel," the "church-splitters." Numerous times in his writings he mentions the lack of a charitable spirit which characterizes all those who would leave the Catholic Church. He pleads for a mind which has "spit out all the bitterness of division, and which loves the sweetness of charity."[28] In another place Augustine invites the Donatists to "agree to the peace and unity of Christ," to repent of their sins, and to return to their "Head, Christ, in the Catholic peace, where 'Charity covereth a multitude of sins.' "[29] He also appeals to the sacrament of the Lord's Supper as a sign of unity. "For, the one bread is the sacrament of unity. . . . Therefore the Catholic Church alone is the Body of Christ. . . . But the enemy of unity has no share in the divine charity."[30]

No amount of appeals to love can be a proper basis for disobeying God in an unholy alliance. Love obeys God. Augustine did not emphasize this.

His argument from the wheat and the tares.

One of Augustine's favorite Scriptures to use against the Donatists was the parable of the wheat and the tares (Matt. 13:24-30). He deducted from this that since the Lord stated that the wheat and the tares should grow together until harvest (the end of the world), we had no right to try to separate them in this age, but rather let them grow together in the church until the Lord Himself would divide them. This argument appears many times in his writings.

> As to those whom we are not able to amend, even if necessity requires, for the salvation of others, that they share the sacraments of God with us, it does not require us to share in their sins, which we should do by consenting to or condoning them. We tolerate them in this world, in which the Catholic Church is spread abroad among all nations, which the Lord called His field, like the cockle among the wheat, or on this threshingfloor of unity, like chaff mingled with the good grain; or in the nets of the word and the sacrament, like the bad fishes enclosed with the good. We have them until the time of harvest.... Let us not destroy ourselves in evil dissension, because of evil men....[31]

He says in another letter that we should "bear with the chaff on the threshingfloor and, because it is destined for the fire at some future time, we do not for that abandon the Lord's threshingfloor."[32]

Donatists, to Augustine, were heretics. They complained to him and other authorities of the Catholic Church about the unjust persecution which they suffered. It is true that the Donatists were persecuted by the Catholics. Donatist property was confiscated, and some of their churches were closed. "The Catholic Church's first great and inhuman persecution against other Christians was against the Donatist free church."[33] How did Augustine justify this? He felt it was perfectly proper for extraordinary measures, yes, forceful measures, to be used against those who had departed from the "true church."

His defense of the persecution of heretics.

> Why, then, should the Church not compel her lost sons to return if the lost sons have compelled others to be lost? ... Is it not part of the shepherd's care when he has found those sheep, which have not been rudely snatched away, but have been gently coaxed and led astray from the flock, and have begun to be claimed by others, to call them back to the Lord's sheepfold, by threats, or pain of blows if they try to resist? ... As the

Donatists . . . claim that they ought not to be forced into the good . . . the Church imitates her Lord in forcing them. . . .[34]

Evaluations

Important, lasting and scriptural lessons can be learned from the Donatist controversy. The Donatists were not models of theological or personal perfection. We are not claiming such. Nor are we pleading that all the views they held be adopted by contemporary believers. But where they stood for a scriptural principle we should take note and be instructed. They believed that God wanted a pure testimony on earth. They believed that men and women associated with a church should live exemplary lives. They believed that the state had no right to interfere in the church's business. They denounced the apostasy and impurity which characterized much of the visible church in their day. Donatism represents an early example of separatism. In Donatism were the seeds of later separatist movements. So strong was the memory of these Donatists that later separatist bodies such as the Waldensians and the Anabaptists were often described as Donatists. The principle for which they stood we must now proceed to trace, if possible, through the Dark Ages.

Notes:

1. Frederic Farrar, *Lives of the Fathers* (Edinburgh: Adam & Charles Black, 1889), I, 183.

2. Gunnar Westin, *The Free Church Through the Ages* (Nashville: Broadman Press, 1958), p. 17.

3. Philip Schaff, *History of the Christian Church* (Grand Rapids: Wm. B. Eerdmans Publishing Co., 1910), I, 91.

4. H. D. McDonald, "Novatianism," *The New International Dictionary of the Christian Church*, p. 717.

5. St. Cyprian, trans. Maurice Bevenot (London: Longmans, Green, and Co., 1957), p. 47.

6. Ibid., pp. 52, 53.

7. Ibid., p. 65.

8. Ibid., p. 58.

9. Augustus Neander, *General History of the Christian Religion and Church*, trans. Joseph Torrey (Boston: Houghton, Mifflin and Co., 1871), II, 216.

10. R. A. Markus, "Christianity and Dissent in Roman North Africa: Changing Perspectives in Recent Work," *Schism, Heresy, and Religious Protest,* ed. Derek Baker (Cambridge: University Press, 1972).

11. W. H. C. Frend, *The Donatist Church* (Oxford: The Clarendon Press, 1952), pp. 112, 113.

12. "Donatism," *Westminster Dictionary of Church History,* p. 275.

13. Frend, *The Donatist Church,* p. 319.

14. Ibid., p. 106.

15. C. A. Scott, "Donatists," *Encyclopedia of Religion and Ethics,* III, 844, 845.

16. Walter Nigg, *The Heretics,* ed. and trans. Richard and Clara Winston (New York: Alfred A. Knopf, 1962), p. 110.

17. Albert Henry Newman, "Donatism," *The New Schaff-Herzog Encyclopedia of Religious Knowledge,* III, 488.

18. Neander, *General History of the Christian Religion and Church,* II, 238.

19. Leonard Verduin, *The Reformers and Their Stepchildren* (Grand Rapids: Wm. B. Eerdmans Publishing Co., 1964), p. 40.

20. Schaff, *History of the Christian Church,* I, 153, 154.

21. Nigg, *The Heretics,* p. 112.

22. Ibid., p. 113.

23. "Donatists," *Cyclopedia of Biblical, Theological and Ecclesiastical Literature,* II, 863.

24. Schaff, *History of the Christian Church,* I, 153, 154.

25. Augustine, Letter 185, *The Fathers of the Church,* ed. Joseph Deferrari (New York: Fathers of the Church, Inc., 1953), XXX, 185.

26. Ibid., Letter 141, XX, 139.

27. Frend, *The Donatist Church,* p. 333.

28. Augustine, Letter 142, XX, 149.

29. Augustine, Letter 141, XX, 146.

30. Augustine, Letter 185, XXX, 189.

31. Augustine, Letter 238, XVIII, 209, 210.

32. Augustine, Letter 142, II, 149.

33. Westin, *The Free Church Through the Ages,* p. 22.

34. Augustine, Letter 185, XXX, 164, 165.

Lights
in the Dark Ages

2

THE DONATIST Church continued for several centuries, though its strength gradually declined. As Europe passed into the Dark Ages (approximately 500-1500 A.D.), the light of the true gospel grew dim. During this period of time the Roman Catholic Church held sway both ecclesiastically and politically. Religious freedom as is now enjoyed by many was unknown in that day. The minds of men were shackled by religious superstitions innumerable but disseminated in the name of Jesus Christ. Here and there, however, were individuals and groups who dared to study the Scriptures and to preach them. What exactly did they believe? What were their modes of worship? How did they contribute to the separatist testimony? The answer to these questions is not easy to discover, but the study of these groups is most rewarding.

Problems, Guidelines and Dangers

It is with great difficulty that a proper evaluation can be given of the various "heretical" groups which existed during the Middle Ages. It seems clear (though difficult to establish from written evidence) that the beliefs of the Donatists were perpetuated in some hearts long after the Donatist Church as such had passed from the scene. Verduin observes: "This Donatist concern [for the purity of the church] ... continued to be heard long after the Donatist rebellion had been suppressed. It runs, refinement and all, through the literature dealing with the 'heretic' of the Middle Ages."[1] In another place he states: "Donatism as a movement in the fourth century was successfully repressed; but the ideas of

Problems.

27

Donatism lived on. They recurred in wave upon wave of dissent against the medieval sacralist order."[2] Moeller sees, running through various sects of the Middle Ages, the "Donatist conceptions" of the church with a "tendency towards separation on principle from the Romish hierarchy."[3]

To obtain accurate information concerning these dissident groups as given in their own words is practically impossible. They were considered enemies of both the state and the established church, and hence their writings were systematically destroyed. Most of the literature on which researchers must base their judgments was written by their enemies.

One writer, in commenting on the difficulty of correctly assessing the Albigenses, a "heretical" group of the Middle Ages, comments:

> What these Albigenses were it cannot be well gathered by the old Popish histories: for if there were any who did hold, teach, or maintain against the Pope or his papal pride, or withstand or gainsay his beggarly traditions, rites, and religions, etc., the historians of that time, in writing of them, do, for the most part, so deprave and misrepresent them (suppressing the truth of their articles), that they make them and paint them to be worse than Turks and infidels.[4]

Correct identification and evaluation are further hindered by the loose and imprecise use of names in that period. Epithets were hurled about with little regard for exactness. Persons were called Donatists or Petrobusians or other names, but little attempt was made to distinguish them. Some groups were more orthodox theologically than others, with differences of belief and emphasis between members of the same group.

Guidelines.

We approach this study with the conviction that God has had His people in every age though we may be frustrated in our efforts to trace them. Through the darkest periods of human history, God has protected His Word and has had a witness on the earth. "It is an error to believe that Christianity did not exist before the Reformation, save under the Roman-Catholic form, and that it was not until then that a section of the church assumed the form of Protestantism."[5]

In this brief review we are concerned primarily with important truths held by the groups cited and not with their errors. Many of them were not completely orthodox in every detail of doctrine. On the other hand, not all charges of heresy brought against them were accurate. For instance, in many discussions of these groups the ancient charge that they were Manicheans is brought forth. (Manicheans were dualists who believed in two eternal principles in the universe—good and evil.) Investigation seems to indicate that this charge was originally formulated by Augustine in his writings against the heretics. Verduin feels this is an unfair charge.

> In any event, we may by and large dismiss the charge of dualism as a feature of the medieval 'heretics,' although it is a little too sweeping to say that there was not a trace of dualism anywhere. . . . The orthodox 'heretics' seem to have been aware of the dualism, which they put far from themselves.[6]

When one remembers that these people lived and labored in an era of abysmal spiritual darkness, a more sympathetic view of them may be warranted. Given limited access to the copies of the Bible and hunted and hounded at every turn, it is a wonder that they possessed as much light as they did.

Dangers. While treating these groups with fairness, we must also guard against being carried away with unrealistic enthusiasm concerning their beliefs and practices. We may attribute to them more light and knowledge than they really possessed, thus adopting too rosy-hued a viewpoint. Or we may go to the other extreme (as many have done) and denounce them as completely hopeless heretics. Again, some have sought to find in them the particular distinctives of their own denomination. This view has been particularly true of some Baptists who have followed the "trail of blood" from the Donatists forward, and have discovered all of these groups to be fundamental Baptists.[7] While some modern Christians would share cherished principles with these who have gone before, we would be forced to repudiate some aspects of their beliefs as unscriptural.

Two Anti-Catholic Groups
with Questionable Doctrine

Keeping in mind all that has just been said, we look at a few groups that existed during the Dark Ages. Their mention does not constitute their endorsement in toto, but it will serve to show that throughout this period of spiritual darkness some sought to be lightbearers of the truth.

Albigenses (Cathari).

Not all bodies in the Middle Ages were thoroughly orthodox, but we include them in our discussion as those who were apart from Romanism, or in protest to it. Prominent particularly in southern France and northern Italy was a group known as the Albigenses (possibly from a city in southern France—Albi—where they centered in great numbers). They were also known as the Cathari (pure ones). Certainly many of the Albigenses were dualists, having imbibed the teachings of Mani, a Persian teacher of the third century. These, of course, would not be part of the heritage of Biblical separatists. Dualists believed in two eternal forces, Light and Darkness, who struggled for dominance.

The question is, To what extent did all persons called Albigenses hold to dualistic thought? An earlier scholar suggests the possibility that "many who held the simple truths of the Gospel, in opposition to the corruptions of Rome, were included in the title by Romish authorities, from whom our knowledge of these sects must be chiefly derived."[8] He goes on to state that some have claimed too much for the Albigenses, and yet some "have gone too far in admitting the trustworthiness of . . . Romanist sources of information."[9] A more recent writer discusses the problem of the doctrinal integrity of those called Albigenses and offers the opinion that, while some among them were Manichean, these probably did not represent all. "Yet their existence, however thinly scattered, would be sufficient to afford a pretext for branding the whole, agreeably to ancient custom, with the odium attaching but to the opinions of a part."[10] Clouse does not make any distinctions in various shades of belief among them but treats them as Manichean.[11]

The name Cathari derived from the emphasis of

these people upon purity of life and of the church. Adherents were placed into various categories. The leaders were called "the perfect," and, prior to their initiation into office, underwent a rite called "the Consolamentum," a form of confirmation, confession and the laying on of hands. Possibly they also took vows of abstinence and chastity. Those not called "leaders" were simply referred to as "believers."

These peoples were separatists. Wakefield describes their churches, which were organized completely independent of Rome. They emphasized "the contrast between the spirituality of the church of Christ, preserved in the apostolic succession of the Good Men [a name given to them], and the actuality of the Roman organization, described as an institution of the world and its evil maker. . . ."[12] An Albigense "heretic" was observed at his trial by St. Dominic, a Catholic clergyman. The "heretic" declared that "the Roman Church is the devil's church and her doctrines are those of demons. She is the Babylon whom St. John called the mother of fornication and abomination."[13] Because of their separation from Rome, they were forced to worship in caves and other remote locations, some of which may still be seen in southern France.[14] Crusades of persecution were launched against the Albigenses by the Roman Church, and they suffered terribly.

Bogomils.

The exact origin of this group is lost in antiquity. Some think that, similar to portions of the Albigenses, they sprang from the teachings of Mani, but this is not clear. We do know that they were viewed as heretical by the Eastern Orthodox Church. "Much that is known about them comes from hostile writers sympathetic to the established church of the day."[15] They were prominent in the area of Bulgaria, being first mentioned in literature around the tenth century.

The Bogomils gathered in congregations separate from the Roman Church. They held that "Christ had not instituted the established church, whose teaching about images, saints, infant baptism . . . was all false."[16]

> In 1140 supposed Bogomil error was
> found in the writings of Constantine
> Chrysomalus and condemned at a synod
> held in Constantinople. The teaching ob-
> jected to was, that Church baptism is not ef-
> ficacious, that nothing done by unconverted
> persons, though baptized, is of any value,
> that God's grace is received by the laying on
> of hands, but only in accordance with the
> measure of faith.[17]

Again, as with so many of these groups, people
with varying beliefs were called by the same name.
Latourette says there was more than one "stream" of
Bogomils, but that most of them were dualistic.[18]
Another summarizes some of their views:

> Their views of the sacraments were in
> some ways similar to several Protestant
> groups in later centuries both in western
> Europe and in America. The Bogomiles op-
> posed the sacramental materialism of the
> church. They rejected water baptism. . . .
> Likewise, the Lord's Supper was to be prac-
> ticed spiritually, for the bread and the wine
> could not be transubstantiated into the body
> and blood of Christ.[19]

Their heretical views apparently included a belief that the flesh was intrinsically evil, and that birth
is the imprisonment of the spirit in a corporeal body.

If what we know of the majority of people called
Bogomils is accurate, they would not be an example
of the purest strain of separatist bodies. Since the
chief source of information about their teachings
comes from a bitter opponent, the Catholic Cosmas
and his *Sermon Against the Heretics*, and since, as
was mentioned earlier, "heretics" were grouped together under convenient labels, we should be cau-
tious in evaluating the Bogomils.

Groups of Clearer
Doctrinal Persuasion

Paulicians.

Another group which spread quite widely during the Middle Ages was known as the Paulicians.
The name is thought to have been derived either
from (1) Paul of Samasota, bishop of Antioch around
260 A.D., or (2) the apostle Paul.

Of the origin of the sect we are not entirely

sure. They may have been in lineal descent from some of the dualistic Christian bodies of the first centuries. It has often been asserted, but without adequate foundation, that the Paulicians were an offshoot of Manichaeism. Probably they were not. Their Christology was adoptionists. . . . The Paulicians professed to base their teachings on the New Testament, all of which they accepted. . . . Admission to the church, they held, could be only by adult baptism. . . . They abhorred monasticism. They did not accept the intercession of the saints or the kind of honors paid by the Orthodox to Mary. They repudiated the use of images, crosses, relics, incense, and candles. . . .[20]

Another scholar reinforces this impression by stating that the Paulicians, while often accused of being Manichean, were really "men who were disgusted with the doctrines and ceremonies of human invention, and desirous of returning to the apostolic doctrine and practice."[21]

The reputed founder of the group was one Constantine. About 657 he entered into lengthy preaching journeys which carried him up the Euphrates and across into Asia Minor, founding many churches as he went. It is obvious from this activity, and also from their beliefs just cited, that the Paulicians were separatists and not in happy harmony with the established churches either east or west. They were an "evangelical antihierarchical sect"[22] whose teachings spread far and wide, and whose disciples multiplied. Savage persecution under Empress Theodora (842-857 A.D.) reportedly resulted in the martyrdom of 100,000 Paulicians. If this be anywhere near accurate, it shows that their ministry had been successful and that there were large numbers of them.

Peter of Bruys and the Petrobusians.

Little is known of Peter of Bruys except that he was a priest who appeared in southern France around 1105. He opposed the Catholic Church and was burned to death about 1126. A bit more is known about Henry of Lausanne, Peter's successor, who carried on his work. He was a Benedictine monk who apparently had considerable preaching ability. His itinerant preaching and the great response it received brought his imprisonment and, we assume, his death, though this is not recorded. Followers of Peter became known as Petrobusians.

What was it about the doctrine of these two men that stirred the animosity of the Roman ecclesiastics so? We are dependent upon Peter the Venerable, abbot of Cluny and Peter of Bruys' chief opponent, for an outline of his teaching. The Venerable lists five objectionable beliefs of Peter of Bruys: (1) believer's baptism only; (2) the uselessness of church edifices and consecrated altars; (3) the necessity of breaking up crosses and burning them; (4) the meaninglessness of the Mass; and (5) the powerlessness of prayers, alms and other good works to help the dead.[23]

Schaff notes something else which certainly was contrary to the accepted beliefs and practices of the day.

> Peter and Henry revived the Donatistic view that piety is essential to a legitimate priesthood. The word "Church" signifies the congregation of the faithful and consists in the unity of the assembled believers and not in the stones of the building.[24]

Peter and Henry had a "remarkable emphasis upon personal faith as the sole means of salvation."[25]

Disdaining as they did the formal ordination at the hands of the Catholic Church, and believing evangelical doctrines so fervently, these preachers of Christ had only one end. Their followers, the Petrobusians, were officially condemned as heretics by the Synod of Toulouse in 1119. To what extent their followers retained a nominal affiliation with the established church is not always clear from the information we have, but certainly their teachings were not welcomed within the church.

Bohemian Brethren. Out of the mind and heart of an eloquent bishop of the Roman Church, John of Rokycana (c.1390-1471) came the seeds that were to sprout into a breakaway movement from Rome. While he became increasingly vocal in his criticism of papal corruption and in his expression of the ideal of primitive Christianity, he himself did not wish to pay the price of a complete cleavage from Rome. His followers, however, gathered themselves to another teacher,

Peter Chelcicky (c.1390-1460) who, while not formally trained in theology, had a good grasp of it and exhibited leadership abilities. He began to speak and write forcefully in favor of the separation of church and state and the authority of the New Testament as over against the authority of the church. "For Chelcicky the fall of the church came with the 'poisoned embrace' of Constantine the Great."[26]

As Chelcicky and others began to teach the Scriptures, many listened. At first they determined to remain with the established ecclesiastical structure though they did set up a fellowship called *Unitas Fratrum,* the Unity of Brethren, which they hoped would provide spiritual fellowship within the Catholic system. The wrath of the established church began to descend upon them, and the logical results of their scriptural convictions began to motivate them. In 1467 they established themselves as a separate body from Rome. Some contact was made with certain of the Waldensians. Later, when the Protestant Reformation broke out, the Brethren established contact with some of the Reformers and had discussions with them. The Brethren, however, were disappointed in the lack of emphasis on church discipline on the part of the Reformers, and the Reformers in turn were unhappy with the Brethren practice of adult baptism.

Waldensians.

One of the largest and most prominent of the more evangelical groups in the Middle Ages was the Waldensian Church. Where did they originate? The Waldensians viewed themselves as but the continuation of a long line of witnesses to the truth which had come through the centuries. Neander comments:

> But it is not without some foundation of truth that the Waldenses of this period [1100-1200 A.D.] asserted the high antiquity of their sect, and maintained that from the time of the secularization of the church— that is, as they believed, from the time of Constantine's gift to the Roman bishop Silvester—such an opposition as finally broke forth in them had been existing all along.[27]

To what extent this was true we will leave for the moment to comment on the portion of Waldensian history that is recorded. The movement takes its name from a wealthy merchant of Lyons (France), Peter Waldo, who lived about 1170-1215 A.D. Waldo had a life-changing spiritual experience, renounced his materialistic ways and began to preach Christ. His followers were known as "Poor Men" since they advocated giving up earthly possessions and becoming servants of the Master. They believed in lay preachers, a concept almost unheard of in that day, and one for which they were especially denounced by Rome. Their ministers knew the Scriptures, preached in itinerant ministries, established churches throughout Europe, and, with such activities, brought upon themselves considerable persecution. (The small remnant of Waldensians remaining in Italy today are ecumenical and not of the same spirit as their ancient counterparts.)

Most certainly the great majority of Waldensians were separatists. Mosheim feels certain groups of the Waldensians had differing opinions concerning the extent of the apostasy of the Roman Church. He is of the opinion that the Italian Waldensians acknowledged the Roman Church as a true church though much corrupted, while Waldensians in France and elsewhere disagreed. A look at some of their official statements, however, makes a strong case for their separatism. In a document entitled "The Articles of the Waldenses," produced by them around 1160 A.D., they stated:

> Now it is evident, as well in the *Old* as in the *New Testament*, that a Christian stands bound, by express command given to him, to separate himself from Antichrist [Roman Church]. . . . Be it known unto everyone in general and in particular, that the cause of our separation is this, namely, for the real Truth's sake of the Faith, and by reason of our inward knowledge of the only true God. . . .[28]

One of their ancient disciplines instructs believers "not to communicate at all with wicked ,works, and more especially with those which favour of Idolatry or the service belonging to it [false church] and so of other things."[29] In one of their catechisms is found these words:

Minister: What is that which thou believest concerning the Holy Church?

Answer: I say, that the Church is considered two manner of ways, the one Substantially, and the other Ministerially. As it is considered Substantially, by the Holy Catholic Church is meant all the Elect of God, from the beginning of the world to the end, by the grace of God through the merit of Christ, gathered together by the Holy Spirit and foreordained to eternal life; the number and names of whom are known to him alone who has elected them; and in this Church remains none who is reprobate. . . .

Minister: By what mark knowest thou the false ministers?

Answer: By their fruits, by their blindness, by their evil works, by their perverse Doctrine, and by their undue administration of the Sacraments. . . .

Minister: By what marks are those people known who are not in truth within the Church?

Answer: By public sins, and an erroneous faith. For, we ought to fly from such persons, lest we be defiled by them.[30]

The Waldensians were not bashful about identifying error, nor were they hesitant in prescribing the Biblical response to error as it had embodied itself in the established church. They did not rationalize about "opportunities to witness" within the bosom of the monstrous harlot. Their attitude is plainly seen in further citations from their catechism:

Minister: By what marks is the undue administration of the sacrament known?

Answer: When the priests, not knowing the intention of Christ in the sacraments, say that the grace and truth are included in the external ceremonies, and persuade men to the participation of the sacrament without the truth, and without faith. But the Lord chargeth those that are his to take heed of such false prophets, saying, "beware of the pharisees," that is to say, "of the leaven of their doctrine." Again, "believe them not, neither go after them." And David hates the church or the congregation of such persons, saying, "I hate the church of evil men." And the Lord commands to come out from the midst of such people, Num. XVI, "Depart from the tents of these wicked men, and touch nothing of theirs, lest ye be consumed in their sins. And the apostle also, 2 Cor. 6:14. . . .[31]

The Waldensians were bitter foes of the Roman Church whom they felt had ensnared the souls of thousands and had spilled the blood of many of God's people. Lea in his great work on the Inquisition says of Waldensian beliefs:

Theirs was the true Church, and that of the Pope was but a house of lies, whose excommunication was not to be regarded and whose decrees were not to be obeyed. They had a complete organization, consisting of bishops, priests, and deacons. . . .[32]

Durnbaugh says the same: "Eventually a complete underground structure rivaling the institutional church formed along sectarian lines."[33]

How do Roman Catholics view the Waldensians? Bernard Gui, a leading inquisitor for the Roman Church (c. 1261-1331), wrote of them:

Disdain for ecclesiastical authority was and still is the prime heresy of the Waldenses. . . . The misled believers and sacrilegious masters of this sect hold and teach that they are in no way subject to the lord Pope or Roman Pontiff, or to the prelates of the Roman Church. . . .[34]

A later Catholic writer said:

But contempt for the power of the Church, which was the basis of the heresy, led the Waldenses into a much more radical attitude. In their view, priests of the Roman Church had lost their authority; churches were useless; religious chants were superfluous; and it was futile to observe the feasts of the saints and to pray to them. They also violently attacked the doctrine of purgatory and its consequences, and scoffed at indulgences.[35]

It seems evident that the Waldensians stand as one of the strongest groups of the Middle Ages in doctrine and practice.

While neither John Wycliffe nor John Hus were themselves separatists, we mention them here because their teachings spawned separatist movements in their respective countries.

Through the ministry of John Wycliffe in England from about 1370 A.D. on, some began to reject various teachings of the Roman Catholic Church. Wycliffe's followers were called Lollards. (The origin of the name is disputed.) Under his leadership the Bible was not only translated into English, but was distributed far and wide. At the Council of Constance (1415) Wycliffe was condemned as a heretic. His writings and influence had a wide impact. Turberville, an apologist for the Roman Catholics, notes that "separation tendencies" showed themselves early among Wycliffe's followers, the Lollards, and that they began to "develop into a separate sect."[36]

A contemporary of Wycliffe, John Hus, lived and ministered in Prague, where he was a professor at the university. He was greatly influenced by Wycliffe's writings. He openly opposed the Roman Church and was finally martyred in 1415. While not directly responsible for any separatist movement, the seeds of discontent against the papal system which he sowed no doubt bore fruit in the Bohemian Brethren under Peter Chelcicky and others.

Summary Thoughts

In the study of these dissident groups, the doctrine of the "gathered" church, that is, the church of the regenerate only, comes to the fore time and again. As men embraced this concept, they were driven farther and farther away from the sacramentarianism of Rome. An ancient Catharist document, "A Vindication of the Church of God," declared: "But this Holy Church is the assembly of the faithful and of holy men in which Jesus Christ is and will be until the end of the world. . . ."[37] The Paulicians believed in "separation from the nominal Christian populace."[38] A proper view of the nature of the local church will lead one to a proper view of purity in ecclesiastical relationships.

These groups loved the Scripture. In an age when the Scriptures were all but forgotten, buried under the ecclesiastical trappings and opinions of men, a remnant dared to study them, and, upon the basis of what they found, to challenge the reigning powers. It was risky business. The Waldensians, for example, rejected the popular fanciful and allegorical interpretations of their day in favor of a more literal approach. One of the chief objections raised against Peter of Bruys was the fact that "he rejected the authority of the Fathers and of tradition, adhering to the Scriptures alone."[39] Significantly, some, such as Peter Chelcicky, contended that the form of the church should be determined from the New Testament alone, thus rejecting the Old Testament concepts which undergirded the generally accepted ecclesiology of the day.

These groups also had an emphasis upon practical godliness in an age when the godlessness of even the religious leaders was the subject of open mockery. They believed that Christians were to be honest, pure and Christlike in their daily deportment. While we would not necessarily condone all of their views, we do honor them, that in such a wicked and apostate age they sought as best as they could to bear the testimony of the risen Lord.

Some Abiding Lessons

What can we learn from a perusal of these little-known and much-maligned peoples? Certainly we can know that in the darkest hours of human history, God, through His Spirit, has prompted some to search the Scriptures and to yearn after Himself. Amidst the pagan darkness and unbelievably dead sacramentarianism, the light of the Lord shines into some hearts.

Modern-day separatists can rejoice that they do not walk alone. Others have paid a price in days gone by for the truth of God. An examination of the witness of such groups of believers reminds us again that the principle of separation, with its corollary, the believers' church, brings upon its adherents tremendous opposition.

> These churches, carrying on the New Testament principles in large measure, though no doubt in varying degrees in different places, called by their adversaries Manicheans, Paulicians, and other names, suffered for centuries with patience and without re-

taliation the dreadful wrongs inflicted on them.[40]

The record stands for all to see what it has cost men and women to be separated from the established but apostate church, to accept the Bible   one as authority for faith and practice, and to repudiate the fellowship of those who deny the truth.[41]

Notes:

1. Verduin, *The Reformers and Their Stepchildren*, p. 96.
2. Ibid., p. 32.
3. Wilhelm Moeller, *History of the Christian Church in the Middle Ages*, trans. Andrew Rutherford (London: Swan Sonnenschein Co., 1893), p. 395.
4. George Townsend (ed.), *The Acts and Monuments of John Foxe* (New York: AMS Press, 1965), II, 586.
5. J. H. Merle D'Aubigne, *History of the Reformation of the Sixteenth Century* (New York: American Tract Society, n.d.), I, 98.
6. Leonard Verduin, *The Anatomy of a Hybrid* (Grand Rapids: Wm. B. Eerdmans Publishing Co., 1976), p. 134.
7. Authors maintaining such a view in varying degrees are J. M. Carroll, *The Trail of Blood* (Lexington, KY: Ashland Ave. Baptist Church, 1931); S. J. Ford, *The Origin of the Baptists* (Nashville: Southwestern Publishing House, 1860); Roy Mason, *The Church That Jesus Built* (Tampa: Central Ave. Baptist Church, n.d.); G. H. Orchard, *A Concise History of the Baptists* (Lexington, KY: Ashland Ave. Baptist Church, 1956).
8. "Albigenses," *Cyclopedia of Biblical, Theological and Ecclesiastical Literature*, I, 134.
9. Ibid.
10. Robert Vaughn, *The Life and Opinions of John de Wycliffe* (New York: AMS Press, 1973), I, 148, 149.
11. Robert Clouse, "Albigensians," *The New International Dictionary of the Christian Church*, p. 22.
12. Walter Wakefield, *Heresy, Crusade, and Inquisition in Southern France: 1100-1250* (Los Angeles: University of California Press, 1974), pp. 32, 33.
13. Joseph R. Strayer, *The Albigensian Crusades* (New York: The Dial Press, 1971), p. 22.
14. Nigg, *The Heretics*, pp. 186, 187.
15. George Giacumakis, "Bogomiles," *The New International Dictionary of the Christian Church*, p. 140.
16. Wakefield, *Heresy, Crusade, and Inquisition in Southern France: 1100-1250*, p. 28.

17. E. H. Broadbent, *The Pilgrim Church* (London: Pickering and Inglis, 1931), p. 60.

18. Kenneth Scott Latourette, *The History of the Expansion of Christianity* (Grand Rapids: Zondervan Publishing House, 1970), II, 442.

19. Giacumakis, "Bogomiles," p. 140.

20. Latourette, *The History of the Expansion of Christianity*, II, 440.

21. "Paulicians," *Cyclopedia of Biblical, Theological and Ecclesiastical Literature*, VII, 836.

22. J. G. G. Norman, "Paulicians," *The New International Dictionary of the Christian Church*, p. 755.

23. Schaff, *History of the Christian Church*, V, 484.

24. Ibid.

25. C. Peter Williams, "Peter de Bruys," *The New International Dictionary of the Christian Church*, p. 768.

26. Donald F. Durnbaugh, *The Believers' Church: The History and Character of Radical Protestantism* (London: Macmillan Co., 1968), p. 55.

27. Neander, *General History of the Christian Religion and Church*, IV, 605.

28. Samuel Morland, *The History of the Evangelical Churches of the Valleys of Piedmont* (London: Henry Hills, 1658), pp. 151, 155.

29. Ibid., p. 93.

30. Ibid., pp. 81, 82.

31. *The Waldenses* (Philadelphia: Presbyterian Board of Publication, 1853), pp. 382, 383.

32. Henry Charles Lea, *A History of the Inquisition of the Middle Ages* (New York: Russell and Russell, 1958), II, 150.

33. Durnbaugh, *The Believers' Church*, p. 45.

34. Bernard Gui, "The Manual of the Inquisition," *The Development of Civilization*, ed. Harry Carroll, et. al. (Glenview, IL: Scott, Foresman and Co., 1969), I, 313.

35. Y. Dossat, "Waldenses," *New Catholic Encyclopedia*, XIV, 771.

36. Arthur S. Turberville, *Medieval Heresy and the Inquisition* (London: Archon Books, 1964), p. 93.

37. Walter Wakefield and Austin Evans (trans.), *Heresies of the High Middle Ages* (New York: Columbia University Press, 1969), p. 238.

38. Westin, *The Free Church Through the Ages*, p. 24.

39. Albert Henry Newman, *A Manual of Church History* (Philadelphia: The American Baptist Publication Society, 1948), I, 562.

40. Broadbent, *The Pilgrim Church*, p. 55.

41. For an astounding accumulation of testimonies and records describing the terrible sufferings of Christians who stood against the Roman Church, read *The Bloody Theater* or *Martyrs Mirror* by Thielman J. Van Braght, trans. Joseph Sohm (Scottdale, PA: Herald Press, 1950).

Separatism and the Anabaptists

3

UNTIL FAIRLY recent years the term *Anabaptist* was one of strong disapproval. Historians and authors used it to describe a wide variety of persons opposed to the establishment in the ecclesiastical world. To many, the Anabaptists are the fanatics of Munster who, around 1533, committed excesses in the name of the Lord. Fortunately, in the last generation or two, scholars have given more attention to the movement; as a result more accurate information and evaluation has been forthcoming. Rather than using the term indiscriminately to refer to "a variety of heresies and revolutionary malcontents,"[1] it has been discovered that there were various kinds of Anabaptists, many of them with solid Biblical convictions and responsible deportment.

The Rise of the Anabaptists

The Anabaptist movement arose during the sixteenth century at the time of the Reformation. It is sometimes referred to as the "Radical Reformation."

The name *Anabaptist* originated with those who viewed anyone rejecting Catholic baptism as "guilty of rebaptizing." An Anabaptist was a "rebaptizer." This, of course, was considered a very serious offense because it signified rejection of the supposedly efficacious baptism of Rome, and of the Protestant groups as well. It also constituted, in principle, a repudiation both of church and state. It was seen as subversive of the entire societal and ecclesiastical structure of the day, which viewed the church and the state as inextricably interwoven and interdependent. Thus, those who dared to rebaptize were

The significance of the name.

thought of as seditious and worthy of the harshest punishment. They were challenging the divinely established order of things. They were separatists, made so by the very fact that they rejected the church-state concept and thus could not fellowship within its framework. The term Anabaptist was "applied by Lutherans, Zwinglians, and Catholics to all radicals indiscriminately who would own allegiance to none of these communions. . . ."[2]

The beginnings and growth of Anabaptism.

Newman, in a helpful discussion, distinguishes five different groups of Anabaptists.[3] Whether all agree with every distinction made, at least it is important to recognize that there were differences among the people known by this name. We are not concerned with efforts to delineate all the differences; rather, we want to see where the more Biblical groups of Anabaptists fit into the total flow of separatist testimony through the centuries.

The most Biblical segment of the movement began in Switzerland as an outgrowth of the ministry of the noted Reformer Ulrich Zwingli. Zwingli became convinced of certain segments of Biblical truth and began to preach them with conviction in the cathedral in Zurich. In the process, he became troubled over the Roman Catholic doctrine of the Mass, finding no scriptural support for it. He presented arguments to the Zurich city council in favor of the Lord's Supper instead of the Mass. (The civil authorities were in charge of religion within political jurisdictions in that day; hence Zwingli's approach to the council.) Zwingli declared he was going to celebrate a Biblical observance of the Lord's Table, but the city council opposed it; so he backed down, explaining to his followers that the Reformation would be hindered if the matter were pressed.

By this time, however, Zwingli, through his emphasis upon the Scriptures, had created convictions in the minds of some of his followers that caused them to oppose his acquiescence to the city council. Such young men as Conrad Grebel (1495-1526) and Felix Manz (c. 1498-1527) felt that if the Scriptures taught something, it should be obeyed—regardless of what the city council thought. They remonstrated with Zwingli, but to no avail. Since they felt Zwingli lacked the courage of his convictions, they began to break with him.

These young men and others whom they influenced began to consider seriously the nature of a true gospel church. What should be its organization and membership? What ordinances should it observe and in what manner? As they studied the Scriptures, they became convinced that a church, if organized after the New Testament pattern, should be composed of believers only, and that, if this be true, only the baptism of believers was acceptable.

Basically, then, we could say that Anabaptism arose out of the renewal of Bible study which characterized the Reformation period. The major Reformers (such as Luther and Calvin) stopped short of complete obedience to the Word of God, particularly in reference to the composition and ordinances of the local church. They could not bring themselves to accept the radical (for that day) teachings which would have brought them into immediate conflict with the entire ecclesiastical-political system so entrenched in society. Their failure to adopt scriptural principles created in their hearts a tremendous antagonism for those who did. Zwingli, for instance, could not abide the teachings of Felix Manz, his former friend. Manz was executed by drowning in Zurich, the very city that Zwingli supposedly was creating into a model of a Christian state. What was the official reason given for Manz's execution? The answer to that gives a great insight into the hatred that the Reformers (and others following them) had for the separatists.

> Because he has, contrary to Christian order and custom, become involved in rebaptism . . . has confessed to having said that he wanted to gather such as want to accept Christ and follow him, to unite himself with them through baptism . . . so that he and his followers have separated themselves from the Christian Church, to raise up a sect of their own . . . such doctrine being harmful to the united usage of all Christendom and tending to offence-giving, to insurrection and sedition against the government.[4]

Very interesting is the charge of Donatism brought against the Anabaptists by their opponents.

In seeking to refute the teachings of Bernard, an Anabaptist leader, an old German Lutheran wrote:

> Aha, here Bernard resorts to a genuinely Donatist trick. They too condemned and abandoned Christendom on account of some evil and false Christians. . . . We don't want to rend the net because there are some bad fish in it, as the super-saintly Anabaptist Bernard is doing. He gives himself away at this point and shows that he has the same Anabaptist devil in him which blinded also the Donatists in Africa. . . . They proceeded to go off by themselves, apart from Christendom, and made off that they wanted to raise up a truly Reformed church, one in which there were nothing but saints. . . . They scolded Augustine for staying on in the assembly of the wicked. . . . Let Bernard consider himself told off, for he is a neo-Donatist . . . and he has . . . gone about to raise up a holy and unspotted church . . . he and his company cut loose from Christendom.[5]

Melancthon was a strong opponent of Anabaptism. He had a different view of the church than did the Anabaptists.

> Time and again Melancthon accused the Anabaptists of destroying the church, which to him constituted heresy. Clearly he understood the church to be both the occasion and the instrument of God's grace. . . . It was unnecessary and wrong to cause divisions from the true church.[6]

Clearly, the separatist tendencies of the Anabaptists, a result of their doctrine of the church, brought them into direct conflict with not only the Catholics but also the Reformers.

A Survey of Some Anabaptist Distinctives

Our purpose would not be served in seeking a complete survey of Anabaptist teachings. We are concerned only with their convictions which bear directly upon the question of separation.

The Word of God— divine and final authority.

The Anabaptists felt strongly that the Bible was the final authority for the believer's faith and practice. They rejected the authority of men, church councils, the Pope or man-made creeds. This stubborn adherence to what the Bible said cost them heavily. It led them to reject the commonly accepted concepts about the church and its ordinances and to endure great hardship for their convictions. "They preferred to make a radical break with fifteen hundred years of history and culture if necessary rather than to break with the New Testament."[7]

The Anabaptists studied the Bible. They used the Bible in their preaching and teaching. They often confounded their opponents by citing the Word of God which gave clear teaching on some disputed point. They believed implicitly that the Bible was God's holy Word.

This is not to say that they made no mistakes or were faultless in their theology. But, particularly in the area of ecclesiology, they made a tremendous contribution. They enunciated clearly the concept of the "gathered (believers') church," and indebted themselves to many who have followed them and likewise have embraced that doctrine.

Baptism only for the true believer.

Not all Anabaptists immediately (or even later) embraced immersion as the proper mode. They did come to see, however, the importance of baptism as a personal confession of one's faith in Christ, as a free, conscious act on the part of a person knowledgeable as to his actions.

The Roman Catholic Church, of course, taught and practiced infant baptism, which they saw as necessary to salvation. The Reformers were also pedobaptists (infant baptizers). Baptism was mandatory for all infants born into political states where either Catholicism or the Reformation ruled. To refuse to have one's baby baptized was considered a serious offense.

As the Anabaptists progressed in their study of the Scriptures, they saw the entire picture much more clearly.

It is interesting to note how zeal for Bible study gradually led the forces of the opposition further and further. In the summer of 1523 the issue was a separatist church, and its advocates sought to have Zwingli join them. A year later there was the debate over the question of antipedobaptism, which resulted in sharp conflict. At the beginning of 1525 the practice of the new baptism was initiated.[8]

Church discipline to be exercised.

Since the Anabaptists believed strongly in the purity of the church, it was important to them that impure persons—persons who were not living like Christians should—be barred from church fellowship. They called it "the ban." We refer to it today as church discipline. These hardy believers taught that church membership, being a free response in obedience to Christ, had certain obligations. Members who were living loose lives should be banned from participation in the Lord's Table, or be completely removed from the church fellowship.

> Repeatedly, when Anabaptists were questioned by state church leaders . . . as to the reason for their separation from the official church they cited the lack of discipline. The state church could not be the true church of Christ because it tolerated in its midst all kinds of sin.[9]

It was this emphasis upon purity which also caused them to avoid interchurch fellowship with those who tolerated evil doctrine and practice.

Separatists continue to see a connection between maintaining church purity through church discipline and maintaining that purity through separation from contaminating interchurch fraternization. (This is why current attempts on the part of some to find links between Anabaptists and the modern ecumenical movement seem so incongruous. Anabaptists were certainly not ecumenical either in spirit or practice.[10])

The Roman Church apostate.

The Anabaptists made no effort to hide their feelings about the Church of Rome. One of their writers said:

> For the Babylonian harlot who sits on the seven hills, I mean the Roman Church, a synagogue of the living devil, only spits out all the children of God and drives them into wastelands, into their byways.[11]

They made no attempt to "build bridges" with Rome. They preferred to establish independent congregations built upon the Scriptures alone.

The Doctrine of the Church:
Reformers vs. the Anabaptists

Particularly in the area of ecclesiology, the Anabaptists strongly disagreed with Calvin, Luther and the other Reformers.

The major Reformers believed that the *invisible* church was inclusive of all true believers. Perhaps they inherited this emphasis upon the *invisible* church from Augustine, who found it a useful concept in contradicting the Donatists.

Views of the major reformers regarding the church.

As for the visible church, the major Reformers defended stubbornly the concept that both believers and unbelievers were included *and that it was wrong to seek to correct that situation*. Berkhof has a penetrating analysis of Luther's position. "His [Luther's] insistence on the invisibility of the Church served the purpose of *denying* that the Church is *essentially* an *external* society with a visible head, and of affirming that the essence of the Church is to be found in the sphere of the invisible. . . ."[12] Luther defended an outward ecclesiastical society which included "the number or multitude of the baptized and believing who belong to a priest or bishop, whether in a city, or in a whole land, or in the whole world."[13]

This church visible, according to the Reformers, was entered by infant baptism. While they differed regarding the details of the meaning of baptism, they agreed on this point—infants should be baptized. They taught (except Zwingli) that baptism was a sacrament, conferring grace upon its recipients.

> In opposition to the Anabaptists who laid the emphasis in the sacrament upon their own act as against the act of God and saw in baptism nothing but a sign that the new birth has already taken place, and consequently rejected infant baptism, Luther maintained the right and necessity of infant baptism. Children are to be baptized as well as adults, for baptism is essential to salvation.[14]

One dogma of the Reformers is especially hard for many modern Christians to grasp. They believed that the visible church should be defended by the civil powers. As has already been stated, they firmly held to an interlocking relationship between the church and the state. "The prince should tolerate in his realm only the One Church of the pure Word."[15] This belief drove them to persecution with the sword of those who disagreed with them, and of Anabaptists in particular.

Views of the Anabaptists regarding the church.

Anabaptists felt that the emphasis of the New Testament was upon the church as visible in local congregations. They did not accept the Reformers' attempts to escape the New Testament implications of a gathered (free) church by fleeing to the doctrine of the invisible church.

> The Anabaptists were not pleased with the Reformers' distinction between a visible church which is earthly and impure and an invisible church which is heavenly and pure. Their practical concern was the actualization of a visible and true body of Christ on earth, which would be in accord with the New Testament pattern. They did make a sharp distinction, however, between the "true church," by which they meant themselves, and the "church of the antichrist," by which they meant the Roman Church.[16]

The Anabaptists completely rejected the concept of the established church, "replacing the monopoly of the authoritarian and compulsory state church with independent, voluntary congregations. . . ."[17]

There was another point of disagreement as well. The Reformers had a much wider concept of the composition of the church than did the Anabaptists. As one has pointed out, Zwingli was "willing to assume that everyone in Zurich was, in some sense, a Christian." The Anabaptists, however, came to conclude "that such a 'mass church' idea is alien to the New Testament."[18] In one of their doctrinal statements, the Schleitheim Confession (1527), the Anabaptists stated: "Baptism shall be given to all who have learned repentance and amendment of life . . . and to all those who walk in the resurrection of Jesus Christ. . . ."[19] We cannot refrain from quoting Bender's fine summary of the distinctions.

> But the most characteristic feature of the Anabaptist contribution following inevitably from its concept of discipleship, is its insis-

tence upon a new church of truly committed and practicing believers in contradistinction to the prevailing concept of the "Volkskirche," or inclusive church of the Reformation and subsequent periods, held by Catholics and Protestants . . . alike, with a church maintained by the powerful patronage of the State, and to which, by birth and infant baptism, the entire population belonged. Grebel and his associates saw this issue clearly and dared to challenge Zwingli directly on it. . . . Zwingli . . . deliberately rejected the Swiss Brethren call for a church of true believers only and established "a church in which all professing Christians, the nominal, lukewarm, and indifferent ones as well as the really live and active Christians are kept together, a church to which the entire population belongs and which is not the church of genuine believers, but only the imperfect human institution."[20]

Naturally, on the basis of the information already cited, the Anabaptists held tenaciously to the doctrine of the separation of church and state. This was one of the principal reasons they were considered so heretical in their day. With their emphasis, however, they paved the way for the introduction of religious freedom in later years and other lands.

Apostasy and separation.

For our consideration, one of the most important of the Anabaptists' beliefs concerning the church was that of "the fall" or "ruin" of the church.[21] They believed that the professing church had fallen away from the truth—apostasized—and that a restoration of true churches was necessary. They differed among themselves as to when this "fall" occured. Some felt there had been no true church for centuries.[22] Most seemed to hold that the apostasy set in with the reign of Constantine. Pilgrim Marpeck, an influential Anabaptist leader, thought that the ruin of the church began with the acceptance of infant baptism. Most of them agreed that there had been true churches scattered throughout "Babylon" (the apostate state church). They saw the marks of the fall as being dependent upon the state, the condoning of the spirit of the age, the acceptance of false doctrines such as the Mass and infant baptism, and the general laxity toward Biblical truth.

What, in light of this apostasy, was the duty of an obedient Christian? The Anabaptists were not bashful in answering that question. They felt that a true New Testament church could be established "only after a decisive separation from the established Roman Church had been made...."[23] Menno Simons, in a section of one of his writings entitled "The Duty of Shunning Babylon," remarked:

> We also teach and admonish from the Word of God that all genuine children of God, born again of the incorruptible living seed of the divine Word ... must according to the Scriptures shun all seducing and idolatrous preachers in regard to doctrines, sacraments, and worship. They must avoid all who, of whatever belief, doctrine, sect, or name, are not in the pure doctrine of Christ....[24]

One student of the movement observed, "In reviewing the records, the reader is struck with the Anabaptists' acute consciousness of separation from the 'fallen' church—in which they included the Reformers as well as the Roman institution."[25]

Numerous statements by Anabaptists underscore their convictions regarding separation from apostasy. The Schleitheim Confession drawn up by the Swiss Brethren Conference, February 1527, was written chiefly by Michael Sattler.

> We are agreed [as follows] on separation: a separation shall be made from them and from the wickedness which the devil planted in the world: in this manner, simply that we shall not have fellowship with them [the wicked] and not run with them in the multitude of their abominations.... For truly all creatures are in but two classes, good and bad, believing and unbelieving, darkness and light ... God's temple and idols, Christ and Belial; and none can have part with the other.

> To us then the command of the Lord is clear when He calls upon us to be separate from the evil and thus He will be our God and we shall be His sons and daughters.

> He further admonishes us to withdraw from Babylon and the earthly Egypt that we

may not be partakers of the pain and suffering which the Lord will bring upon them.

From this we should learn that everything
which is not united with our God and Christ
cannot be other than an abomination which
we should shun and flee from. By this is
meant all popish and antipopish works and
church services, meetings, and church at-
tendance. . . . From all these things we
should be separated and have no part with
them for they are nothing but an abomination. . . .[26]

The Anabaptists believed in both personal separation from ungodliness and also from the apostasy.
Sometimes the two concepts combined in their use
of the term "separation." Dietrich Philips, in discussing the various marks (ordinances) of a true church,
wrote, "The fourth ordinance is evangelical separation, without which the congregation of God cannot
stand or be maintained."[27] For their separatist stand
they were roundly criticized by the leaders of the
Reformation.

Conrad Grebel, one of the Swiss Anabaptist
leaders, wrote in a letter in 1524:

Christ must suffer more in his members. . . . Our shepherds are so furious and
enraged against us that they rail at us from
the pulpit, calling us boys and Satans [dis-
guised as] angels of light. . . . Do not act,
teach, or set up anything according to
human notions, yours or that of others, and
that which is set up, abolish. Set up and
teach only the clear Word and rites of
God. . . .[28]

Conclusion

The Anabaptists made a great contribution to
the continuing separatist testimony. We recognize
their weaknesses (we have not tried to enumerate all
of these here). We also hail their strengths. In an age
when their doctrine of the church was most unpopular, they did not shrink from declaring it and practicing it. From their courageous example modern
separatists should derive encouragement.

Notes:

1. C. Norman Kraus, "Anabaptist Influence on English Separatism as Seen in Robert Browne," *The Mennonite Quarterly Review*, XXXIV (January 1960), 5.

2. Newman, *A Manual of Church History*, II, 149.

3. Ibid., II, 156ff.

4. H. S. B. Neff, "Felix Manz," *The Mennonite Encyclopedia*, III, 473.

5. Verduin, *The Anatomy of a Hybrid*, pp. 165, 166.

6. John Oyer, "The Writings of Melancthon Against the Anabaptists," *The Mennonite Quarterly Review*, XXVI (October 1952), 275.

7. Harold S. Bender, "The Anabaptist Vision," *The Recovery of the Anabaptist Vision*, ed. Guy Hershberger (Scottdale, PA: Herald Press, 1957), p. 41.

8. Westin, *The Free Church Through the Ages*, p. 57.

9. Harold S. Bender, "Church," *The Mennonite Encyclopedia*, I, 595.

10. See discussion on ecumenism in Franklin Littell, "The Free Churches and Ecumenism," *The Free Church* (Boston: Starr King Press, 1967), pp. 132-148.

11. Franklin Littell, *The Anabaptist View of the Church* (Boston: Starr King Press, 1958), p. 130.

12. Louis Berkhof, *History of Christian Doctrine* (Grand Rapids: Wm. B. Eerdmans Publishing Co., 1959), p. 243.

13. Ibid., p. 244.

14. E. H. Klotsche, *The History of Christian Doctrine* (Burlington, IA: The Lutheran Literary Board, 1945), p. 182.

15. Ibid., p. 187.

16. Erland Waltner, "The Anabaptist Conception of the Church," *The Mennonite Quarterly Review*, XXV (January 1951).

17. Claus Peter Clasen, *Anabaptism: A Social History, 1525-1618* (Ithaca, NY: Cornell University Press, 1972), p. 89.

18. John L. Ruth, *Conrad Grebel: Son of Zurich* (Scottdale, PA: Herald Press, 1975), p. 128.

19. Durnbaugh, *The Believers' Church*, p. 73.

20. Harold S. Bender, *Conrad Grebel* (Scottdale, PA: Herald Press, 1971), p. 211.

21. For a good discussion of this matter, see Frank Wray, "The Fall of the Church" in "History in the Eyes of the Sixteenth Century Anabaptists" (doctoral dissertation, Yale University, 1953), pp. 167-206.

22. Franke held this. See Sebastian Franke, "A Letter of John Campanus," *Spiritual and Anabaptist Writers*, ed. George H. Williams (Philadelphia: The Westminster Press, 1957), p. 149.

23. John Oyer, "The Reformers Oppose the Anabaptist Theology," *The Recovery of the Anabaptist Vision*, p. 206.

24. Menno Simons, *The Complete Writings of Menno Simons*, trans. Leonard Verduin, ed. John C. Wenger (Scottdale, PA: Herald Press, 1956), pp. 158, 159.

25. Littell, *The Anabaptist View of the Church*, p. 79.

26. John C. Wenger (ed.), "The Schleitheim Confession of Faith," Appendix III, *Glimpses of Mennonite History and Doctrine* (Scottdale, PA: Herald Press, 1940), p. 209.

27. Deitrich Philips, "The Church of God," *Spiritual and Anabaptist Writers*, p. 246.

28. John C. Wenger (trans.), *Conrad Grebel's Programmatic Letters of 1524* (Scottdale, PA: Herald Press, 1970), p. 41.

The Puritans and the Separatist Principle

4

MUCH OF the current debate over the question of separaton from an unsound church was foreshadowed in the rather spirited discussions that took place among the Puritans hundreds of years ago. While the Puritans agreed on some things, they disagreed on many others. One of their points of disagreement concerned the relationship they should sustain toward the Church of England. Before considering this, however, the discussions should be set in their historical perspective.

The Rise of Puritanism

Puritanism was a movement that began within the Church of England during the reign of Elizabeth I (1558-1603). A longing arose among some to reform the Church of England, the state church of the land. Bible study was encouraged, and regular Biblical preaching was practiced. As the Scriptures were perused, the dissatisfaction with some of the forms and ecclesiastical trappings of Anglicanism grew greater. There was controversy over the rituals of the church. Such items as vestments were called by some "the trappings of popery." Many Puritans felt that the prayer book was too Catholic. Actually, the name Puritan denoted a desire to purify the existing church and a commitment to purity of personal living as would befit a child of God. As the movement took hold, more and more issues came into focus: the supremacy of the Scriptures over human authority; the freedom of the church from the state; and the proper nature of church government.

Did those more radical Puritans who espoused a

separatist position obtain their ideas from the Anabaptists? Or, to ask it differently, to what extent were the separatist Puritans influenced by the Anabaptists? There is considerable debate about the matter. Some scholars have supported the idea that Robert Browne (separatist Puritan) was influenced by the Anabaptists.[1] Others maintain a contrary position.[2] Kraus, after a discussion of the matter, concludes that there was "a minimum of direct relationship" between Anabaptists and English Separatists.[3] As we shall see, however, some Puritans eventually made their way to an Anabaptist position.

Some Characteristics of Puritanism

The authority of the Scriptures.

The Puritans were people of the Book. They prized the Bible as "the only valid source from which doctrine, liturgy, church polity, and personal religion should be constructed."[4] They catechized their children, making them memorize long portions of Scripture in the process. Lengthy sermons, expounding passages and books of the Bible, were the regular fare in Puritan assemblies. Some of the interpretation was a bit fanciful and allegorical at times, but much was solid, doctrinal and Christ-honoring teaching.

Calvinistic theology.

Most Puritans were Calvinists. These had imbibed largely of the theology of the continental Reformer, John Calvin. "It [Calvinistic theology] largely dominated the thinking of the Church of England into the seventeenth century, forming the core of Puritan thought which was transplanted to New England."[5] (It should be noted, however, that a non-Calvinistic branch of Puritanism came to fruition in the General Baptists.)

Division over the nature of church government.

Some Puritans, while not approving all that went on in the established church, felt that the basic form of church government was acceptable. Others, such as Thomas Cartwright, Lady Margaret's professor of divinity at Cambridge, argued that the form of church government must be found in the Scriptures regardless of tradition. Episcopacy was not found there, he said. Presbyterianism was. And some Puritans came to the conviction of complete autonomy of local congregations. Such a concept was radical for the England of that day.

The Puritans emphasized personal piety. Much of the literature which they penned on the subject is still read with profit by believers today. They sought to cultivate a deep love for God and His Son, and to exhibit that love in personal devotion and daily good living. While the term *puritanical* is used in a negative connotation today, all who truly know the Lord can be thankful for the emphasis on individual holiness which characterized these people.

Personal godliness.

The Controversy over Separation

As Durnbaugh indicates, two groups arose within English Puritanism. The basic issue that divided them was the question of separation.

> ...Two factions had formed within Puritanism. The first was hopeful that a Church of England reformed after Biblical authority could be secured within the existing order.... The second party, convinced that obedience to Christ demanded "reformation without tarrying for any" (Browne), began to call for separation from the establishment.[6]

Many able men among the Puritans defended the position that one ought to remain within the Church of England.[7] What were some of their arguments? Even though unbelievers are present, a church can still be a true church of Christ, said this branch of Puritanism. While deploring the excesses and faults of the Church of England, they still maintained that she was a true church.

The "stay-in" reformers.

One of their principal arguments was that the truth had survived for centuries within the church and would continue to do so (reminiscent of Augustine's appeal to order and antiquity?).

> The problem of the non-separating reformers in England was to demonstrate that a strain of purity had survived and would continue to do so. To show that Christ's true church lived amidst the Antichristian degeneracy, they resorted to a history of church polity which had the pure Church surviving unseen within the impure.... They did so

out of a commitment to one of the oldest beliefs about Church history: the Church of Christ would survive to the end of the world.[8]

Believing as they did in the interrelationship of church and state, the nonseparating Puritans argued that through appeals to the civil power the church could be acceptably reformed. For many years they valiantly made an attempt to do this. In 1572 they drew up the "Admonition to Parliament." This first open manifesto of the Puritans said, in part:

> May it please your wysedomes to understand, we in England are so fare of, from having a church rightly reformed, according to the prescript of God's worde, that as yet we are not come to the outwarde face of the same.[9]

In the "Second Admonition to Parliament" (written by Cartwright), they complained, "And of all the greevous enormities laide upon this churche of God in England this is the greatest, that it is not lawful to utter that which we learn truely out of the scriptures."[10]

Both "stay-iner" and "come-outer" complained, but the differences were there.

> To the Puritan and Separatist alike, the Church as established was obnoxious on account of its abuses. But the one sought its reformation by an act of Parliament, looking forward to the time when his form of worship and discipline should be established for the nation. The other thought that a reformation would never come, that the whole system of a State Church was inherently wrong and that the only duty before the true believers was to leave the Church to its abuses, and to set up independent congregations.[11]

Those who sought to purify the church hoped, of course, that the impure could be driven out. This was why they felt they should remain inside. How could they have an influence for good, a reforming purge, unless they were an integral part of the organized body? Many reasoned as William Bradshaw, who felt that the "English church was substantially pure enough for them to remain in it in the expectation of finally extruding from it all but the pure."[12]

Besides this, to separate from the established church was an act of schism and therefore heretical. This attitude was brought to the New World by the majority of Puritans, and on both sides of the Atlantic the separatists were condemned by their brethren.[13]

Noble and good men contended that believers obedient to God should come out of the Church of England. In a moment we shall observe something of their growth and influence. However, it is vital at this point to mention some of the reasons given for such separation. Early separatists in England (around 1575) issued a defense of their position. They asked those who would stand with them to accept the truth of this statement:

The "come-out" separatists.

> Being thoroughly persuaded in my conscience, by the working and by the Word of the Almighty, that these relics of antichrist are abominable before the Lord our God. . . . Therefore I come not back again to the preaching of them that have received the marks of the Romish beast.[14]

Neal then discusses the reasons given for such separation. Here is a summary of them: (1) because God commands us to go unto perfection; (2) because idolatrous worship is an abomination to God; (3) because it is wrong to "communicate" with other men's sins; (4) because false teachers give offense; (5) because false teachers strengthen the papists and grieve the godly; (6) because they persecute Jesus Christ in the members of His Church; (7) because popish practices are idolatrous and take the place of the Bible; (8) because believers should separate from idolatry.[15]

It is evident from a perusal of the literature of the separatists that it was their desire to follow Scripture, and that they felt obedience to God's Word led them out of apostasy.

The Growth and Influence of the Separatist Puritans in England

Who were some of the men who advocated separation from the Church of England, and what were they like?

Leaders of the separatists.

Separatists were often called Brownists, a term of derision, after the name of the man usually looked upon as the first proponent of separatist principles, Robert Browne (c. 1553-1633). He attended Cambridge where he was influenced by Thomas Cartwright, noted Puritan leader. He began to preach in some English churches without the bishop's permission since he held that that authority for the ministry lay in local congregations, not in the bishopric. He and a friend organized local independent congregations around the Norwich area, and this brought about several imprisonments since it was contrary to ecclesiastical law. He and some of his followers finally moved to the Netherlands, where he pastored for several years. Unfortunately for the separatist cause, he later renounced some of his views, returned to England, and became sufficiently acceptable to the establishment so as to be ordained and serve as a pastor of one of their churches.

Browne was a somewhat unstable personality, and, of course, nonseparatists played upon this fact to discredit the entire separatist cause. Henry Dexter has a good study on Browne and an evaluation of his personality and ministry. He attributes many of his deviations (whether rightly or wrongly) to physical and mental weakness aggravated by the intense persecutions which he underwent.[16] Browne was the author of a famous treatise in which he set forth the separatist principles. Its full title was: *A Treatise Of Reformation without tarrying for anie, and of the wickedness of those Preachers which will not reforme till the Magistrate commande or compell them.* While Browne had his eccentricities, serious students should not judge the validity of the separatist position upon the character of one of its advocates, but rather upon its conformity with Scripture.

Amen

The pastor of the Pilgrim Fathers, John Robinson (c. 1575-1625), was a man of spiritual depth and balanced leadership. He was born in England and possibly attended Cambridge. Details of his early life are not clear. In the early 1600s he adopted Puritan views and joined a separatist congregation. He fled to Holland amid persecution and settled at Leyden. Many of the members of his church went with him, and they called and ordained him as their pastor. Robinson advocated Calvinistic views as over against the Arminians, and was also a strong supporter of the autonomy of the local church. While he urged the members of his flock to immigrate to the New World, he himself did not. However, his influence upon those who sailed on the *Mayflower* was great, and he made his imprint in the New World though never seeing it. One of the most moving Puritan documents is the farewell message which he gave before the *Mayflower* set sail.

In 1610 Robinson wrote *Justification for Separation*, in which he elaborated on the reasons for separating from the Church of England. One of his reasons was the fact that so many in the church were merely professors:

> But this I hold, that if iniquity be committed in the Church, and complaint, and proof accordingly made, and that the Church will not reform, or reject the party offending, but will on the cotrary maynteyn presumptuously, & abet such impiety, that then by abetting that party & his sin, she makes it her own by imputation, & enwrapps her self in the same guilt with the sinner. And remayning irreformable, eyther by such members of the same Ch:, as are faithful, (if there be any) or by other sister Churches, wypeth her self out the Lords Church-rowl, and now ceaseth to be any longer the true Church of Christ. And whatsoever truthes, or ordinances of Christ, this rebellious rowt still reteynes, it but vsurpes the same, without right vnto them, or promise of blessing vupon them, both the persons and sacrifices are abhominable vnto the Lord. Tit. 1:16; Prov. 21:27.[17]

Another graduate of Cambridge, Henry Barrowe (d. 1593), was influenced by his close friend, the separatist John Greenwood; and both men admired the writings of John Browne. Barrowe was imprisoned for selling seditious literature and aiding the cause of separatism. He was finally martyred. He was the author of several books, including *A Brief Discovery of the False Church*. In a controversy with Anglican divines over separation, he also produced the work entitled *A Brief Summe of the Causes of Our Separation*.

John Smyth, an English Cambridge graduate, was ordained and ministered in the Church of England, but he was dismissed from his post in a dispute over his preaching. He pastored a separatist congregation which moved to Amsterdam in 1607. He remained apart from existing separatist bodies because he held different views of the church, and he was in the process of adopting the view of believer's baptism. In 1608, finding no one whom he felt qualified to baptize him, he baptized himself (so-called "Se-baptism"), and then baptized others upon their confession of faith. (Thomas Helwys was included in this number.) John Smyth embraced Arminian views in his latter years, and he is now remembered as the father of the English General Baptists. Before his death he wrote an interesting book in which he made a plea for maintaining a proper spirit in the midst of controversy, and lamented his lack of the same in his earlier years.[18]

Principles of the separatists.

The leaders of the separatists were men of deep conviction, else it would have been impossible for them to have weathered the fiery trials through which they passed. Nor have the writings of later historians placed them in any better light. "Much as the Puritans have been vilified in history, their treatment has been mild compared with that which has been accorded to Separatists."[19]

The whole framework of separatist thought began with the belief that the Church of England was apostate. Robert Browne declared that "the Church of England was radically impure" and that it was the plain duty of true Christians "to gather themselves from its defilements into separate churches."[20] In correspondence with a friend, John Smyth thanked God that He had "brought us out of Babylon the mother of abominations."[21] Henry Barrowe felt the same.[22]

At least four reasons were given for denominating the Church of England as apostate and calling for separation: (1) the church included many wicked and profane persons; (2) its ministry was anti-Christian; (3) its worship was superstitious and idolatrous; (4) its government was Romish.

Having established their convictions regarding

the fact of the apostasy, the separatists went on to the logical and scriptural conclusion that true Christians could not remain within an apostate body and be honoring to God. They believed that there was a "clear command of God implicit in the New Testament to rise and rebuild."[23]

Dexter summarizes Browne's arguments as follows:

1. It is necessarily the first duty of every true Christian to endeavor the highest attainable purity of faith and life. . . .

2. The Church of England was inwardly corrupt, and outwardly so under subjection to an unscriptural hierarchy, that every true Christian ought to strive at once to obtain its reform, or failing that, to separate from it to follow Christ elsewhere.[24]

The whole question of the nature and extent of apostasy entered into the controversy. When is a church apostate? At what point should believers leave it (if they should)? It is the same issue which has reappeared through the history of the church. It is summarized thusly:

. . .Their chief difference was in their attitude to the Church of England as it then appeared. The Separatists believed that Canterbury was so defiled by Rome as to be a false Church; the Puritans believed that, while evidence showed the Church of England to be inadequately reformed, it was sufficiently reformed for it to be, or at least to become, a true Church. Once their contrasting judgments, arrived at on the basis of evidence, about which they were largely agreed, are appreciated, the contrasting policies of the two groups can be readily understood. Since they despaired of the "false" Church the Separatists believed in withdrawal and reform "without tarrying for any" while the Puritans of various shades of opinion, on the other hand, were prepared to recognize that the "true" Church in some measure appeared even in Elizabeth's ecclesiastical patchwork, and were prepared to wait, again with varying degrees of impatience, for further reformation imposed from above by the godly magistrate.[25]

Another important point of disagreement concerned the autonomy of the local congregation. In the Church of England no individual congregation was autonomous. They were interlocking under the episcopal system of church government. Separatists began to see that when congregations are tied together by some ecclesiastical bond other than a common faith it becomes increasingly difficult to practice scriptural separation. Barrowe in particular argued for the autonomy of each church. He declared that each church is independent of human control, should not be connected to the state, and should be free to worship God as it sees fit.[26]

Separatists saw in the New Testament the truth of a regenerate church membership. The congregation was a voluntary association of those who were truly born again. As did the Anabaptists, they rejected the concept of a church created by infant baptism and including all within a given locale.

Nonseparatists vigorously opposed the views of their brethren. They emphasized the presence of the true believers who were within the state church and minimized the presence of the false professors who were there. The presence of the true believers made it a valid church. As one has pointed out, the nonseparatist Puritans themselves were not completely consistent with their own views. "Thanks to their deft stratagems they were always prepared to protest that they were not Separatists, even at the very moment when they were erecting independent churches in England or gathering them on foreign shores."[27]

Then, as today, one of the favorite allegations made against the separatists was that they were "schismatics" and were rending the Body of Christ. Edwin Hall, in his interesting lectures on the Puritans, remonstrates with those who would call the separatists "schismatics."

We shall find there [in Scripture] no allusion to such thing as schism, consisting in breaking away from the domination of Popes, Councils, Prelates, or of the "Catholic" Church. The Word of God charges no schism upon those who follow simply the ordinances of the Lord Jesus Christ, and reject the mere ordinances and commandments of men. It does not forbid us to separate from false teachers, whatever be their official character; but, on the contrary, requires us to reject such a teacher, though he were an Apostle or an Angel from Heaven. The Schism of which the New Testament speaks is *internal dissension, within the bosom of the same Church.*[28]

Many separatist Puritans carried the newly discovered truths to conclusions which seemed to them proper and scriptural. Thus it was that the early English Baptist congregations were formed. John Smyth was the first to propound such conclusions "when he became convinced that the baptism of believers was the only true Christian baptism in spite of the chorus of shocked horror from his former friends as well as his acknowledged foes."[29]

Resultant Baptist congregations.

As many of the separatists pored over the Scriptures, it became increasingly clear that the doctrine of separation was entwined with the truth of believer's baptism. "It may be noted that Baptist roots lay within the Puritan Separatist movement."[30] They began to see that "true religion must be voluntary to be valid."[31]

John Smyth in his introduction to the book *The Character of the Beast* shows the logical conclusion to which he came:

Finally, they that defend the baptism of infants cannot with any truth or good conscience separate from England as from a false Church, though they may separate for corruptions. And they that separate from a false Church must of necessity separate from the baptism of England and account the baptism of infants false baptism. Therefore, the Separation must either go back to England or go forward to true baptism; and all that shall in time come to separate from England must separate from the baptism of England, and if they will not separate from the baptism of England there is no reason why they should separate from England as from a false Church. . . .[32]

In other words, Smyth said the baptism of the Church of England is a part and parcel of its falseness, its unscriptural character. Separation from it requires separation from all that is false within it, including its baptism. (It should be noted, however, that many separatist leaders, while maintaining complete official separation, did allow for personal Christian fellowship with those remaining within the apostasy.)

In concluding our discussion of the Puritans and separatism, let us contemplate the problem as set forth in one of their own statements "A True Confession," drawn up in 1596. Excerpts from it read as follows:

> 29. That the present ministerie reteyned & vsed in Englad . . . are a strange & Antichristian ministerie & offices; & are not that ministerie aboue named instituted in Christs Testament, or allovved in or ouer his Church. . . .

> 31. That these Ecclesiasticall Assemblies, remayning in confusion and bondage vnder this Antichristian Ministerie . . . neither can bee in this estate, (whilest wee iudge them by the rules of Gods word) esteemed the true, orderly gathered, or costituted churches of Christ. . . .

> 32. That by Gods Commandment all that will bee saued, must vvith speed come forth of this Antichristian estate. . . .

> 33. That beeing come forth of this antichristian estate vnto the freedom and true profession of Christ, . . . they are vvillingly to ioyne together in christian communion and orderly couenant, and by confession of Faith and obedience of Christ, to vnite themselues into peculiar Congregatios. . . .[33]

Separatism in the New World

The English colonists. Thousands of Puritans emigrated to New England under the reign of Charles I of England (1625-1649). They first settled in Massachusetts. In early days they claimed to be loyal churchmen and talked of the dear "mother church" of England (Church of England). However, their remoteness from England, plus the influence of the Pilgrims who landed at Plymouth in 1640, gradually brought them into a more separatist position.

An early separatist in the colonies was a man

now chiefly remembered for his strong denunciation of church-state relationships and his advocacy of the complete separation of the two: Roger Williams. In some of his spirited pamphlet exchanges with John Cotton, he occasionally referred to the separatist principle. In one letter he deals with the question of church membership:

> Secondly, I aske, Whether it be not absolutely necessary to his uniting with the true Church, that is with Christ in true Christian Worship, that he see and bewaile, and absolutely come out from that false Church or Christ, and his Ministrie, Worship, etc. before he can be united to the true Israel, must come forth of Egypt before they can sacrifice to God in the wilderness.[34]

In another he declares that the people of God are "Nazarites" who are "separated unto Him" and, as a result, they "ought to touch no uncleanness" and should "separate from Religious Idolatry. . . ."[35] After migrating to Boston, he was offered a position as a teacher, but he refused because the church was not separated from the Church of England.

As the Congregational churches multiplied in the New England states, laxness, compromise and spiritual coldness began to develop. The Halfway Covenant was adopted in 1662. This, basically, was an effort to placate those persons who did not have a clear experience of salvation themselves, but who wanted their children baptized and received into a church fellowship. It brought into the churches more and more unsaved members. The churches became more and more lax. More authority was placed into the hands of the clergy (through the Saybrook Platform passed in 1708). The combination of lowered standards for church membership plus increasing denominational hierarchy spelled nothing but trouble for the Congregational churches of the day.

The Great Awakening

About 1700 Increase Mather wrote:

> If the begun apostasy shall proceed as fast in the next thirty years as it has done these last, surely it will come to pass that in New England . . . the most conscientious people

therein will think themselves concerned to gather churches out of churches.[36]

Little did Mather know how accurate his prediction was. In 1733 a tremendous spiritual revival began which swept through New England under the preaching of Jonathan Edwards, George Whitefield and others. It is called the Great Awakening. The individuals who were saved and the congregations that were revived during this time became thoroughly dissatisfied with the established religion of the colonies as found particularly in the staid Congregational churches. These New Lights (as they were popularly called) began to separate from the old-line denomination and to form new congregations. They became known as Separates or Strict Congregationalists. They wanted a more evangelistic ministry (though within the theological framework of sovereign grace which they emphasized). They contended for stricter requirements for church membership, limiting such membership only to those who had a personal experience with Christ. They stood for the practice of church discipline in order to maintain purity of the congregation. They also believed that truly saved persons should possess the assurance of their salvation.

It can be readily seen by the brief description above that these separatists (or Separates) shared basic convictions with other separatist bodies already studied. They felt they were merely returning to the original concept of the church which the earlier Puritans had had before 'spiritual decline had set in. One of the chief apologists for the Separates was Ebenezer Frothingham (1719-1798), who wrote a major work entitled *The Articles of Faith and Practice*. Among other things, he sought to answer the objections raised against the Separates. They sound very familiar: (1) separatism splits churches; (2) good and learned men repudiate separatism; (3) disorder and confusion among the churches results from separatism; (4) separatists have an uncharitable, un-Christian spirit.[37]

The Separate Baptists. One of the problems the Strict Congregationalists or Separates had to face was the matter of baptism. Repudiating as they were the concept of a

church composed of a "mixed multitude," and es-
pousing strongly the Biblical concept of a regenerate
church, what should they do about the question of
infant baptism? So potent was the issue that, after
studying it, considerable numbers of Congregationalists became Baptists. They received the name
Separate Baptists.

> "Gone to the Baptists" is a frequent entry
> in the record books of the Separate churches
> beside the names of former members who
> had adopted the principle of believer's, as
> opposed to infant's baptism. Few Separate
> consciences escaped turmoil over this point,
> and as a result their churches earned the
> epithet, "nurseries of baptists."[38]

The great preacher and theologian Jonathan
Edwards wrestled with this question. He came to see
the necessity of a pure church composed of regenerate people, but he wavered on the implementation of
it, largely because he clung to the concept of infant
baptism.

> All of the Separates agreed with Edwards
> at the point of insisting on experimental
> faith as a term of communion in the visible
> church. . . . Those who adopted Baptist
> views, however, regarded his position on
> baptism as groundless sophistry, and deter-
> mined that if the fruits of the new reforma-
> tion [Great Awakening] were to be preserved
> it must be done by a strict adherence to the
> concept of the gathered church. Isacc Backus
> wrote that the great tragedy of the whole
> Awakening had been that many of its con-
> verts flocked into churches "very much
> blended with the world," and did not see
> that infant baptism was the root of the evil
> which had deadened them in the first
> place.[39]

The Separate Baptists spread to the south under
the ministry of Shubal Stearns (1706-1771) and
Daniel Marshall (1706-1784). Great blessing attended their witness in Virginia, the Carolinas and
other places. Through mergers with other Baptist
groups, their distinctive existence was finally lost;
but the lessons gained from their activities are retained for those who will receive them.

This brief look at separatism and Puritanism

should serve to remind students, among other things, that separatists, keen as they are on doctrinal commitment and ecclesiastical purity, can fall victim to spiritual lethargy. Thus they can lose the very distinctives which originally brought them into existence. They can become so spiritually lifeless that some future generation will of necessity separate from them.

Notes:

1. Ernest Troeltsch, *The Social Teaching of the Christian Churches* (New York: Macmillan, 1949), II, 661-664.

2. Williston Walker, *A History of the Christian Church* (New York: Scribner's, 1947), pp. 461, 462.

3. Kraus, "Anabaptist Influence . . . as seen in Robert Browne."

4. Peter Toon, "Puritans; Puritanism," *The New International Dictionary of the Christian Church*, p. 815.

5. W. S. Reid, "Calvinism," *The New International Dictionary of the Christian Church*, p. 181.

6. Durnbaugh, *The Believers' Church*, p. 95.

7. Some books defending the "stay-in" concept were: Henry Jacob, *A Defence of the Churches and Ministry of England* (1599); John Paget, *An Arrow Against the Separatism of the Brownists* (1618); John Cotton, *The Way of the Congregational Churches Cleared*; Thomas Hooker, *A Survey of the Summe of Church Discipline*.

8. Robert Middlekauff, *The Mathers* (New York: Oxford University Press, 1971), p. 43.

9. Walter Freve and Charles Douglas (eds.), *Puritan Manifestoes* (London: SPCK, 1954), p. 9.

10. Ibid., p. 93.

11. Douglas Campbell, *The Puritans in Holland, England, and America* (New York: Harper Brothers, 1892), II, 181, 182.

12. William Haller, *The Rise of Puritanism* (New York: Harper and Row, 1938), 192.

13. Larger Ziff (ed.), *John Cotton on the Churches of New England* (Cambridge, MA: Harvard University Press, 1968), p. 3.

14. Daniel Neal, *The History of the Puritans* (New York: Harper Brothers, 1843), I, 132.

15. Ibid.

16. Henry Martyn Dexter, *The Congregationalism of the Last Three Hundred Years* (New York: Burt Franklin, 1970), I, 119ff.

17. John Robinson, *Justification for Separation* quoted by Dexter, *The Congregationalism of the Last Three Hundred Years*, I, 393.

18. The title of his work: *The Last Book of John Smyth Called the Retraction of His Errours, and the Confirmation of the Truth*.

19. Campbell, *The Puritans in Holland, England, and America*, II, 177.

20. Dexter, *The Congregationalism of the Last Three Hundred Years*, I, 104.

21. Champlin Burrage, *The Early English Dissenters* (New York: Russell and Russell, 1912), II, 172.

22. Barrington R. White, *The English Separatist Tradition* (London: Oxford University Press, 1971), p. 76.

23. Ibid., p. 74.

24. Dexter, *The Congregationalism of the Last Three Hundred Years*, I, 98, 99.

25. White, *The English Separatist Tradition*, p. 33.

26. Barrowe's work was entitled *A True Description of the Visible Congregation of the Saints*.

27. Perry Miller, *Orthodoxy in Massachusetts: 1630-1650* (Gloucester, MA: Peter Smith, 1965), p. 92.

28. Edwin Hall, *The Puritans and Their Principles* (New York: Baker and Scribner, 1846), p. 279.

29. White, *The English Separatist Tradition*, p. 116.

30. Robert Torbet, *A History of the Baptists* (Valley Forge, PA: Judson Press, 1973), p. 54.

31. Ibid., p. 57.

32. John Smyth, "Introduction to *The Character of the Beast*," *The Baptist Treasury*, comp. and ed. Sydnor Stealey (New York: Thomas Crowell Co., 1958), p. 5.

33. William L. Lumpkin (ed.), "A True Confession," *Baptist Confessions of Faith* (Philadelphia: Judson Press, 1959), pp. 90-92.

34. Roger Williams, "Mr. Cotton's Letter, Lately Printed, Examined and Answered," *The Complete Writings of Roger Williams* (New York: Russell and Russell, 1963), I, 354.

35. Roger Williams, "The Examiner Defended in a Fair and Sober Answer," *The Complete Writings of Roger Williams*, VII, 252.

36. Newman, *A Manual of Church History*, II, 675.

37. Ebenezer Frothingham, *The Articles of Faith and Practice* . . . (Newport, CT: no publisher given, 1750), pp. 100ff.

38. C. C. Goen, *Revivalism and Separatism in New England: 1740-1800* (New Haven, CT: Yale University Press, 1962), p. 208.

39. Ibid., p. 210.

The Rise and Impact of Modern Religious Unbelief

5

EVEN WHILE the Puritan theology was at its height, forces were at work which were to spell its demise as a leading system of thought. The Puritans (non-separatist and separatist) brought their beliefs to the New World and were, in large measure, responsible for laying the foundations of the United States. The seventeenth and eighteenth centuries, however, witnessed the beginnings and growth of systems of thought which were antithetical to Biblical Christianity and to that for which the Puritans and Pilgrims stood. Gradually these ideas began to dominate, particularly in some institutions of higher learning, and "modern religious liberalism" (modernism) was born. As a result, a tremendous religious conflict arose between those who accepted the Bible as absolute authority, as did the Puritans, and those who did not.

The Roots of Modern Religious Liberalism

Many tributaries helped to form the great stream of religious liberalism—in particular, English deism, French naturalism and German rationalism. These schools of thought rose to prominence in the seventeenth and eighteenth centuries. Our concern is to mention a few of the leading concepts—those which had an influence on the rise of modern religious unbelief (i.e., the denial of historical, orthodox Christianity)—of these philosophical systems.

The Bible presents a faith which, while not irrational, is not the product of human reason, nor sustained by it. John Locke (1632-1704), an English

Preeminence of human reason.

thinker, contested this. Locke declared that Christianity must be acceptable to human reason. The truths of divine revelation must be believable, that is, rational according to human standards. This emphasis became more and more noticeable in religious circles as the writings of Locke and others like him began to have circulation and acceptance. The supernatural and the miraculous were rejected by professed proponents of the Christian faith. If it was not believable and explainable, it was not valid.

Religion— a natural development, not a supernatural revelation.

Perhaps no one man was more vitriolic in his denunciation of Christianity than Francois Marie Arouet whom we better know as Voltaire (1694-1788). Voltaire totally rejected the unique origin of the Christian faith. He said it could be explained on purely natural grounds. Religion, said he, arose out of the ignorance and fear of primitive peoples and was in no wise a revelation from a personal, all-wise God. He undertook to find analogies between Christianity and other world religions, thereby aiming to discredit Christianity as a distinctive system of thought coming from God. Voltaire's concepts became popular. In later years courses on "Comparative Religions" were introduced into the curriculum of many colleges and universities. Students were taught that each religion had its good points and that the Christian faith was not to be thought of as anything unique, but simply embodying, for the most part, concepts to be found in other religions of the world.

The ability of man.

One of the greatest philosophers who contributed much to the rise of modern unbelief was a German named Immanuel Kant (1724-1804). Among other things, Kant emphasized the innate ability of man. This was expressed in his well-known maxim, "We ought; therefore we can." In other words, "If I am supposed to do it, I have the ability to do it." Kant underscored the moral precepts of Christianity, but he did not have a supernatural gospel by which men could implement these precepts. Obviously, he did not accept the scriptural doctrine of total depravity and inability. He saw man as a creature able to do right if he would. He also taught that God cannot be truly known, and this concept had a great influence on following generations of theologians.

One man is especially noted for his emphasis upon religious experience—Friedrich Schleiermacher (1768-1834). To him religion was basically a feeling of dependence upon God; it was an inner experience. The more intense these feelings are, the more religious a person is. Doctrinal matters and formulated theology are of little importance. It is the joy of "experiencing God" which is at the heart of Christianity. The influence of Schleiermacher was great, and this strand was an important one in the total tapestry of the old modernism (liberalism). Believing this, one can reject cardinal doctrines of the faith as objectively revealed in Scripture and still be a very "religious" person, loving and enjoying God.

The essence of religion is the inner consciousness of God.

Orthodox Christianity believes that the Christian faith was delivered by God to His people and that it is fixed and stable. Modern views of theology, however, are quite different, and many of them have been influenced by Georg Hegel (1770-1831). Hegel was a pantheist and did not believe in a personal, omnipotent God such as the Bible presents. For him, God was constantly changing; thus there were no absolutes. His philosophy was the evolutionary concept applied to theology. We have no final word from God. We have no fixed and authoritative faith, but one that is constantly developing. This approach naturally appealed to the minds of men and was particularly popular, coming as it did at a time when men were looking at the entire universe as a gradually developing entity which had no personal Creator nor any personal Director.

The continuous change and development of theology.

Men and women who imbibe such concepts as these could not possibly accept the Bible as divinely inspired and authoritative. During the period of time under discussion, a radical and unbelieving approach to higher criticism had developed. (Higher criticism is the study of the authorship, purpose, date and occasion of writing of Bible books. It can be a legitimate pursuit, but when utilized by unbelieving, anti-supernatural minds, it can be devastating.

A humanistic view of the Bible.

So it was in these centuries.) The Bible was viewed as a merely human book and was treated as any other piece of literature. The critics did not appreciate its uniqueness and, as a result, popularized the idea that it was full of errors, both scientific and otherwise.

These are some of the ideas that were spawned by men who were "by nature the children of wrath" (Eph. 2:3). They were eagerly received by many others whose minds were in spiritual darkness as well.

Modern Unitarianism

About the same time as the rationalistic philosophers began promulgating their anti-Christian theories, another very devastating system of thought arose. It was destined to have a considerable impact upon religious life and thought, particularly in England and the United States. It was known as Unitarianism, so named because it was the opposite of Trinitarianism, the orthodox and Biblical position. A Unitarian denied the doctrine of the Trinity and, as a result, the deity of the Lord Jesus Christ.

The beginnings of Unitarianism are usually traced to John Biddle (1615-1662), an Englishman. The first actual Unitarian congregation on record, however, was not organized until 1774 in England.

Unitarianism began developing in America among the Congregational churches of New England in the late 1700s. Since it bears upon the general subject of apostasy and separation which we are studying, it would be well to ask the question, How did it begin? Is it not strange that a system such as Unitarianism would spring up among the churches which were founded by the Puritans? An author friendly to Unitarianism has a startling answer. *It began because of a mood of compromise.* In the introduction to his volume which describes the great Unitarian leaders, he writes, ". . . They loved to emphasize the points of agreement rather than the points of difference. They were willing to make concessions for the sake of the peace of the churches."[1] Obviously they found persons in the more orthodox churches who bought their affable and winsome approach and did not recognize the venomous poison hidden in the outstretched hand. We could well beware of those who make unwarranted concessions, ostensibly to gain the "peace of the churches."

Some locate the roots of Unitarianism in America in that system known as Arminianism. One says that Arminianism was "democracy in religion" and its essence was faith in man and the declaration of human equality and liberty. Arminianism, according to Cooke, was "the theological expression of the democratic spirit, as Calvinism was of the autocratic."[2]

Once started, how did Unitarianism make such spectacular progress? Was it not immediately spotted for what it was and denounced by orthodox leaders? In a most interesting chapter, "The Silent Advance of Liberalism," Cooke seeks to answer that question also.

> The progressive tendencies went silently on, and step by step the old beliefs were discarded, but always by individuals and churches and not by associations or general official action. . . . Something of this tendency was also due to the spirit of free inquiry and the rational interpretation of religion that were beginning to make themselves felt. . . .[3]

Unitarian proponents point with pride to the fact that Unitarianism arose in New England without an open fuss (until it was already entrenched). Many churches became Unitarian instead of Trinitarian and "crossed the boundary without knowing it."[4] In many churches "there was not even any debate over theological changes. It was a natural, peaceful evolution."[5]

By the time any public and official notice was taken of Unitarianism, it was too late to stem the tide of its advance. Henry Ware, a Unitarian, was appointed Hollis Professor of Theology at Harvard University in 1805. This open move finally galvanized some conservatives into action, and there was a struggle. The opponents of the appointment of Ware lost, but their reasons for opposing him were published by Jedediah Morse. It was this action that precipitated a public controversy which lasted for a number of years. While it eventually brought about the separation of the Unitarians as a distinct body from the Congregationalists, it did not undo the tragic results which had come from years of Unitarian teaching in the churches. The American Unitarian Association was finally formed in 1825. One of the leaders of New England Unitarianism was the popular and able William Ellery Channing (1780-1842), pastor of the Federal Street Church of Boston.

Modern Religious Liberalism Challenges Orthodoxy

The second half of the nineteenth century saw a rapid coalescing of the forces already described plus others which appeared. No dramatic change in the outward face of church life was immediately visible. It was more subtle and gradual. Charles Darwin's *The Origin of Species* appeared in 1859, and the thoughts expressed in it caught the imagination of the scientific community. Darwin's later book, *The Descent of Man*, was even more controversial and openly challenged the Genesis account of man's creation.

In both America and Europe, religious liberals began to write and speak more openly. An effort was made on the part of some to make the new intellectualism respectable by calling it "evangelical liberalism" or something of the sort. The early part of the twentieth century saw the rise of Horace Bushnell with his evolutionary view of Christian education in which he denied the necessity of the new birth. Men such as Washington Gladden, Phillips Brooks and Shailer Mathews emphasized the social aspects of religion and denied the great fundamental doctrines of the faith. All of these had been influenced in either subtle or more open ways by the many humanistic and evolutionary patterns of thought that were prevalent. Not only was this true in America but in Britain as well. It was actually in England that one of the earliest and most notable challenges was raised to the encroachments of modernism by one of the great separatists of all time— Charles Haddon Spurgeon.

The Issue of Separation
in the Down Grade Controversy
of England

Because it illustrates so well important principles and serves as a hallmark in the conflict between inclusivism and separatism, let us look more closely at the famous Down Grade controversy.

Religious liberalism began gradually and increased in strength as the eighteenth century progressed. A liberal spirit was abroad in society in general which had its effect within the religious community. The Bible was no longer looked upon as an authoritative book, the final revelation from God. Man was not hopeless in his sin, but was progressing little by little upward. The doctrine of an eternal Hell was denied by many, a number of whom were thought of as respectable evangelical scholars (such as R. W. Dale). The leaven of unbelief crept steadily into more and more pulpits of most of the denominations without much ballyhoo.

The issues.

The first public challenge to the hitherto surreptitious spread of heterodox teaching was among the Baptists. Liberalism was present among the Baptists of the British Isles, but it was covered over by professions of loyalty to the evangelical faith and not publicly debated. Charles Spurgeon, pastor of the largest Baptist church in the world at that time— Metropolitan Tabernacle in London, was not easily fooled by outward appearances, however. Not only was he a great preacher, but he possessed a deep understanding of doctrine and a strong commitment to the old-fashioned faith of the apostles. It was his growing uneasiness about the "downgrade" trend of some of his Baptist brethren that precipitated the controversy that bears that name. They were going "downgrade" in the sense that they were departing from the "higher ground" of faith in the inspired Word of God and the fundamental doctrines therein presented. They were accepting lower, more humanistic views of Scripture.

In March and April of 1887, two articles were published in Spurgeon's paper, *The Sword and Trowel*. The articles dealt with the presence of

The controversy itself.

liberalism and warned of its dangers. In subsequent issues Spurgeon came even closer to home and expressed his concern about liberalism within the Baptist camp. This specific attack was the spark which ignited the controversy in the Baptist Union (the association of Baptist churches in the British Isles).

Perhaps the major issue (at least *a* major one) was the nature of Biblical inspiration. As is always true, lowered or weakened views of Biblical inspiration finally result in weakened views in other areas of theological thought. Spurgeon declared that some Baptist ministers held incorrect views of doctrine because they did not accept the complete inspiration of Scripture.

> The charges of Spurgeon put his evangelical contemporaries into a difficult position. It was impossible to deny that eternal punishment was no longer held by many evangelicals. On the other hand, they sincerely felt that the evangelical faith was held in all essentials as strongly as ever. That was the question: What are the essentials? Spurgeon saw very clearly that inspiration in its traditional sense meant inerrancy. To talk about the divine inspiration of an erring record was to use the term in an entirely different sense, and this simply bred confusion. But other evangelicals preferred to be confused.[6]

Well-known men such as the great pulpiteer Joseph Parker were not clearly committed to an inerrant Scripture. The Baptist Union itself was of such a nature that "free spirits" could exist within it happily. One of Spurgeon's biographers describes it:

> The Baptist Union was composed of Baptists and Congregationalists and was a very free and liberal organization which did not attempt to hold any person very strictly to doctrine or creed. Yet many of the strongest preachers in the Baptist denomination in and about London were members of that Association. In the membership there were also a number of pastors who taught in their pulpits some of the modern ideas of science—so called—and who advocated the theories of the higher criticism and a more liberal and loose construction of the old Testament records.[7]

In order to "smoke out" those who were hiding within the fellowship of the Baptist Union, Spurgeon wanted the Union to draw up a doctrinal platform similar to that which the Evangelical Alliance had in those days. However, there was strong resistance to this. Questions were raised of the violation of Baptist liberty, but one wonders in viewing the scene in perspective if this was not a calculated method of covering up the orthodox beliefs of men who did not want them too openly exposed. Similar arguments were raised in later years when fundamentalists prodded the old Northern Baptist Convention toward a more definite doctrinal commitment but without success. Liberals and their defenders are ever the foes of clear doctrinal statements. Spurgeon pinpointed an issue which people have grappled with for centuries:

> It now becomes a serious question how far those who abide by the faith once delivered to the saints should fraternize with those who have turned aside to another gospel. Christian love has its claims, and divisions are to be shunned as grievous evils; but how far are we justified in being in confederacy with those who are departing from the truth?[8]

In October 1887, Spurgeon announced his withdrawal from the Baptist Union. He could no longer fellowship where unbelief was tolerated. His reasons were more fully stated in *The Sword and Trowel*:

> Believers in Christ's atonement are now in declared union with those who make light of it; believers in Holy Scripture are in confederacy with those who deny plenary inspiration; those who hold evangelical doctrine are in open alliance with those who call the fall a fable, who deny the personality of the Holy Ghost, who call justification by faith immoral, and hold that there is another probation after death. . . . Yes, we have before us the wretched spectacle of professedly orthodox Christians publicly avowing their union with those who deny the faith, and scarcely concealing their contempt for those who cannot be guilty of such gross disloyalty to Christ. To be very plain, we are unable to call these Christian Unions, they begin to look like Confederacies in Evil. . . .

It is our solemn conviction that where there can be no real spiritual communion there should be no pretence of fellowship. *Fellowship with known and vital error is participation in sin.*[9]

Perhaps no concise statement better expresses the convictions of separatists in all ages than the last sentence just quoted from Spurgeon. This is the heart of the matter.

Spurgeon lived in an era which was witnessing profound changes in society in general and in the religious world. Not all were as perceptive and far-seeing as Spurgeon in analyzing the current situation and its implications for the future. Many of his contemporaries and not a few later observers have asked the question, Was Spurgeon right in separating from the Baptist Union? Naturally one's answer will reflect one's theological and ecclesiastical perspective. Glover says:

Spurgeon's insight into the religious life of his own times was proved by subsequent events. He *did* stand on the eve of a great evangelical depression, and unquestionably the theological confusion of his day and the disturbance to the religious traditions wrought by higher criticism had a great deal to do with the decline of evangelicalism.[10]

Though leaders in the Baptist Union professed loyalty to the faith, Spurgeon's instincts proved to be absolutely accurate in the matter of encroaching apostasy. Only thirty-eight years later an out-and-out liberal was elected to the highest office of the Baptist Union.

The tide which Spurgeon sought in vain to stem swept steadily outward. The tolerance of advanced views in the Baptist churches reached its climax in 1925 when, . . . Dr. T. Reaveley Glover was elected to the presidency of their Union. The event was a landmark in the progress of Modernism in Dissent. . . .[11]

The withdrawal of Spurgeon made it necessary for the officials of the Baptist Union to do something. One of the world's leading Baptist preachers had withdrawn from fellowship with his own denomination. Why? The question was naturally asked by many. After several meetings of the leaders of the

Union to discuss the problem, a public gathering of the Union was announced. Amidst great fanfare (the auditorium was crowded), they met and passed what amounted to a censure of Spurgeon by a large—almost unanimous—majority.

What an unusual meeting it was! The motion was made by an outspoken advocate of modernism, Charles Williams, who, in making the motion, declared that he felt it represented a vindication for liberal theology and a repudiation of Spurgeon's position. Oddly enough, the motion was seconded by none other than James Spurgeon, Charles's brother (who did not withdraw from the Union with his brother). James's part in the controversy is not always clear, and his motivations and position are confused. History records only seven votes against the motion and about two thousand in favor. The resolution was clearly understood as one censuring Mr. Spurgeon, though it was not officially worded in that fashion. A firsthand account of the meeting by Henry Oakley is most instructive and heart-sickening:

> "I was present at the City Temple . . . when the motion was moved, seconded, and carried. . . . I listened to the speeches. The only one of which I have any distinct remembrance was that of Mr. Charles Williams. He quoted Tennyson in favour of a liberal theology and in justification of doubt. The moment of voting came. Only those in the area were qualified to vote as members of the assembly. When the motion of censure was put a forest of hands went up. 'Against,' called the chairman, Dr. Clifford. I did not see any hands, but history records that there were seven. Without any announcement of numbers the vast assembly broke into tumultuous cheering, and cheering and cheering yet. From some of the older men their pent-up hostility found vent; from many of the younger men wild resistance of 'any obscurantist trammels,' as they said, broke loose. It was a strange scene. I viewed it almost with tears. I stood near a 'Spurgeon's man,' whom I knew very well. Mr. Spurgeon had welcomed him from a very lowly position. He went almost wild with delight at this censure of his great and generous master. I say it was a strange scene, that that vast assembly should be so outrageously de-

lighted at the condemnation of the greatest, noblest, and grandest leader of their faith."[12]

Need we say it? It is this kind of price that many men cannot pay. Far too many want to profess the faith of Spurgeon without undergoing the agony of Spurgeon. Therefore, they rationalize their ungodly allegiances and remain with the crowd. It has always been so and will continue to be until the end of time.

And what was the doctrinal confession so roundly cheered? It was brief and fuzzy, which was the purposeful desire of its creators. It presented six doctrines which were said to be "commonly held among the churches of the Union." These were: (1) the divine inspiration and authority of Holy Scriptures; (2) the fallen and sinful state of man; (3) the person and work of Jesus Christ; (4) justification by faith; (5) the work of the Holy Spirit; and (6) the resurrection and judgment at the Last Day, "according to the words of our Lord in Matthew 25:46." To this last statement was appended a note which was written to cover the presence of those who denied an eternal Hell, and which illustrates more clearly than any comments the tragic situation into which the Union had fallen. The explanatory note read:

> It should be stated, as an historical fact, that there have been brethren in the Union, working cordially with it, who, while reverently bowing to the authority of Holy Scripture . . . have not held the common interpretation of these words of our Lord.[13]

The statement was neither definitive nor binding. Many within the Union could have been the "uncommon" who did not hold the things stated to be "commonly held." It would make no difference. They were not required to hold any particular doctrines. The statement was a farce and proved only what Charles Spurgeon had been saying all along: there was a mixed multitude within the Union.

Lessons to be learned. How was it that men who claimed (and in many cases actually did possess) belief in the orthodox doctrines of the faith stood against a man who was defending them? Certainly one great lesson leaps out from the study of this controversy. *The spirit of accommodation can lead to compromise on vital is-*

sues. Very often, doctrinal aberrations are born in a *mood* which eventually develops into a more tangible expression, given the right conditions.

The spirit of accommodation is perhaps no better illustrated than in the life and ministry of the man who was the main leader of the Baptist Union at the time of the Down Grade controversy. We refer to John Clifford, who at that time was the vice-president of the Union. Because of the frequent absences of the president, Clifford was, in reality, the leader. He chaired the meeting just described. Who was he? What did he believe? What influence did he have?

John Clifford represented the opposite pole from Spurgeon within the Baptist Union. He pastored for the larger portion of his life at Praed Street Chapel, Paddington (later the congregation moved to Westbourne Park). He possessed great oratorical abilities and was of the more liberal, social-action variety of pastor. He was liberal in political views. He had such an interest in this, he was frequently urged to run for Parliament. He was a leader among the General (Arminian) Baptists who were a part of the Baptist Union.

Clifford had quite early given up belief in the inerrancy of Scripture. He was part of the "Broad School" nonconformists, "broad" in the sense that they defied theological restrictions and opened their minds to a wide variety of theological views. Clifford was persuaded that "his liberal—not to say lax—interpretation of Evangelicalism was the truth of God. It is in this fact that the explanation of much that would otherwise be wholly obscure is to be found."[14] Within the councils of the Baptists of that day he had considerable influence, and his winning personality and apparent largeness of spirit swayed many in his favor.

> He brought to their discussions the widest tolerance of the views against which Spurgeon protested; they were to him no more than the necessary "adjustment of theological belief." His ideas of doctrinal soundness were so flexible and so optimistic that at the very moment when Modernism was daily increasing its hold of the Baptist ministry he declared that in his opinion it was "sounder

than it had been for the last twenty or thirty years."[15]

Another writer reinforces this impression, when he says of John Clifford:

> He did not believe that what the conservatives called "Modern Thought" was undermining the faith once for all delivered to the saints, but he made it his business to bring it into captivity to Christ. For him, theology was a progressive science. . . . Clifford's attitude was that the acceptance of new light and knowledge was perfectly consistent with loyalty to Christ. . . . An ardent evangelical, he thus exercised a liberalizing influence upon the denomination.[16]

Clifford's tremendous influence, brought to bear in private meetings and personal encounters with the Baptists of his day, was most clearly illustrated in the meeting earlier described in which the position of Spurgeon was repudiated. ". . .The famous Resolution in which the crowded assembly declared, by two thousand votes to seven, that the Baptist body was Evangelical to the core was the triumph of his ability to impose his delusion upon others."[17] Clifford and others were not unaware of the defections from the faith, though they made much of the fact that Spurgeon would not document his charges and name the offenders. Some of them were the chief offenders.

> Clifford and his supporters (Alexander Maclaren and Charles Williams) were in a difficult position. They had themselves rejected the doctrine of the inerrancy of the Scriptures and were well aware that one distinguished Baptist minister, Samuel Cox, had made himself one of the best-known and ablest exponents of universal restoration.[18]

Something else can be learned from this heartrending tragedy. Denominational loyalty can undermine one's loyalty to Christ. That is ever a danger facing God's people. Many, if not most, of the Baptists of Spurgeon's day held convictions very similar to his. They, however, were so loyal to the Baptist Union that they were blinded to what was going on around them. Spurgeon observed what others have seen in succeeding generations:

Brethren who have been officials of a denomination have a paternal partiality about them which is so natural, and so sacred, that we have not the heart to censure it. Above all things, these prudent brethren feel bound to preserve the prestige of "the body," and the peace of the committee. Our Unions, Boards, and Associations are so justly dear to the fathers that quite unconsciously and innocently, they grow oblivious of evils which are as manifest as the sun in the heavens.[19]

The problem to which Spurgeon referred has been a recurring one over the centuries. "Stay-iners" in whatever age are generally quite concerned over the "peace of Zion," the retention of the status quo and the preservation of denominational ties. Separatists tend to be more concerned about doctrinal correctness, loyalty to the truth and the preservation of a pure witness regardless of denominational groupings. (This is not to say that separatists have no problems in this area. In a later chapter these will be discussed.)

Why did not the Council of the Baptist Union and the Union itself take more appropriate action? Influences were abroad which militated against that, as has already been discussed. Glover has analyzed the matter:

It was Spurgeon's resignation that first brought the issues of the Down-Grade controversy officially before the Council of the Baptist Union. They had to consider the reasons for his resignation. The Council was in a difficult position. They were not prepared to admit the general charge of a lost evangelical faith, and they were afraid that any admission of his specific charges would lead to unnecessary and fruitless controversy within the Union. The policy which they adopted was to attempt to put the responsibility for disturbing the peace of the Union back on Spurgeon. They took the position that his charges were too vague to merit serious investigation, that he had failed to substantiate them by naming ministers who were guilty. However useful this policy might have been politically, it can only be described as dishonest trifling with the subject. Spurgeon's resentment was well-founded.[20]

In other words, the Union did not face the issue squarely and fairly. They dodged, manipulated and fudged. "A further noticeable feature of most allusions to Spurgeon's protest is the tendency to dwell upon relatively small details in such a way as to divert attention from the major issue."[21]

The Down Grade controversy warns us that lack of spiritual discernment can result in catastrophe for churches. It is evident that most of the men in Spurgeon's day did not discern what was happening. They were lulled to sleep by the constant assurances that all was well. The doctrinal issues were far-reaching. Unfortunately, many of God's shepherds were blind.

Obedience to God in separation often brings abuse even from those who claim to love the Lord and be evangelical. Spurgeon suffered tremendous criticism. Those who should have been his friends and stood with him turned against him. On one occasion the celebrated London pastor, Joseph Parker, wanted Spurgeon to cooperate in a certain evangelical conference. Spurgeon graciously but definitely refused, citing the fact that he and Parker did not hold the same evangelical faith (particularly with regard to the inerrancy of Scripture). Parker vented his displeasure rather openly in an article in the *British Weekly* entitled "Parker to Spurgeon, An Open Letter." He wrote, in part:

> You bring sweeping charges against your brethren for want of orthodoxy, but I will not join you in what may be anonymous defamation. . . . The universe is not divided into plain black and white, as you suppose. It is not your function to set some people on your right hand, and the rest on your left. . . . I cannot but think that any man who expells the whole Baptist Union must occupy a sovereign place in some pantheon of his own invention.[22]

Such scorching reactions from those who were purportedly evangelicals caused Spurgeon great heartache. They no doubt contributed to some degree to his physical deterioration which was in progress at the time.

Spurgeon did not hesitate to do what he felt was right regardless of the price he must pay. He believed separation from apostasy was right. He acted in accordance with these convictions, born in his heart by a study of the Word of God. He was not optimistic regarding a possible purge of unbelief.

> I have taken a deep interest in struggles of the orthodox brethren, but I have never advised those struggles, nor entertained the slightest hope of their success. My course has been of another kind. As soon as I saw, or thought I saw, that error had become firmly established, I did not deliberate, but quitted the body at once. Since then my counsel has been, "Come out from among them." I have felt that no protest could be equal to that of distinct separation.[23]

Certainly many have and do share Spurgeon's convictions and rejoice in the fact that, despite ridicule and ostracism, he was willing both to enunciate them and to implement them.

Notes:

1. Samuel Eliot, *Heralds of a Liberal Faith* (Boston: American Unitarian Association, 1910), I, intro.

2. George Willis Cooke, *Unitarianism in America* (Boston: American Unitarian Association, 1902), pp. 37, 38.

3. Ibid., p. 55.

4. Eliot, *Heralds of a Liberal Faith*, I, intro.

5. Ibid.

6. Willis B. Glover, *Evangelical Nonconformists and Higher Criticism in the Nineteenth Century* (London: Independent Press, 1954), p. 167.

7. Russell H. Conwell, *Life of Charles Haddon Spurgeon* (Philadelphia: Edgewood Publishing Co., 1892), pp. 468, 469.

8. Ian Murray, *The Forgotten Spurgeon* (London: The Banner of Truth Trust, 1966), p. 149.

9. *The Sword and Trowel* (November 1887).

10. Glover, *Evangelical Nonconformists. . .* , p. 168.

11. E. J. Poole-Conner, *Evangelicalism in England* (London: The Fellowship of Independent Evangelical Churches, 1951), p. 249.

12. Ibid., pp. 247, 248.

13. Ernest Payne, *The Baptist Union* (London: Carey Kingsgate Press, 1958), p. 140.

14. Poole-Conner, *Evangelicalism in England*, p. 249.

15. Ibid., p. 242.

16. A. C. Underwood, *A History of the English Baptists* (London: Carey Kingsgate Press, 1947), pp. 232, 233.

17. Poole-Conner, *Evangelicalism in England*, p. 242.

18. Underwood, *A History of the English Baptists*, p. 230.

19. Glover, *Evangelical Nonconformists*. . . , p. 170.

20. Ibid., p. 172.

21. Poole-Conner, *Evangelicalism in England*, p. 237.

22. Glover, *Evangelical Nonconformists*. . . , p. 245.

23. Cited in John Horsch, *Modern Religious Liberalism* (Scottdale, PA: Fundamental Truth Depot, 1920), pp. 198, 199.

The Exodus from Mainline Denominations

6

CONFLICTS ENSUED between those who accepted the "new thought" and those who adhered to time-honored Biblical orthodoxy as alien liberal systems of thought began to make more and more impact upon the churches. This struggle within the denominations in the United States became known as the fundamentalist-modernist controversy. It was at its height in the period which encompassed roughly the first third of the twentieth century. In this chapter we are not attempting an exhaustive account which would include all denominations affected, but rather choosing examples which serve to illustrate the issues involved.

Conflicts Among Northern Presbyterians

The Presbyterian Church as a whole had represented a bastion of orthodoxy in the seventeenth and eighteenth centuries. Great conservative scholars arose within their ranks, and we still profit today from their writings. Princeton Theological Seminary in particular was looked to as a strong, Biblically-oriented training ground for ministers. Distinguished men such as Francis Patton, B. B. Warfield, Charles and A. A. Hodge and others graced its faculty. They held and taught a strong view of Biblical inerrancy.

The specter of modernism arose to public view in the last few years of the nineteenth century.[1] In 1893 Charles Briggs was suspended from the Presbyterian ministry for heresy after a much-discussed ecclesiastical trial. The matter, however, was far

Disturbing trends.

93

from settled. Leaven works its way and spreads, leavening the whole lump. In 1922 three Presbyterian churches in New York City merged, continuing the name of First Church. The church called the notorious liberal, Harry Emerson Fosdick, as their pastor. Though ostensibly a Baptist, he began serving the church without transferring his membership. In May 1922 he delivered a message entitled "Shall the Fundamentalists Win?"—a stirring confrontation to the forces of Biblical fundamentalism and a call for the toleration of more liberal views within Christian churches. Fosdick's message created a storm of protest on the part of conservatives. "Dr. Fosdick's basic contention was that liberals also were Christians and therefore could not rightfully be excluded from the Christian churches."[2] Naturally, conservatives did not believe that men were Christians who denied such great doctrines as the inspiration of Scripture, the virgin birth of Christ and the necessity for blood atonement.

More disturbing trends began to arise with the Northern Presbyterian Church. A committee had been appointed to revise the Westminster Confession. While changes at that time (1903) were slight compared to the later revision, they portended some dissatisfaction and more changes on the horizon. Some Presbyterians were using and approving literature denying Christ's deity, such as *The Never Failing Light* by James Franklin. The Presbyterian Board had approved some books like this. In India the Presbyterians cooperated with groups denying the inerrancy of Scripture. Liberals such as A. E. Marling and J. M. Speers served on the Presbyterian Mission Board.

When Francis Patton resigned as president of Princeton Seminary, J. Ross Stevenson was appointed to the position (1914). While professing to be evangelical, his operating philosophy was one of accommodation to those who held various theological positions within the denomination. (One declares, however, that Stevenson was "less orthodox in theology than his predecessor."[3]) His softer personal convictions plus his desire to accommodate persons of conflicting views spelled disaster for the great heritage of Princeton Seminary.

In 1923 about 1,300 Presbyterian ministers signed "An Affirmation," now popularly known as the "Auburn Affirmation" (because it was drawn up in Auburn, New York). It was intended as a response to the five-point doctrinal delivery made by the General Assembly of the Presbyterian Church in 1910 (and thereafter repeated in 1916 and 1923) which declared that such doctrines as inerrancy, the virgin birth of Christ, His vicarious blood sacrifice and His physical resurrection were "essential doctrines" of the Word of God. The heart of the statement is as follows and shows the general tenor of the whole:

> Furthermore, this opinion of the General Assembly attempts to commit our church to certain theories concerning the inspiration of the Bible, and the Incarnation, the Atonement, the Resurrection, and the Continuing Life and Supernatural Power of our Lord Jesus Christ. We all hold most earnestly to these great facts and doctrines; we all believe from our hearts that the writers of the Bible were inspired of God; that Jesus Christ was God manifest in the flesh; that God was in Christ, reconciling the world unto Himself, and through Him we have redemption; that having died for our sins He rose from the dead and is our ever-living Savior; that in His earthly ministry He wrought many mighty works, and by His vicarious death and unfailing presence He is able to save to the uttermost. Some of us regard the particular theories contained in the deliverance of the General Assembly of 1923 as satisfactory explanations of these facts and doctrines. But we are united in believing that these are not the only theories allowed by the Scriptures and our standards as explanations of these facts and doctrines of our religion, and that all who hold to these facts and doctrines, whatever theories they may employ to explain them, are worthy of all confidence and fellowship.[4]

With many Presbyterian ministers possessing wishy-washy views such as these, the doom of the Presbyterian denomination in the north was sealed. There were plenty of "theories" abroad to explain whatever needed to be explained; and if they were all equally acceptable, a theological mishmash would result. And so it did.

Protest and separation.

Matters grew worse, not better. The brilliant young scholar and professor at Princeton Seminary, J. Gresham Machen, wrote articles and books championing the cause of Biblical truth as over against the growing liberalism. His book *Christianity and Liberalism* was a clear and masterful statement of the difference between the two approaches. He and those that stood with him (including notable fellow faculty such as Robert Dick Wilson and Oswald Allis) were vilified unmercifully. Finally, acting upon their convictions and the Biblical teaching concerning separation from apostasy, Machen and his followers left Princeton (and the old Presbyterian denomination) and formed a new school, Westminster Theological Seminary near Philadelphia.

At this time Machen still retained the support of some of the notable pastors and leaders within the Presbyterian Church, such as Clarence Macartney, then pastor of historic Arch Street Presbyterian Church, Philadelphia (and later First Presbyterian, Pittsburgh) and Mark Matthews, pastor of First Presbyterian Church, Seattle, the largest Presbyterian church in the world. However, in 1933 when Machen and others led in the formation of the Independent Board of Presbyterian Foreign Missions, they lost the support of a number of men, including Matthews and Macartney. They represented a good many men, found in every denomination, who are themselves evangelical in their faith, but are not prepared for various reasons to sever their connections with apostate denominations and to attempt to lead their churches to do so.

For their militancy, several of the leaders in the separatist movement, including Machen, were unfrocked (their ordination was removed). This fact is often mentioned in unfavorable accounts written about these men as though it were a mark of disgrace, but rather it was a badge of honor for those who had obeyed the truth. These men organized the Orthodox Presbyterian Church, a small denomination presently composed of about 125 churches.

It was not long until this infant group divided. Under the leadership of Carl McIntire, Allan MacRae and J. Oliver Buswell, the Bible Presbyterian Church was begun (1938). A later defection of some leaders from this group produced (for a time) a second Bible Presbyterian Church, but eventually (through a merger) the Reformed Presbyterian Church, Evangelical Synod was formed. Today it has approximately 150 churches.

Probably no more capable spokesman for the separatist position has ever arisen than J. Gresham Machen. Even his enemies conceded that he was a tremendously able man with a keen mind and a facile pen. He was gracious and gentlemanly, but offered no quarter to unbelief. He is an example of one who, though endowed with unusual gifts of scholarship and possessing renown for his effective ministry, was willing to lay all at the feet of Christ and obey what he felt to be a clear, Biblical injunction to quit the ranks of the ungodly and those who tolerated them. Perhaps we can feel the pulsebeat of this soldier of the cross as we read his words:

> Again, men tell us that our preaching should be positive and not negative, that we can preach the truth without attacking error. But if we follow that advice we shall have to close our Bible and desert its teachings. The New Testament is a polemic book almost from beginning to end. . . . It is when men have felt compelled to take a stand against error that they have risen to the really great heights in the celebration of the truth.[5]

Conflicts Among Northern Baptists

Various autonomous but cooperating Baptist groups existed prior to 1907 in the northern half of the United States. In that year they merged organizationally to form the Northern Baptist Convention (now called the American Baptist Churches in the U.S.A.). From the very inception of the denomination liberals were within it, such as social-gospel exponents Walter Rauschenbusch and Shailer Mathews. It was an exercise in futility from its very first hour of existence to expect such a convention to give testimony to clear Bible truth. One is reminded of the mixed multitude in Israel's day.

After perusing the following pages, one might inquire as to why such space is devoted to the controversy within the Northern Baptist Convention and to the problems of the Conservative Baptists. It is because we believe this controversy clearly illustrates certain principles which are crucial to the whole question of separation. In particular, it reveals the significant distinctions between the gradual approach to separation and the clear-cut approach, and it amply demonstrates the implications and resultant attitudes of each.

The problems within the Convention.

Conservatives within the Convention early recognized the problems caused by the University of Chicago Divinity School (where Shailer Mathews was dean). As a liberal institution, it was filling the pulpits of the Convention with men trained in unbelief. At that time separation was unthought of by most. (The large Wealthy Street Baptist Church in Grand Rapids, Michigan, did withdraw in 1909.) In an effort to counteract the effects of the liberal school, Northern Baptist Seminary was organized in 1913. Eastern Baptist was started later in hopes of furthering Baptist orthodoxy.

Internal ecclesiastical battles marked the years just preceding and following 1920.[6] Bible-believing men tried in vain to get the Convention to adopt a doctrinal statement which would positionalize it on matters of importance. In 1920 the Convention's Board of Education, reporting to the Convention meeting in Buffalo, openly admitted that the Convention was a gathering place for "birds of all feathers" when it said:

> In Chicago, we have the Divinity School of the University and the Northern Baptist Seminary. . . . This institution [Chicago Divinity School] is largely a graduate school for advanced work. Only a small percentage of its students are preparing for the pastorates of our churches. Moreover, this school frankly and unequivocally represents only one group of churches in our denomination. This group is large and important and must have a school for the adequate training of its ministry.
>
> On the other hand, the great majority of our churches in the Middle West are of the conservative type and they have a right to an institution which shall train ministers for their churches.[7]

What a sad state of affairs is here exposed! A

convention seeks to work together for the glory of God with men and churches who believe the Bible banded together with those who do not. It was a sorry spectacle indeed, but one that many hoped would be changed through rigorous efforts on their part.

Conservatives became increasingly disturbed when, in 1919 at the meeting of the Convention in Denver, it was voted to participate in the Interchurch World Movement. This was a liberally motivated scheme to unite about thirty denominations in an effort to alleviate the social ills of the postwar world. Its goal was to raise several million dollars for this purpose. John D. Rockefeller pledged to give one million dollars to each of the American Baptist mission societies if they would in turn raise several million. Fundamentalists saw in the total program a furtherance of the social gospel and a step toward ecumenical alignments.

As a result of the concern of fundamental leaders in the Convention, a call went out to interested persons to attend a preconvention conference in Buffalo, New York, in June 1920 to hear messages on the theme "The Fundamentals of Our Baptist Faith." Signers of the call were men such as J. C. Massee, Curtis Lee Laws, J. Whitcomb Brougher, Russell Conwell, A. C. Dixon, Frank Goodchild, W. B. Hinson, Clarence Larkin, Cortland Myers, William Pettingill, W. B. Riley, Cary Thomas and numerous others. Many fine messages were delivered, and Baptists were alerted to the frightening progress of liberal thought within their own ranks. It was to be a precursor of many such meetings of conservatives within the Convention.

Out of that Buffalo meeting came the Fundamentalist Fellowship which for almost a quarter of a century held preconvention gatherings. It was their aim to rid the Convention of objectionable liberalism and to retain its structure, churches, societies and schools for the old-fashioned faith of the Bible. They were not of a separatist bent of mind, but were reformers in the sense that they desired to reform the existing structure. The Fundamentalist Fellowship continued under that name until 1945 when it be-

Two attitudes and movements within the Convention.

came known as the Conservative Baptist Fellowship, one segment of the emerging Conservative Baptist movement.

Existing alongside the Fundamentalist Fellowship was another body, organized in 1923 and called the Baptist Bible Union. Organizers included R. E. Neighbour, O. W. Van Osdel, William Pettingill, W. B. Riley and J. Frank Norris. The Baptist Bible Union was, in general, more militant in their protests against apostasy in the Convention, though they had in their membership men who were not in the Convention; so their activities were somewhat broader than those of the Fundamentalist Fellowship. While one may not agree with every detail of the assessment, the remarks of Frank Goodchild, long active in the Fundamentalist Fellowship, give somewhat of the flavor of the differences that existed between the two bodies. He noted six differences:

> 1) The Union embraced certain Northern, Southern, and Canadian Baptists while the Fundamentals Conference worked only in the Northern Convention. 2) The Union had a membership, the Fundamentals Conference did not. 3) The Union attempted to boycott the schools by non-support while the Fundamentalists tried to purge and rescue the institutions "from the pernicious influence of rationalism." 4) The Union was a fellowship of pre-millenarians (later denied by the Union) while the Fundamentalists received both pre- and post-millenarians. 5) The Union was an exclusive fellowship while the Fundamentals Conference sought to preserve denominational unity "while recognizing the incongruity of attempting to walk with those with whom we have little agreement." 6) The Unionists were ready to start new institutions and agencies while the Fundamentalists attempted to rescue the old agencies from Modernism.[8]

Thus two attitudes or approaches formed within the Convention with relation to the problems caused by liberalism. One approach was the softer one—complain, speak out, but try hard to maintain the denominational unity. The other approach was more militant, less willing to cooperate with denominational programs and more separatistic in character.

The first approach culminated in the Conservative Baptist movement, and the softer views were still present in the minds of many of its founders. The second approach culminated in the General Association of Regular Baptist Churches, which took a stricter, more clear-cut position regarding the problems of the Convention. As one has put it, the Fundamentalist Fellowship was marked by "more optimism and less agitation."⁹ The Baptist Bible Union, while starting with the same philosophy of "cleaning up the mess" within the Convention, changed to a more separatistic philosophy as the struggle within the Convention proved more and more hopeless.

It is important to notice, however, that the Fundamentalist Fellowship and the Baptist Bible Union were distinguished from one another, not so much by doctrinal position (for both were nearly identical), but by a *mood* and *attitude* toward the apostasy within the Convention. Moods and attitudes are sometimes difficult to delineate in words, but they may be crucial when it comes to establishing positions. Those within the Fundamentalist Fellowship had a mood which was characterized by a great desire to maintain the denominational unity. They wanted to be loyal to the Scriptures, but to do so within the Convention framework. The Union men, on the other hand, were more independent-minded, less inclined to be overly concerned about the denominational unity, and more concerned about the doctrinal purity of the churches. It is a distinction which can be noted throughout church history wherever "stay-iners" and "come-outers" are compared.

Both movements that had operated within the Convention eventually operated outside the Convention. The one came out much earlier than the other. The Baptist Bible Union was marred in its fellowship by the personal idiosyncrasies of some of its leaders, as well as the fiasco involving the Des Moines University (which we will not take time to review).¹⁰ Following the sorry tale of the University involvement, the Union began to decline in membership and influence. Men within it realized both from the study of Scripture and the firsthand observance of

Two attitudes and movements outside the Convention.

the Convention situation that all further attempts to purge the ranks of modernism were futile. They made plans to quit the ranks of the Convention and to form a new association of churches. This they did at the final meeting of the Union in the Belden Avenue Baptist Church in Chicago in May 1932. The change of name was accomplished in such a way as to make the General Association of Regular Baptist Churches the legal successor of the Baptist Bible Union. Since that time, of course, the GARBC has grown to its present strength of approximately 1600 churches and has continued the separatist testimony of the men who were its founders.

The members of the Fundamentalist Fellowship, in contrast, remained within the Convention for many more years, vocalizing their protest, but getting nowhere as far as changing the Convention. They finally decided to organize a missionary agency which would be competitive with the American Baptist Foreign Mission Society. In a meeting in Chicago in 1943 the Conservative Baptist Foreign Mission Society was launched. The same attitude toward separation which had characterized these men all along was evident in this effort as well. The minutes of the organizational meeting record the intent:

> ... A Conservative Baptist Foreign Mission Society be formed within the Northern Baptist Convention in order to channel the gifts of such individuals and churches which were no longer willing to make their contributions undesignated to the American Baptist Foreign Mission Society. The sentiment was expressed that churches which had satisfactory missionaries that they were supporting through designations would do well to continue this, lest these missionaries be forced to depend upon liberals for their support, and that churches could continue to give to the Unified Budget by designating the proportion of their gifts AWAY from the ABFMS as they now do away from the Federal Council of Churches.[11]

Tulga pinpoints their aim in beginning the mission society: "*The intentions of the founders of the Conservative Society was to create a society which*

would, like the Conservative seminaries, be within
the Convention fellowship but not under Convention
control." [12] Shelley declares:

> Regardless of the outcome, the hopes of
> the conservatives at that time are noteworthy
> because they show that the leaders of this
> movement did not initially embrace separa-
> tion as a basic principle of action. In fact,
> they did not at that time want separation at
> all. They wanted rather a theologically
> grounded means of channeling their mis-
> sionary volunteers and dollars to the mission
> fields of earth, and they had hopes that this
> could be done under the recognition, if not
> the benediction, of the Northern Baptist
> Convention. To them this position was not
> so much a compromise as a genuine attempt
> at Christian toleration and unity without the
> sacrifice of truth. [13]

Shelley goes on to state that "this original intention of the Conservatives accounts for the refusal of
some later to adopt a strict separatist policy which
takes no account of the biblical injunctions toward
unity." [14]

Earle V. Pierce, while leader of the Fundamentalist Fellowship in 1943, wrote an explanation concerning the organization of the CBFMS which
clearly reveals the outlook of these men at that point
in time:

> This action seemed to be necessary to pre-
> vent a serious and complete division of the
> forces of the Northern Baptist Convention.
> We have not yet given up hope of seeing our
> Convention controlled by the conservatives
> who are in the great majority, as it ought to
> be. . . . We are not "pulling out" and leaving
> them (the liberals) in full control of all the
> invested funds and income, for, cooperating
> in the general work of the denomination, we
> are voting members of all its societies and
> must plan on attending the conventions and
> working for the right people on the
> boards. . . . We should pray and work that
> the time may come when a separate mis-
> sionary society will not be longer necessary.
> If this is all rightly handled it will mean for
> purification, and purity leads to peace. [15]

An evaluation of the issues represented in the CBA and GARBC.

Unfortunately, in the controversies that erupted between the CBA and GARBC and also between the two factions that developed within the CBA, personal bitterness and clashes of leadership created a smoke screen for some and blurred the real issues at stake. It is not a question of personal character or love for the Lord which we are discussing, but, in the final analysis, which position most closely represents the teaching of the Word of God. In a later chapter the scriptural teaching on separation will be examined and, hopefully, clarified. For now, we confine ourselves to an evaluation of the two viewpoints on separation as represented in this controversy within the Convention.

The foundations of the Conservative Baptist movement were laid by at least three types of persons: (1) some were separatist "in spirit and objective," and, as they progressed in their thinking and experience, became more convinced of the necessity of organizational separation; (2) some were never separatist at heart, but became so reluctantly through the pressure of circumstances or for other reasons; (3) some were never separatists at heart and never did become so organizationally, but they had considerable influence on the minds and attitudes of men who did eventually separate from the Convention.

Because a spirit of tolerance toward unbelief had been cultivated on the part of many of those who remained within the Convention, this spirit of broadness or toleration came with some of them when they separated from the Convention. Their philosophy of coexistence with the enemy produced in them a mind-set which is difficult to define, but which was nonetheless real. Probably the best way to describe it is by saying that numbers of Conservative Baptists had a separatist position organizationally, but not deep separatist convictions which rested upon Scripture and which they were willing to implement consistently. This explains why a number of CBA leaders became enamored with the National Association of Evangelicals and its affiliates. The NAE represented the attitude toward separation from apostasy which they had always held. The fact that they were reluctant separatists from the Convention did not change their basic attitude toward the matter.

The argument that some Conservative Baptists gave was this: "We want to separate from the Convention with the faith and the furniture." By this they meant they not only wanted to come out, but to bring with them the agencies, state associations and other parts of the denominational "furniture" which they had helped to build. Regrettably, they later found that the "furniture" had termites in it and was not sound even though separated organizationally.

Twice in 1947 special committees appointed by the GARBC Council of Fourteen and the Committee of Fifteen of the Conservatives met to discuss a possible merger between the Conservatives and the GARBC. The meetings proved fruitless. Shelly tells why:

> As we have observed, the differences between the Fundamentalist Fellowship and the Baptist Bible Union were revealed as early as 1923. These differences were not so much in theology . . . as in attitude toward separation from other Christians. The fact that the churches forming the GARBC separated from the Northern Baptist Convention earlier than the Conservatives underscored the fact that they were more negative in their view of separation. This difference, revealed so early, persisted and was the one major reason why the merger attempts proved fruitless.[16]

It is interesting that early separation from the Convention would be noted as exhibiting a "more negative" view of separation. Does the descriptive adjective *negative* connote "unsound" or "undesirable"? How can separation be other than negative? Does it not require the repudiation of something? Is that not negative? Is such negative action not required by Holy Scripture?

When the Conservative Baptist Association was formed in 1948, the differences between the CBA and the GARBC were brought sharply into focus by the requirements for church fellowship in the CBA as given in its constitution: "The affiliates of the Association shall consist of: (1) Autonomous Baptist churches *without regard to other affiliations.*" The GARBC, on the other hand, stated: "Any Baptist church in the U.S. *which is not in fellowship or cooperation* with any national or local convention, association or group which permits the presence of modernists or modernism. . . ." In other words, a church could still be in the Northern Baptist Convention and also be in the Conservative Baptist Association. Not so with the GARBC. They required a church to be completely out.

Arguments Conservatives used to support their philosophy were several: (1) it created competition for the ABC as well as harrassing them as much as possible; (2) it avoided having to begin with a small handful; (3) it made it easier for a church to change affiliations; (4) it helped to save church properties and other ecclesiastical assets; (5) it left the matter of affiliation in the hands of the local church where it properly should be.

This last argument has been especially emphasized by some Conservatives.

> Unlike the GARBC, matters of affiliation were not allowed to exclude one from the "fellowship" of the CBA. These provisions were undoubtedly aimed at attracting as many of the conservative men within the Northern Baptist Convention as possible.[17]

Separation, however, does involve affiliations. This goes to the very heart of the matter. You cannot be a consistent separatist while retaining un-Biblical affiliations. This was one of the basic problems which hounded the Conservative Baptist movement throughout its days of internal struggle. Some wanted to be separatists on paper but not in action. Separation requires severance from that which is wrong.

There developed within the Conservative Baptist movement a group of men and churches strongly committed to separation. The CBA, under the able leadership of Myron Cedarholm, its general director for many years, grew, multiplying churches mostly by the planting of new ones. Cedarholm became more separatistic as he went along and stood fast for a consistent separatism much to the annoyance of many Conservatives. Many able leaders of the more separatist group such as Archer and Arno Weniger, Bryce Augsburger and Richard Clearwaters were

forthright in their exposure of compromise and in
their call to a Biblical position. Seminaries true to
the separatist conviction were formed (Central Conservative Baptist Seminary and San Francisco Conservative Baptist Seminary). Pillsbury Baptist Bible
College stood in this tradition as well. However,
their noble efforts did not stem the tide. Most of the
more separatistic men have since left the Conservative movement along with the schools mentioned
above and are either totally unaffiliated, associated
with small local or national groups, or in the
GARBC.

Conflicts Among
Baptists in the South

The separatist movement among Southern Baptists centered primarily around the stormy and controversial personality of J. Frank Norris, pastor of
the First Baptist Church in Fort Worth, Texas.[18] In
addition to his own ministry at the church, where he
built what he hailed as "the world's largest church,"
Norris also had a worldwide influence. He established the Premillenial Baptist Missionary Fellowship (later renamed the World Fundamental Baptist
Missionary Fellowship). He became a thorn in the
side of the Southern Baptist Convention, exposing
liberalism among its leaders and agencies and holding competing meetings with the Convention. Actually, he was trained at Baylor University, a Southern
Baptist school, and pastored in the Convention for
several years before finally departing from it. His
school—Bible Baptist Seminary—was located in his
church and was basically a Bible institute. Through
the pages of his widely read paper, *The Fundamentalist*, he reached multitudes with his message. He
was a highly capable pulpiteer, but, sadly, his ministry was marred throughout by many unsavory elements which often made him an embarrassment to
other fundamentalists, and which eventually
brought the demise of his empire.

The fellowship which Norris started grew, and
many pastors and churches interested themselves in
its work. Among these churches were some very
large and successful ones. Internal conflicts with
Norris grew in intensity, however, until mature

leaders who had worked with him for years had finally had enough. In 1950 they severed their connections with the World Fundamental Baptist Missionary Fellowship and organized the Baptist Bible Fellowship. Leaders in this action were such men as G. Beauchamp Vick, Wendell Zimmerman, John Rawlings, Al Janney and Scotty Alexander. The mantle (if such there was) that had been upon Frank Norris fell upon G. Beauchamp Vick, a capable leader who had been chiefly responsible for building up the Sunday schools at Norris's churches and who pastored until his death the Temple Baptist Church in Detroit. Vick's leadership was much wiser and steadier than had been Norris's, and the new fellowship and its school, Baptist Bible College, Springfield, Missouri, progressed. The growth of the fellowship has come primarily through new churches which they have started rather than from defections from the Southern Baptist Convention (though there has been some of this).

Another fellowship, centered principally in the southern United States, is called the Southwide Baptist Fellowship. It began originally under the impetus of Dr. Lee Roberson and others, and continues to hold regular Bible conference meetings which feature music and preaching. While some of the men active in its beginnings were in the Southern Baptist Convention, more and more it has included those who are not in the Convention and is, for all practical purposes, a separatist testimony today. This group is premillennial, committed to the inerrancy of Scripture and strongly evangelistic. The pastors and churches of this fellowship are also concerned about world missions.

Other Separatist Bodies

We make no effort here to list all those groups, denominations or bodies which might be considered separatist in their convictions. Numbers of totally unaffiliated churches exist all across America and in other lands which have no fellowship with unbelief. They are called by various names—tabernacles, fellowships, Bible churches, etc. While not counted in any organized body, they make a significant contribution to the total separatist testimony.

In 1930 a farsighted and deeply convicted pastor, William McCarrell (Cicero Bible Church, Cicero, Illinois), led in the formation of a new separatist body. Its inception came as some Congregational churches, particularly in the Chicago area, became disenchanted with the liberalism in their denomination and decided to obey God and get out. At the same time a small group of independent churches, the American Conference of Undenominational Churches, was foundering and needed help. McCarrell and others succeeded in gathering these various churches together into a new organization, the Independent Fundamental Churches of America. They continue as a separatist testimony today, publishing a magazine, *The Voice*, and forming a focus of fellowship for autonomous fundamental congregations.

The Methodist denomination never experienced the large-scale theological battles that rocked Presbyterians and Baptists. Liberalism took over rather early and with little fanfare within Methodism. What protest was given was earnestly done but had little impact within the denomination as a whole. Robert Shuler, pastor of Trinity Methodist Church in Los Angeles, was well-known during his ministry there for his stand for the faith. Regrettably, Shuler never left the Methodist Church and, while his paper, *The Methodist Challenge*, exposed unbelief, it did not produce a separatist testimony. Some Methodists left the denomination in 1940 and formed the Southern Methodist Church. Other groups organized by separatist Methodists were the Evangelical Methodist Church and the Bible Protestant Church.

There are several bodies of Brethren name. One of these is well-known as Grace Brethren (or National Fellowship of Brethren Churches) with headquarters in Winona Lake, Indiana. This group originated in a protest against the growing liberalism within the Brethren Church. In 1939 a number of pastors, teachers and churches left the parent group and formed their own fellowship. They operate Grace College and Grace Theological Seminary. Until his death, Alva McClain was one of this group's most illustrious leaders.

Some other bodies of separatist convictions and not already named are associated with the American Council of Christian Churches. They are as follows: Asbury Bible Churches, Congregational Methodist Church, Fundamental Methodist Church, Independent Churches Affiliated, Independent Fundamental Bible Churches, Tioga River Christian Conference, Ukranian Evangelical Baptist Convention, Westminster Biblical Fellowship, and the World Baptist Fellowship.

Notes:

1. For the history of the struggle within the Presbyterian Church between modernism and fundamentalism, see Edwin Rian, *The Presbyterian Conflict* (Grand Rapids: Wm. B. Eerdmans Publishing Co., 1940) and Lefferts Loetscher, *The Broadening Church* (Philadelphia: University of Pennsylvania Press, 1954).

2. Loetscher, *The Broadening Church*, p. 109.

3. Norman J. Furniss, *The Fundamentalist Controversy: 1918-1931* (Hamden, CT: Archon Books, 1963), p. 189.

4. Loetscher, *The Broadening Church*, p. 118.

5. J. Gresham Machen, *What Is Christianity?* ed. Ned Stonehouse (Grand Rapids: Wm. B. Eerdmans Publishing Co., 1951), pp. 132, 133.

6. For detailed information concerning the struggles within the Northern Baptist Convention from about 1910 to 1948, see the following: Robert Delnay, *A History of the Baptist Bible Union* (Winston-Salem, NC: Piedmont Bible College Press, 1974); Chester E. Tulga, *The Foreign Missions Controversy in the Northern Baptist Convention* (Chicago: Conservative Baptist Fellowship, 1950); George Dollar, "The Big Baptist Battle" and "Fundamentalist Fellowships," *A History of Fundamentalism in America* (Greenville, SC: Bob Jones University Press, 1973).

7. Joseph M. Stowell, *Background and History of the General Association of Regular Baptist Churches* (Hayward, CA: J. F. May Press, 1949), p. 8.

8. Bruce L. Shelley, *Conservative Baptists* (Denver: Conservative Baptist Theological Seminary, 1960), p. 23.

9. Ibid., p. 24.

10. Robert Delnay has an entire chapter on this.

11. Tulga, *The Foreign Missions Controversy. . .*, pp. 107, 108.

12. Ibid., p. 108.

13. Shelley, *Conservative Baptists*, p. 47.

14. Ibid.

15. Tulga, *The Foreign Missions Controversy*. . . , p. 108.

16. Shelley, *Conservative Baptists*, p. 61.

17. Ibid., pp. 67, 68.

18. For information on J. Frank Norris, see Billy Vick Bartlett, *A History of Baptist Separatism* (Springfield, MO: Baptist Bible Fellowship Publications, 1972); Billy Vick Bartlett, *The Beginnings: A Pictorial History of the Baptist Bible Fellowship* (Springfield, MO: Baptist Bible College, 1975); E. Ray Tatum, *Conquest or Failure? A Biography of J. Frank Norris* (Dallas: Baptist Historical Foundation, 1966).

Separatism in Non- and Interdenominational Bodies

7

THE INROADS of religious unbelief into the denominations brought about internal strife for many of them. However, separatist influences were abroad that were not directly related to any specific denomination, but were nevertheless significant.

Separatist Concepts Inherent in Fundamentalism

New evangelical writers in particular have long complained that separatism was (and is) inherent in the very warp and woof of fundamentalism, and this is one of the reasons they oppose fundamentalism as a system or position. No doubt they are correct in their assessment. Within the fundamentalist position as a whole, there are elements which tend to separatism, that is, to severance from fellowship with organized groups that permit the presence and propagation of error.

The term "fundamentalism" arose from a series of booklets published in the first part of the twentieth century under the title *The Fundamentals*. (These have since been republished in two volumes.) Noted fundamentalist scholars and leaders wrote articles dealing with such great topics as the virgin birth, the deity of Christ, the inspiration of Scripture and the bodily resurrection of the Lord. Those who held these doctrines to be essential became known as "fundamentalists." As we have already seen, some fundamentalists were not separatists (such as those in the Fundamentalist Fellowship in the Northern Baptist Convention). However, the definite *tendency* on the part of those who embraced fundamental views was to separate eventually from denominations and groups tolerating modernism. It was a *tendency*, but it was not true of *all* fundamentalists. What was there in the fundamentalist position that resulted in many fundamentalists separating from groups in which apostasy was found?

A sense of supreme loyalty to the Word of God.

In the fires of conflict with modernism, fundamentalists developed more than ever a deep commitment to the authority of Scripture. It was, of course, at this very point that modernism was making its challenge. The Bible was being discredited in the public eye, and its message reduced to the level of other so-called "holy books." Fundamentalists rose up to defend the Scriptures from attack and to enunciate clearly their authority and uniqueness.

Questions arose in the minds of many fundamentalists. If the Bible is true and authoritative, and if my denominational leaders and others disparage its truth, what is my responsibility? On the one hand were those who pleaded for denominational unity. It was a sin to "rend the Body of Christ," said they. Yet other thoughtful fundamentalists saw clearly that loyalty to Scripture was more important than loyalty to a denomination. If there was a conflict between the two, the Scripture must be followed, even when that led to rupture with a religious body.

There was another factor also. The average family man, greatly concerned for the spiritual welfare of himself and his children, sensed that spiritual needs were not being met in the cold, liberal atmosphere of many of the denominational churches. While perhaps not totally oblivious to the scriptural teaching on separation, for many the choice was a very practical one. "Am I going to remain within a church that gives me no spiritual food, or am I going to seek out a ministry that offers me what I need?" Many made the latter choice, thus leaving the denomination where they had been. They sought a Bible-teaching ministry where they would be taught the whole counsel of God and not face constant criticisms and innuendos from the pulpit, reflecting on the Word of God which to them was precious.

The preaching and teaching of early fundamentalists emphasized the doctrine of the apostate church as revealed in the New Testament. Attention was called to the fact that apostasy set in early, has grown throughout the Church Age, and will result eventually in the total leavening of professing Christendom and the rise of the Babylonian church described in Revelation 17.

Contemporary critics of fundamentalism and separatism declare that this particular view of the church arose in the dispensationalism made popular by the Plymouth Brethren and the Scofield Bible. They view it as an unwarranted pessimism and subversive of efforts to help society through some sort of a social gospel.

First of all, we believe it has been amply demonstrated to this point that this concept of an apostate church did not begin with the Plymouth Brethren or C. I. Scofield. Such teaching on apostasy can be traced all the way back through the centuries.

It is true that the teachings and writings of the Plymouth Brethren have had a definite impact upon fundamentalism. It is certainly true that the Scofield Bible has had a tremendous influence as well. We need not seek to deny these facts nor be embarrassed by them. Because fundamentalists have been influenced in some measure by Plymouth Brethren writers is not in and of itself bad, nor does it imply that all fundamentalists embrace all the teachings of the Plymouth Brethren. All of us have been influenced by someone. The question is, Is the influence scriptural? If something is scriptural, let us believe it and obey it. Many believe that the doctrine of the fall (apostasy) of the professing church as expounded by Plymouth Brethren authors is essentially scriptural. (We have seen that the Waldensians, Anabaptists and others taught this as well.) This does not mean that all the deductions that may have been drawn from this doctrine by Brethren scholars are valid, but certainly the New Testament teaches that a pervasive and growing apostasy will be seen within the professing church.

Who were these Plymouth Brethren? They were persons in Ireland and England who began studying the Scriptures, became dissatisfied with the estab-

The view of an apostate church.

lished churches in which they found themselves, and began meeting in separate congregations from about 1830 on.[1] One of their most notable leaders, and the man most commonly associated with the group in the public mind, was J. N. Darby. He, and numerous others associated with the Brethren, were very able students of the Scriptures. Most regrettably, the movement broke into several squabbling factions as time went on. It stands as a warning to all separatists that great care must be taken in implementing the doctrine of separation lest one be shipwrecked on the shoals of human pettiness. More will be said of this at a later time.

J. N. Darby believed that the professing church had fallen into apostasy. He connected this with man's continued failure upon earth due to his sinful nature.[2] He wrote an essay entitled "Separation from Evil: God's Principle of Unity" in which he said, "Separation from evil is the necessary first principle of communion with Him. . . . Separation from evil is His principle of unity."[3]

It would be assumed from this statement that Darby opposed continued communion with apostate denominations. This would be a correct assumption and verified by Darby's own statements. In discussing the apostasy of both Romanism and the churches after the Reformation, Darby contends, "But wherever the body declines the putting away of evil, it becomes in its unity a denier of God's character of holiness, and then separation from the evil is the path of the saint. . . ."[4]

One of the historians of the Brethren movement points out that indeed the Brethren believed in separation from apostate churches, but they believed it should be done, not with glee, but "in an attitude of sorrow and contrition." This same observer maintains that some Brethren had a softer position on separation than others and that perhaps this accounts for the later development of that branch of Plymouth Brethrenism known as the Open Brethren.[5]

That the Plymouth Brethren, through their skillful and widely distributed writings, helped to popularize the dispensational scheme of Biblical interpretation is true. This fact, however, does not in any wise prove that dispensationalism is non-Biblical or merely the late invention of a few Plymouth Brethren teachers. (Some principles of dispensationalism were held by persons who lived long before the Plymouth Brethren. It is a method of Biblical interpretation which arises out of the Scriptures themselves.) Sandeen sees the teaching of dispensationalism regarding the apostasy of the church as critical in the development of fundamentalist views of the church. He writes that in the dispensationalist's view, "The true church could not possibly be identified with any of the large denominations, which were riddled with heresy. . . . It is impossible to overestimate the importance of this ecclesiology for the history of Fundamentalism."[6] (In this same article Sandeen declares fundamentalism to be an alliance between dispensationalism and the Princeton Theology—the general system of theology, particularly in relation to inerrancy, which was taught at Princeton during the days of Hodge, Warfield and others.)

In summary, it can be said that elements of fundamentalist teaching in the latter eighteenth and early nineteenth centuries contributed to the development of a separatist spirit among many. While not all actually separated from apostate groups, large numbers did. Many of them were influenced toward such a step by truth which they learned in interdenominational gatherings of various kinds. These we now examine briefly.

The Fundamentalist, Interdenominational Movement

Dissatisfied with the "husks" they were receiving for spiritual food, many of the Lord's people began looking elsewhere than in their regular churches. From about 1875 through the first third of the twentieth century, great Bible conferences sprang up and flourished throughout America. Among these were those at Montrose, Pennsylvania; Winona Lake, Indiana; Pinebrook, near Stroudsburg, Pennsylvania; Northfield, Massachusetts, and many others. Great Bible-teaching pastors and itinerant Bible teachers were brought to these conferences, and large crowds gathered to hear them. The fundamentals of the faith were emphasized; premillennial truth was taught; and God's people were warned about the encroachments of liberalism. No doubt many who were initially exposed to a solid Bible truth at these conferences later took their stand in separatist testimonies.

City-wide evangelistic campaigns were also popular during this same period. Evangelists such as Dwight L. Moody, J. Wilbur Chapman, R. A. Torrey, Billy Sunday and Bob Jones, Sr., preached to great throngs across America and in other countries. Most of these men excoriated the modernists in their messages and warned Bible-believing Christians to give them no support. Preaching as they did to vast numbers from various denominations, these men had a wide-reaching influence.

As the radio became popular, it was employed by true Bible expositors to spread the truth of the gospel. One of the earliest broadcasts was the "Old-Fashioned Revival Hour" with its beloved teacher, Charles Fuller. Fuller was a fundamentalist (though not all that bears his name today would be so designated). Simply, fervently and powerfully he preached the great truths of Scripture. Many were saved, and the influence for good was immeasurable. Many people who heard his broadcasts wondered why they were not hearing such Bible teaching in their own churches. They were motivated to seek fellowship elsewhere. The same impact came from other broadcasts, such as M. R. DeHaan's "Radio Bible Class."

Independent missionary agencies began to spring up as well. Persons who loved Christ and His Word no longer had to channel their money through denominational mission boards either totally liberal in character or accepting coexistence with liberalism. Now there were such missions as the China Inland Mission, Sudan Interior Mission, Africa Inland Mission and many others. (Not all these missions today accept the scriptural teaching on separation which is being defended in this book.) Much of the financial support of missionaries under these missions came from people who were yet in liberal churches, but who were seeing the need of supporting missionaries true to God's Word.

The Bible institute movement also arose during this period. Such institutions as Moody Bible Institute, the Bible Institute of Los Angeles, Philadelphia School of the Bible and others came into existence to train young people in God's Word because, for the most part, such training was unavailable in denominational schools. The pulpits of many separatist churches today are pastored by graduates from these schools.

Interdenominational fundamentalism, of course, has changed through the years since many of the institutions, agencies and movements mentioned here were founded. Issues are much more complex now than they were in the days when a person was either a modernist or a fundamentalist. Considerable discernment is required to pick one's way through the maze of theological systems abroad today. The rise of the new and young evangelicals has further complicated the matter. Not all organizations stand where they once stood. Care must be taken to examine the position of those who claim the support of Bible-believers, and yet care must also be taken to avoid a nit-picking spirit which can spoil one's spiritual joy and that of others as well.

Two Positions Contrasted: The NAE and the ACCC

The contrasting positions regarding separation that have already been mentioned were organizationally embodied within two groups that came into existence as a result of the fundamentalist-modernist controversy. We speak of the National Association of Evangelicals and the American Council of Christian Churches. (Each of these has their counterparts on the international scene as well.)

In 1942 a call went out, signed by leading evangelicals, inviting interested persons to a conference in St. Louis. The purpose of the meeting was to explore the possibility of organizing an interdenominational evangelical fellowship to promote the common purposes of evangelicalism. The signers of this call were numerous and included such men as Harold Ockenga, Stephen Paine, Robert G. Lee and J.

The organization and position of the National Association of Evangelicals.[7]

Palmer Muntz. Interestingly, some of the signers, in
later days, became more separatist in their convictions and either associated with the American Council or at least did not support the NAE. We refer to
such men as W. W. Breckbill, David Otis Fuller, Bob
Jones, Sr., William McCarrell and William Ward
Ayer. Harold Ockenga, then pastor of the Park Street
Church, Boston, gave one of the principal addresses,
challenging evangelicals to unite.

In 1941 another organization had been launched
called the American Council of Christian Churches.
Its leader, Carl McIntire, was invited to address leaders of the St. Louis conference to explain the purposes and goals of his organization. McIntire urged
them to join with him in his new organization rather
than starting another. The gathering of evangelicals
in St. Louis rejected McIntire's plea because they felt
that the ACCC was not sufficiently constructive and
did not fulfill the purposes they had in mind.

In actuality the basic difference between the National Association of Evangelicals (the movement
arising out of the St. Louis meeting) and the American Council of Christian Churches is in the area of
separation. While there are also some structural and
procedural differences, it is separation that is the
critical issue. One defender of the NAE position put
it this way: ". . . The N.A.E. does not insist that evangelical denominationalists separate from their
churches just because some ministers and leaders of
those denominations have apostasized."[8] The ACCC
required those fellowshiping with it to be completely out of the apostate churches; the NAE did
not. The defense of the NAE position is made vari-
ously.

> Super fundamentalist alliances have casti-
> gated devout men of many denominations
> because they have refused to forsake their
> churches because heretics have invaded.
> Fortunately, Athanasius didn't get out of the
> church when the Arians with their denial of
> Christ's divinity took temporary control of
> it.[9]

Another author opines that "the inclusivist policy of the National Association of Evangelicals has
enabled it to bore from within the major trunk of
American Protestantism, while the exclusivist Amer-

ican Council attacks the liberals from without."[10] Anyone who thinks the two-pronged approach has merit fails to consider what the Scriptures may have to say on the matter.

Perhaps no better source could be found to articulate the position and direction of the NAE than the man who, more than any other, was its guiding spirit in the early years, Harold John Ockenga. He explained the approach of the NAE:

> An up-to-date strategy for the evangelical cause must be based upon the principle of infiltration. . . . The Communists in their battles for Korea, Indo-China, and Tibet used the principle of infiltration. . . . We evangelicals need to realize that the liberals or modernists have been using this strategy for years. They have infiltrated our evangelical denominations, institutions, and movements and then have taken over control of them. It is time for firm evangelicals to seize their opportunity and influence modernist groups. Why is it incredible that the evangelicals should be able to infiltrate the denominations and strengthen the things that remain, and possibly resume control of such denominations? Certainly they have a responsibility to do so unless they are expelled from these denominations. We do not repudiate the Reformation principle, but we believe that a man has a responsibility within his denomination unless that denomination has officially repudiated Biblical Christianity.[11]

In further delineating the distinctions between the National Association of Evangelicals and the American Council, Ockenga stated:

> The specific goals of evangelicalism are definite. It seeks evangelical cooperation. This was expressed in the formation of the National Association of Evangelicals in 1942. The NAE insisted on a positive position toward the Federal Council of Churches and later National Council in distinction from the position later adopted by the American Council of Christian Churches. The NAE gathered evangelicals in fellowship for articulation of the evangelical cause in a score of different fields without attack upon other cooperative movements of diverse the-

ology. . . . Many individual congregations whose denominations were in the Federal Council of Churches were received into the NAE in order to articulate their conviction and give them an opportunity of cooperative action on an evangelical and orthodox base.[12]

With all due respect to Ockenga, who has a brilliant mind and many abilities, these arguments hardly seem to be adequate to support his cause. Where is the principle of infiltration taught in Scripture? We do not believe it is there. Perhaps the communists have used it effectively, but our handbook of operations is the Word of God, which plainly teaches that we should "touch not the unclean thing" (2 Cor. 6:17). The concept is often heard that separation is negative and therefore it is bad. Negative things are not always bad. They may be very good. To be against some things is equally as important as being for others.

The organization and position of the American Council of Christian Churches.

The American Council of Christian Churches was organized under the leadership of Carl McIntire, pastor of the Bible Presbyterian Church, Collingswood, New Jersey. McIntire had been a confederate with J. Gresham Machen and others who left the Presbyterian denomination. Following Machen's death, McIntire split with leaders of the Orthodox Presbyterian Church and formed the Bible Presbyterian Church, in which he has been the guiding spirit through the years. (While not all separatists agree with Carl McIntire's approach, it must be said to his credit that he has exhibited great courage through the years, and, in many cases has stood for that which was right.)

Burdened for a united testimony among those who believed the Bible and stood against the apostasy, McIntire led in the organization of the ACCC. The organizational meeting of the ACCC was held on September 17, 1941, in the building of the old National Bible Institute in New York City. McIntire was the first president of the body (1941-1944). Robert Ketcham was president from 1944-1947. As it grew, it added a number of denominations to its membership, all of which were relatively small. The largest group was the General Association of Regular Baptist Churches, whose churches belonged to the American Council by individual church action, not by virtue of their fellowship with the GARBC.

The doctrinal statement of the organization was fundamental. It excluded Pentecostal and holiness groups, which was a major distinction from the NAE, whose constituency contains a large percentage of such. The position on separation was clear as spelled out in the constitution:

> No national church or association which is a member of the National Council of Churches of Christ in the U.S.A. is eligible for membership in this Council so long as he retains connection with that body, nor shall local churches or individuals connected with national bodies holding membership in the said National Council be eligible for constituent membership.[13]

The preamble to the constitution declares that it is the command of God to His people "to be separate from all unbelief and corruption." The twenty-fifth anniversary brochure published by the ACCC stated that part of its purpose was to "expose the activities" of the National Council of Churches. Herein lies what might seem a subtle but nonetheless important difference between the ACCC and the NAE. It is probably why the NAE leaders often speak of the ACCC as negative. The ACCC spent time and effort documenting and publicly exposing the apostasy of the National Council. This does not mean that they have had no so-called positive programs of mutual cooperation. However, they have been much more precise, insistent and persistent in denouncing the apostasy of the National Council and its affiliated bodies.

In recent years deep-rooted dissension rent the American Council of Churches. Under the leadership of John Millheim, general secretary of the American Council for eight years, the witness of the Council had grown and prospered. However, more and more tensions arose between McIntire and the men who comprised the leadership of the Council. In the ensuing struggle, McIntire lost the leadership of the body; he has subsequently organized a competing group. In a similar conflict with old friends and cohorts (particularly Allen MacRae), McIntire's school, Faith Theological Seminary, was torn asunder, lost almost all its faculty, and spawned a new institution, Biblical School of Theology. Examples of such interpersonal struggles are often thrown up by critics of separatism as inherent in the separatist position. With some knowledge of Christendom as a whole gained through years of experience, we believe it can be accurately said that such problems are not the sole property of separatists. However, separatists have had their share and should mourn rather than rejoice over unnecessary fractures of fellowship and seek to profit from them so as to avoid them in the future.

Since the departure of McIntire from the leadership of the American Council, other brethren have been guiding the organization and seeking to maintain a clear witness for Biblical separation. Regular national and regional conferences continue to be held; literature is published; and God's people are warned concerning the Satanic programs of the day.

The testimony of the International Council of Christian Churches.

In 1948, also under the leadership of Carl McIntire, a worldwide organization was established to counteract the influence of the World Council of Churches. It is the International Council of Christian Churches. Membership in the organization has varied through the years, and conflicts similar to those within the American Council have proved troublesome. Some good conferences have been held in various parts of the world, and the separatist testimony has been strengthened. Such groups as follows have been a part of this organization: Council of Christian Churches of India, Japan Evangelical Council, Korean Council of Christian Churches, Presbyterian Church Orthodox of the Cameroun, Africa Evangelical Presbyterian Church and many other small bodies in various countries.

Conclusion

It is difficult to gather complete information about all the separatist groups that are found in various parts of the world. No doubt some interesting and helpful information could result from such a study. God has maintained a witness to the necessity of a pure church, though much of it is relatively unknown and overshadowed by larger and more popular movements.

Notes:

1. Histories of Plymouth Brethren include Harold Rowdon, *The Origins of the Brethren* (London: Pickering and Inglis, 1967) and W. B. Neatby, *A History of the Plymouth Brethren* (London: no publisher given, 1901).

2. See J. N. Darby, "On the Apostasy" and "The Apostasy of Successive Dispensations," *The Collected Writings of J. N. Darby*, ed. William Kelly (Kingston-on-Thames, England: Stow Hill Bible and Tract Depot, n.d.), I, 112-123 and 124-130.

3. Ibid., I, 361, 362.

4. Ibid., I, 364.

5. Rowdon, *The Origins of the Brethren*, pp. 280ff.

6. Ernest R. Sandeen, "Toward a Historical Interpretation of the Origins of Fundamentalism," *Church History*, XXXVI (March 1967), 66-83.

7. For a history of the NAE, see James DeForest Murch, *Cooperation Without Compromise* (Grand Rapids: Wm. B. Eerdmans Publishing Co., 1956).

8. David Baxter, "Why I Joined the N.A.E.," *United Evangelical Action* (January 1964), p. 16.

9. Ibid., p. 6.

10. Louis Gasper, *The Fundamentalist Movement* (Paris: Morton and Co., 1963), p. 26.

11. Harold J. Ockenga, "Resurgent Evangelical Leadership," *Christianity Today* (October 10, 1960), pp. 14, 15.

12. Ibid.

13. Constitution of the American Council of Christian Churches.

The New and the Young Evangelicals

8

SOME ERRORS are openly evident to true believers. Others are far more difficult to discern. The old modernism was transparently erroneous. God's people saw immediately that men who denied great truths taught in Scripture, such as the virgin birth of Christ and His substitutionary death, were obviously heretics. They were branded as such and duly rejected.

In more recent years, however, systems of thought have been espoused by men thought of as evangelical, teaching in evangelical schools or ministering to multitudes in evangelism. These are more subtle in their compromises and are much more difficult for the average believer to detect. The more truth contained in a specific system of thought the more difficult it is to isolate the errors. So it has been with the system which has been named the new evangelicalism.

The Rise of the New Evangelical School of Thought

Someone has said that the new evangelicalism had its beginnings with a mood. Perhaps this is true, and it makes it the more pernicious because a mood is extremely difficult to describe. You may feel it, but you cannot verbally diagnose it.

After the great struggles between modernism and fundamentalism, a group of younger men arose who had been reared, for the most part, in the homes and churches of fundamentalism. They were intellectually bright and aspiring scholars, many of them trained in either completely secular or liberally oriented religious schools. They were embarrassed by what they viewed as the "backwoodsy" provincialism of fundamentalism. Somehow they wanted to make evangelical truth more "relevant" and acceptable to a larger segment of society. No doubt many of them were sincere in their desire so to do. This mood which characterized them, however, was to lead them into strange paths.

Among these young scholars a more open spirit developed toward liberalism. Not that they openly embraced it, for they did not. But they desired to have more interaction with liberal scholars and leaders, with the hope of learning from them and hopefully imparting some Biblical truth to them as well. It was also their fervent desire that evangelical scholarship have wider recognition. They noted that evangelicalism (fundamentalism) was viewed as unscholarly by society as a whole. Why could not evangelicals win recognition through the writing of books and by securing faculty appointments at prestigious institutions? Of course, to win such recognition before unbelieving scholars, who, for the most part, were bitter enemies of Biblical truth, it would be necessary to show that evangelicals were sufficiently broad-minded and flexible to be able to accept new ideas and work them into their system of thought. Two areas were particularly troublesome to humanistic, unregenerate scholars: the doctrine of Biblical infallibility and the doctrine of creationism. But rising young evangelical thinkers were prepared to make concessions in these areas. Some began to adopt compromising positions regarding creationism. They accepted certain evolutionary premises, using such terms as "theistic evolution" or "threshold creationism." It was an attempt to incorporate at least parts of the theory of evolution into a Biblical framework.

As they moved along in their efforts, the doctrine of the inerrancy of Scripture became more and more of a stumbling block. If the Bible were without error when speaking in areas of biology, cosmology, geology and the like, then evangelicals would have no latitude to formulate views that would accommodate to contemporary scientific theories. So, many evangelicals began to equivocate on the doctrine of infallibility.

There were also the pressures of ecumenicity. Ecumenism is a hot commodity these days. Everyone who is anyone is in favor of getting together. For one to be against all Christians working together is like being opposed to the most sacred things in human life. The ecumenical fever struck many evangelicals. They disdained the isolationism of fundamentalism and longed for wider fellowship and broader horizons. They felt that the evangelical viewpoint should be represented in ecumenical circles. Definite moves were made to see that it was.

With these attitudes prevailing, several historical incidents took place which were important stepping-stones to the public, visible ascendancy of the new evangelicalism. One of the earliest was the organization of Fuller Theological Seminary (1947). Named after Charles Fuller, famous radio preacher, one of its main purposes, according to its first president, Harold Ockenga, was to train young men to go back into the old-line denominations and win a place for evangelicalism. Because millions of people were acquainted with Charles Fuller through the "Old-Fashioned Revival Hour," and because he was a strong Bible believer and preacher, the public naturally assumed that the school which bore his name would also occupy his theological position. In this they were sadly misled. Fuller became one of the major fountainheads for the new evangelical philosophy, and it has drifted farther and farther from the position of the man whose name it bears.

In 1956 articles appeared in *Christian Life* magazine entitled "Is Evangelical Theology Changing?" The conclusion of most of those interviewed was that it was changing. Among those responding to the question were Vernon Grounds, Bernard Ramm and Edward Carnell. They felt that fundamentalism was changing for the better by having a more open attitude toward the gift of tongues, by being less dispensational and by evidencing a more accepting attitude toward science.

In 1956 the magazine *Christianity Today* was begun. It was intended as an evangelical counterpart to the prestigious liberal journal *Christian Century*. In early issues two editorials appeared which showed the direction of the magazine. These were entitled "Beyond the Fundamentalist-Modernist Controversy" and "Dare We Renew the Controversy?" The thought was expressed that too much time has been wasted on fighting the battles with modernism; evangelicals should now progress to more productive efforts. Another editorial, "The Perils of Independency," supported the mediating view of the NAE as over against the views of independency (fundamental separatism) or church unionism (ecumenism). The editors of the periodical expressed the opinion that "the apostasy condemned by Independency is not as clearly discernible as it is assumed."[1]

Interestingly, in the early days of *Christianity Today's* existence, the Conservative Baptist Fellowship submitted a display ad for the famous Case books written by Chester Tulga. These books exposed various forms of modernism and unbelief. The magazine refused to run the ad, explaining the reaction of their editorial committee thus:

> There was a strong feeling, however, that in view of our circulation among many different groups, and of our announced intention to win the liberal, we would be, by running this ad in an early issue, standing the risk of alienating the very persons whom we are trying to win.[2]

The ministry of evangelist Billy Graham also aided the rise of the new evangelicalism since he was one of its chief spokesmen. His crusades, mixed in nature as they were, gave popular expression to the whole philosophy behind new evangelicalism. More is said of this in the next chapter.

Many of the new evangelicals were authors, some of them prolific. Books and articles began to appear from their pens. Edward Carnell, Carl Henry, Bernard Ramm and others produced works which had widespread influence and promoted aspects of the new evangelical position.

The National Association of Evangelicals became an organizational haven for leaders of this movement. The NAE made no official statements about it, but its own approach to the question of the apostasy made it a natural gathering place for the new evangelicals.

The Offspring
of New Evangelicalism:
Young Evangelicalism

Richard Quebedeaux in his definitive study *The Young Evangelicals* popularized the name. The young evangelicals basically are younger persons who have imbibed the general philosophy of the older new evangelicals, but are more radical and feel that the older evangelicals have not gone far enough in some of their viewpoints. They are particularly critical of the new evangelicals in areas of social justice, racial issues and attitude toward the established government. The young evangelicals are radical—theologically, politically and socially. They are activists in politics and in the promotion of various schemes for social betterment. They see these areas as "where the action is." Such persons as Bruce Larson, Tom Skinner, Leighton Ford and Nancy Hardesty are in the forefront of this movement. What are the characteristics of the new and young evangelicals? Let us examine them.

Some Leading Characteristics
of the New and Young Evangelicals

Basically, these people feel that fundamentalists are too narrow, having shut themselves up to very restricted theological positions. This is not to say that new evangelicals have no interest in theology. Some of them have great interest and ability in that area and have produced some works which make significant contributions. But they tend to be more open to diversity and willing to accept persons who hold heterodox views on some things. This is evidenced in the NAE where a wide variety of theological viewpoints are represented, some of which would not be tolerated by stronger fundamentalists. One writer, in analyzing what he called the "green-grass evangelicals" (young evangelicals) described their attitude:

Toleration of a wide diversity of theological viewpoints.

> Green-grass evangelicals are not interested in doctrinal questions like "eternal security.". . .
> Green-grass evangelicals believe that debates over Scripture (infallibility, inerrancy) pay no great dividends. They are more

experience-centered and rest their case for Christianity in the character of their encounter with Christ.[3]

Friendliness toward or acceptance of evolutionary theories.

Many new and young evangelicals have espoused some form of compromise with the theory of evolution. Millard Erickson describes it:

> The new evangelicals hold to "progressive creationism" (Carnell terms it "threshold evolution"). . . . The term "progressive creationism" is a good one. It is progressive in that it denies instantaneous creation and fixity of species. . . . The new evangelical apologist believes that this view fits the scientific data quite well. . . . Ramm and Carnell have both indicated that theistic evolution is not totally contradictory to the Biblical account.[4]

Espousal of or toleration toward questionable views of Scripture.

For a major discussion of just how far some have gone in repudiating orthodox views of the Bible, the student should consult Harold Lindsell's book *The Battle for the Bible*. It is with sadness and not with glee that such a book is read.

Paul King Jewett, a professor at Fuller Theological Seminary, declares in his book *Man As Male and Female* that Paul, in writing concerning the place of woman in Ephesians 5, does not present the infallible teaching of God but only reflects his own personal cultural background. Another professor at Fuller, William LaSor, declared:

> There is in my mind a clear difference between saying that the Bible is entirely without error in all that it teaches, and in saying that the Bible is without error in all matters (such as geology, astronomy, genealogy, figures, etc.) when these matters are not essential to the teaching of the context.[5]

LaSor is presenting a popular view of the Bible now promoted by new and young evangelicals. The Bible is inerrant (without error) when it is teaching us about God and His redemptive works (that is, when instructing in important doctrinal matters), but it may contain errors in other areas about which it speaks. Since it is only essential that the Bible be correct when it speaks about God's saving work and attendant truths, the errors in nonessential portions are of little consequence. In all fairness, it should be said that not all those who would be classified as new evangelicals have scuttled the doctrine of inerrancy. Strong protests against watering down this doctrine have come from such persons as Harold Lindsell, a new evangelical leader and former editor of *Christianity Today*. Nevertheless, there is a definite trend away from inerrancy on the part of numerous so-called evangelical scholars.

> Yet a growing vanguard of young graduates of evangelical colleges who hold doctorates from non-evangelical divinity centers now question or disown inerrancy and the doctrine is held less consistently by evangelical faculties.... Some retain the term and reassure supportive constituencies but nonetheless stretch the term's meaning.[6]

This latter admission is most significant. Evangelical institutions and agencies receive a bulk of their financial support from people who believe the Bible is inerrant. Such people would be greatly upset if convinced that causes they were supporting did not believe this doctrine. Those who hold deviant doctrines are careful not to reveal this clearly and publicly. They place a different interpretation upon the terms "inerrant" or "infallible" than have historically been accepted by fundamentalists or evangelicals.

> ... A surprising array of equally dedicated evangelicals is forming to insist that acceptance of historic Christian doctrines does not require belief in an inerrant book. This latter group maintains that where "inerrancy" refers to what the Holy Spirit is saying through Biblical writers, the word is rightly used; but to go beyond this in defining inerrancy is to suggest "a precision alien to the minds of the Bible writers and their own use of Scriptures," as one statement put it. What has made it a new ball game today is the emergence of a new type of evangelical. These persons accept the cardinal doctrines of Christianity in their full and literal meaning but agree that the higher critics have a point: there are errors in Scripture, and some of its precepts must be recognized as being culturally and historically conditioned.[7]

This is a serious matter. If what one leading

young evangelical says is true, then churches are in trouble. More and more they will have to face the issue of inerrancy and combat those who oppose it. The writer referred to says:

> The position—affirming that Scripture is inerrant or infallible in its teaching on matters of faith and conduct but not necessarily in all its assertions concerning history and the cosmos—is gradually becoming ascendant among the most highly respected evangelical theologians.[8]

Emphasis upon the implications of the social gospel.

The term "social gospel" means different things to different people. The older new evangelicals expressed concern that the church (especially fundamentalism) had neglected its social responsibility and placed all its emphasis upon personal salvation. The young evangelicals have come on even stronger in this area, and many of them see the gospel as two-pronged—individual and social. Mark Hatfield admonishes evangelicals to "turn to the theological problems of social revolution in the present. To do less is to concern ourselves with only half of the gospel."[9] One young evangelical described himself as a "professional social activist," and another announced that traditional orthodoxy "turned him off," but said that "the things that turn us on are social action things."[10]

To find such emphasis upon social action in the teaching of the New Testament would require diligent search and would prove fruitless. Primary place is given to the proclamation of saving grace in Jesus Christ, and the social betterment which surely follows is a by-product but not part of the message. Much of the support for strong social action arises from a misunderstanding and misappropriation of Old Testament passages and excerpts from the Sermon on the Mount.

Enthusiasm over cooperative evangelism.

The concept of large, area-wide evangelistic crusades as currently practiced by many contains an element subversive of Bible truth. It is the principle of combining together in such campaigns those who are truly fundamental in doctrine and those who are not. This approach has become a prominent part of the new evangelical thrust and is discussed in more detail in the next chapter.

Strong exception is taken to separatists who, according to new evangelicals, are guilty of "rending Christ's Body" by separating from denominational alignments. This is a sin against the unity of the church; it is a result of sinful pride, they say.

Separatists, of course, would ask, "What good is a unified church that is not pure?" If open error and blasphemy are tolerated within the bosom of that which calls itself Christ's Church, how can the blessing of God be expected?

> Emphasis upon the unity of the church in preference to its purity.

Edward Carnell was most vociferous in his denunciations. To him the fundamentalist mentality is "rigid, intolerant, and doctrinaire" and fundamentalism is "orthodoxy gone cultic."[11]

> Strong criticism of fundamentalism.

This cry is heard more especially from the young evangelicals, but the older evangelicals uttered it as well. Young evangelicals complain that "Fundamentalists and Evangelicals prefer to treat the symptoms of poverty with benevolence rather than to seek its cure with corporate political action."[12]

> Pleas for more political involvement.

The Bible certainly unfolds definite and important roles for women in the Lord's work. However, what might be called "evangelical women's libbers" have appeared on the scene in recent years, championing certain views of women which have not been normally held by evangelical Christians. It is a reflection within evangelicalism of the turbulence over "women's rights" that has been prominent in our contemporary society. A noted theologian writes, for example, on "Why I Favor the Ordination of Woman."[13] The writings of such women as Sharon Gallagher, Lucille Sider Dayton and Nancy Hardesty are representative of this position.

> Un-Biblical views regarding the place of women.

The Position of
New and Young Evangelicals
with Regard to Separation

Again it must be mentioned that viewpoints vary within the general spectrum of position known as new evangelicalism. As in most movements, there are left and right wings. The profile here drawn is an effort to present a general picture of the attitudes within the movement toward separation and separatists.

Willingness to remain within old-line denominations.

While not all new and young evangelicals find fellowship within the so-called old-line denominations, generally speaking they would defend the concept of doing so. Upon what basis would persons of evangelical persuasion remain in apostate groups? Several years ago L. Nelson Bell, Billy Graham's father-in-law, defended his continuing presence in the apostate Presbyterian Church by writing, ". . .The greatest field for Christian witnessing today is within the Church. . . . The doctrine of separation can lead people to abandon opportunities for witness where it is most greatly needed."[14]

Some have even gone so far as to deny or minimize the fact that the denominations are apostate. Carnell resisted the admission of complete apostasy. He carefully defined apostasy to suit his own tastes. "If a denomination removes the gospel from its creed or confession, or if it leaves the gospel but removes the believer's right to preach it, the believer may justly conclude that the denomination is apostate."[15] He notes, "[The separatist] does not realize that a denomination may be part of the Christian church, even though there are many—clergy and other—who not only reject the gospel, but who take active steps to preach a false gospel."[16]

Broad ecumenical fellowship.

Many new evangelical leaders for years have been active in various ecumenical fellowships and associations. Some of them have become involved in the National and World Council of Churches. Others participate in various dialogues and scholarly exchanges with liberals. For the most part, new and young evangelicals are very favorable toward increased rapport with nonevangelicals at both theological and ecclesiastical levels. Quebedeaux has an entire chapter entitled "Toward a More Effective Ecumenism." Not all his compatriots share the views he expresses (some have criticized him for going too far), but his utterances represent a very definite segment of thought. He feels that young evangelicals and liberals are growing closer to one another. He bases this opinion on:

> . . .The increasing convergence of values and priorities held by Evangelicals (the merging generation, at least) and those espoused in principle by mainstream Ecumenical Liberals. This convergence can best be illustrated by comparing the priorities and values of the Young Evangelicals with the goals established already in 1948 by the founding Amsterdam Assembly of the World Council of Churches.[17]

He then goes on to cite a report of that Assembly to prove his point. In the process of promoting a broader ecumenical spirit, Quebedeaux also urges evangelicals to obtain all or part of their training at liberal universities and seminaries. Thus they can obtain a bit more prestige and status in the eyes of modern society and give evangelicalism more clout.

Ecumenical missionary efforts.

The whole philosophy of infiltration and accommodation has made its way into worldwide missionary effort as well. One who has given impetus to this is Billy Graham. At his conference on evangelism held in Lausanne, Switzerland, in 1974 he declared that he had "warm relationships" with the World Council of Churches.[18] Such a statement coming from such a leader naturally has far-reaching repercussions. Say many, if Billy Graham can be friendly to the apostates in the World Council, so can we. Yet, upon examination, it will be found that some of the bitterest enemies of the true gospel in countries of the world have been representatives and members of the World Council.

Some mission agencies that are respected by evangelicals have fallen prey to new evangelical philosophies. Evangelical mission agencies have been divided over this matter in recent years. Such missions as Wycliffe Bible Translators and the Latin American Mission have been leaders in various ecumenical efforts. One writer, basically favorable to new evangelicalism, writes that both of these missions have been "sharply criticized" for their ecumenical involvements. He says, "The more conservative and traditional evangelical missions affiliated with LAM in the Interdenominational Foreign Missions Association ... question 'cooperative evangelism.' By this they mean cooperation with Pentecostals, Roman Catholics, or main line denominations."[19]

Conclusion

Separatists need to understand and guard against the encroachments of the new evangelicalism. It is a subtle system, propagated as it is by men and women who claim to be loyal to the Scriptures. Many of the things they believe are good and would be shared by separatists. The differences, however, are vital. Courageous leadership is needed on the part of separatist pastors. Solid teaching must be given so that God's people will not be swayed by that which they may imbibe in ignorance.

Notes:

1. Editorial, "The Perils of Independency," *Christianity Today* (November 12, 1956), pp. 20-23.

2. Quoted by R. T. Ketcham, "*Christianity Today*—An Analysis," *Baptist Bulletin*, XXII (March 1957), 8, 9.

3. Bernard Ramm, "Welcome, Green-Grass Evangelicals," *Eternity* (March 1974), p. 13.

4. Millard Erickson, *The New Evangelical Theology* (Westwood, NJ: Fleming Revell, 1968), pp. 160, 161.

5. William LaSor, "Life Under Tension," *The Authority of Scripture at Fuller* (booklet published by Fuller Theological Seminary), p. 27.

6. Carl F. H. Henry, "Conflict Over Biblical Inerrancy," *Christianity Today* (May 7, 1976), p. 24.

7. G. Aiken Taylor, "Is God As Good As His Word?" *Christianity Today* (February 4, 1977), p. 22.

8. Richard Quebedeaux, "The Evangelicals: New Trends and Tensions," *Christianity and Crisis* (September 20, 1976), p. 198.

9. Mark Hatfield, *Conflict and Conscience* (Waco, TX: Word Books, 1971), p. 25.

10. "A Conversation with Young Evangelicals," *Post-American* (January 1975), p. 7.

11. Edward John Carnell, *The Case for Orthodox Theology* (Philadelphia: The Westminster Press, 1959), pp. 113, 114.

12. Richard Quebedeaux, *The Young Evangelicals* (New York: Harper & Row, Publishers, 1974), p. 127.

13. Paul King Jewett, "Why I Favor the Ordination of Women," *Christianity Today* (June 6, 1975), pp. 7-10.

14. L. Nelson Bell, "On Separation," *Christianity Today* (October 8, 1971), p. 26.

15. Carnell, *The Case for Orthodox Theology*, p. 137.

16. Ibid., pp. 134, 135.

17. Quebedeaux, *The Young Evangelicals*, pp. 138, 139.

18. John Millheim, "A Consortium of Compromise," *Baptist Bulletin*, XXXX (October 1974), 10.

19. Russell T. Hitt, "The Latin American Experiment," *Eternity* (November 1975), p. 17.

Ecumenical Evangelism— A Frontal Attack on Biblical Separation

PROBABLY NO issue in recent years has been more vexing to separatists than that of ecumenical evangelism. The reason for this can be easily grasped. Here is a faithful pastor who has taught his people through the years that it is wrong for their church to fellowship with the Methodist and Presbyterian churches in the little suburb where they are located because these churches do not preach the gospel. However, a noted evangelist, in organizing his crusade in the area, requests, yes insists, that these two churches, as well as scores of others like them, be included in the crusade plans.

How is the pastor to explain this? What he has opposed, the glamorous evangelist encourages. Some of his people, enamored with the evangelist, agitate within the church for cooperation with the crusade, either producing tremendous tensions within the congregation by so doing, or, in some cases, even provoking a church split. Such an illustration is not fanciful nor theoretical. It can be documented many times over.

One man more than any other has epitomized this approach to evangelism. His name is a household word not only in the United States but in other countries of the world. We speak of Billy Graham. While other men have engaged in ecumenical crusades (particularly after Graham popularized them), none of them have the prominence in the evangelistic field that Graham does. For this reason his ministry is analyzed as representative of a philosophy and approach that has caused deep grief to Biblical separatists.

The Ministry of Billy Graham

The early ministry of Billy Graham began in a small church in a suburb of Chicago. With the rise of the organization Youth for Christ, he became increasingly well-known as a youth speaker across the country. Still a young man, he became president of a small Christian college in Minneapolis— Northwestern Schools. William B. Riley, noted fundamentalist warrior who had founded the school, personally selected Graham to succeed him. After a few years it became apparent that education was not Graham's field, and he resigned to go into full-time evangelism. In those days he was known as a fundamentalist, and his fellowship and support came from that group.

In 1948 when Graham was editor-in-chief of *The Pilot* (Northwestern's magazine), it declared on its masthead that it took a "militant stand against Modernism in every form." At this same time Graham was a member of the Cooperating Board of the *Sword of the Lord*, a fundamentalist paper edited by John R. Rice. He was honored by a degree from Bob Jones University. Later, when it became evident that Graham was changing his position, the doughty fundamentalist pastor, Robert Shuler, stated:

> None of the great evangelists had ever before accepted the sponsorship of modernists. Billy himself had not only refused to hold a campaign under their sponsorship, but had openly declared that he never would. *In his Los Angeles Campaign I personally saw and heard him turn down and politely decline the approval and cooperation of the Church Federation which represented the Federal Council, now the National Council.*[1]

Clearly, in his early ministry Graham was both fundamental and separated from the apostasy.

The multiplying compromises of Billy Graham.

To offer a complete documentary of all the various questionable involvements of Billy Graham would require space not available here. Gradually over the years he has moved farther from his original position as a fundamentalist. At first fundamentalists such as John R. Rice, editor of the *Sword of the Lord*, endeavored to defend him; but it became quite evident as time went on that it was impossible for a convinced Bible-believer to defend Graham's actions. Rice, Bob Jones, Sr. and Jr., Carl McIntire and many other fundamentalist leaders began to alert the Christian public to the sad compromises Graham was making. A *few* examples follow.

1957, New York Crusade. Liberals, such as the notorious Henry P. Van Dusen, president of Union Theological Seminary, were on the crusade committees. In a magazine interview Billy Graham hailed Van Dusen as one of the "classic examples" of persons "converted by Billy Sunday."[2] At that same time the magazines were announcing Van Dusen's new book *The Vindication of Liberal Theology.* The "convert" of Billy Sunday was not promoting the theology of Mr. Sunday.

1958, San Francisco Crusade. Co-chairman of the crusade was Carl Howie, leading liberal, who, in his book *The Old Testament Story,* reveals a very liberal viewpoint regarding such matters as the creation account, the Noahic flood and the miracles of Elisha. Howie, the liberal, was evangelizing with Graham, the evangelical.

1961. Graham attended (as a friend, not a critic) the New Delhi meeting of the World Council of Churches.

1963, Los Angeles Crusade. Bishop Gerald Kennedy, noted Methodist liberal, was involved as a leader in this campaign.

1965. Graham addressed the college students and faculty at Belmont Abbey, a Roman Catholic institution.

1966. Graham addressed the National Council of Churches in Miami. He praised some liberal ministers, and he spoke no word of rebuke to the multitudes of false prophets who sat before him.

1968. Belmont Abbey, the Catholic institution in Belmont, North Carolina, bestowed an honorary doctorate on Billy Graham, and he was the main speaker at their Institute for Ecumenic Dialogues.

1969. The U.S. Congress on Evangelism met in Minneapolis, sponsored by Graham. The event was complete with rock music and an address by the civil rights leader, Ralph Abernathy. A morning devotional was given by a Roman priest.

1971. A Roman Catholic priest participated in the crusade in Oakland.

1973. Graham, in a message delivered at Leighton Ford's "Reachout" conducted in Milwaukee on October 21, 1973, described what a beautiful experience he had preaching in a Roman Catholic cathedral and participating in a funeral mass.

The problem of Billy Graham is perhaps the toughest one that contemporary separatists have had to face. He is personable. He preaches the old message, "Ye must be born again." His ministry has touched millions and continues to do so. Many have been saved through his preaching. The average believer, hearing him on the radio or seeing his TV programs, only knows there is a stirring call to sinners to receive Christ. Why then are some preachers and others upset with him? Is he not a good man? Does he not preach Christ? These are natural reactions. To criticize a wonderful person like Billy Graham is like criticizing motherhood, the flag and country, or even the Lord Himself. Persons who dare to do so find themselves immediately in an uncomfortable position.

But the issue is not Billy Graham. The issue is far deeper and more far-reaching than merely a person. The issue is a scriptural one—the very one that we have been discussing in this volume. It is not a question of whether or not we like Graham. It is a question of whether or not the philosophy of Christian work which he represents is a Biblical one. It is not a debate over the merits of a particular preacher, but a debate over the teaching of the Bible regarding separation from evil doctrine. Should Bible-believers and non-Bible-believers cooperate in Christian work?

An Examination
of Arguments Used
To Support Ecumenical Evangelism

The method employed by Billy Graham and others has come to be known as ecumenical evangelism. It received this name because it promotes evangelism which gathers together all kinds of churches and people in an effort of evangelism. It is therefore ecumenical. It includes those who believe in the total inspiration of Scripture and the finality of its revelation, and those who do not.

When fundamentalists and separatists began to oppose Graham's new methods, Robert Ferm was commissioned to write a book in his defense. Ferm was at that time the dean of students at Houghton College. The book entitled *Cooperative Evangelism* (1958) was an effort to show that this approach to evangelism was Biblical and also in line with what others had practiced.

Since that time Graham has had many defenders. What are some arguments advanced to support Graham's practice of having a mixed sponsorship of Bible-believers and apostates?

He is winning souls; therefore we ought not criticize him.

This is probably one of the most common arguments heard. It seems especially impressive to the average believer. Fundamentalists through the years have been taught to love evangelism and to be concerned about reaching the world for Christ. With this in their nature, it is no wonder they would look favorably upon anyone who ostensibly is leading thousands to a saving knowledge of Christ.

This argument, however, is based upon an unscriptural premise. Basically, it says that the end justifies the means. If a good result is obtained, then the methods for achieving it matter little. This is religious pragmatism. It cannot be defended from Scripture. A man was struck dead in Old Testament times for doing God's work (moving the ark) in the wrong way (2 Sam. 6:1-11). God does not merely want His work done. He wants it done in the manner which He prescribes according to the rules He has laid down. Cooperation with liberal, Christ-rejecting preachers is not prescribed in Scripture.

Also overlooked is another very important fact. Our first duty as Christians is not to win souls. Our first duty is to do the will of God. Obviously, part of God's will for believers is to witness concerning His Son. But an overarching responsibility must govern all that we do for God. We are responsible to do His will. Saul reported with pride to Samuel that he had done the will of God in destroying the Amalekites.

But he had not done *all* the will of God. He was attempting to obey God while at the same time disobeying Him. He kept back some of the animals he was told to destroy on the pretext that he was honoring God in so doing. Samuel the prophet, however, was not taken in. He declared, "Behold, to obey is better than sacrifice. . ." (1 Sam. 15:22). This is not to say that sacrifice was not good. In its place and according to God's plan, it was good. But if not conducted in obedience to God, it was bad. So it is with soul winning. "To obey is better than to evangelize" (if, in evangelizing, one is disobeying God).

Results prove nothing concerning the validity of the means. Balaam preached some tremendous sermons (Num. 22—24), but we are warned against Balaam's "way" and "error" in the New Testament (2 Pet. 2:15; Jude 11). Balaam was an exceedingly effective preacher, but his ways, his methods, were displeasing to God.

What is the proper way by which to judge religious work? We cannot judge by apparent effectiveness. We must judge *by the standard of God's Word*. How may a believer know whether Billy Graham (or anyone else) is doing the right thing? There is only one infallible yardstick. "Through thy precepts I get understanding: therefore I hate every false way. Thy word is a lamp unto my feet, and a light unto my path" (Ps. 119:104, 105). Falseness is detected as the Word of God is understood and applied. Does God's Word allow us to have cooperative spiritual efforts with those who deny His truth? If so, then we are free to do so. If not, we are bound to refuse.

He obtains a wider hearing for the gospel by inviting liberals to participate.

In other words, one will have bigger crowds if one allows a wider sponsorship. How does this square with the statement of the psalmist, "Blessed is the man that walketh not in the counsel of the ungodly. . ." (Ps. 1:1)? Are we not commanded by such a Scripture to avoid attempted spiritual union with those who do not know the Lord? And what about other specific Scriptures which teach the same? We are to "avoid" those who teach and practice things contrary to apostolic doctrine (Rom. 16:17).

This is truly an argument that brings sadness to the heart of one who believes in the sovereignty of a mighty God. Must we enlist the puny efforts and blessings of vessels of clay (and apostate ones at that) in order to insure the success of an evangelistic crusade? Does the omnipotent God need the help of unsaved preachers to gather for Himself a crowd so that His saving gospel may be heard? Surely the answer to this is self-evident.

Much is made of the various admonitions in Scripture to refrain from judging. "Here is a man who is doing his very best for Christ. It is cruel and unscriptural to judge him." These are the sentiments expressed. This sounds like a pious argument, and it is an emotional one; but it bears examination.

We are not to judge God's servants.

Does Scripture command us to avoid *all* judging? The answer is an emphatic no! We are expressly commanded to judge Christian brethren with regard to certain things. How are we to know if a brother is walking "disorderly" (2 Thess. 3:6)? We must make a judgment. This judgment may lead us to "withdraw" fellowship from him. Would this be wrong? Ought we to avoid such judgment? No, we are told by God to exercise it.

Paul passed judgment on Peter's actions at Antioch and rebuked him because "he was to be blamed," having wandered from the Lord's will (Gal. 2:11-14). John rebuked Diotrephes for unseemly behavior (3 John 9, 10). Paul exposed the false teaching of some who misled people (2 Tim. 2:17, 18).

No, the argument that we are never to judge another believer will not stand up. Local churches must pass judgment on whether or not to receive (or discipline) members. They are to do this according to scriptural standards, *but they are to do it.*

Where in the New Testament does it ever state that either the Lord or His famous apostle accepted the sponsorship of Jewish liberals or any others? When they ministered in synagogues, they did so with no sponsorship. They simply arose and discussed the Scriptures as was the custom in those days. In so doing they in no way condoned the unbelief and modernism of any who were present. The

Jesus and Paul were sponsored by liberals when they preached in Jewish synagogues.

Lord devoted an entire message to the denunciation of false teachers, excoriating them for their spiritual emptiness (Matt. 23). It would not be an acceptable message in a modern ecumenical crusade.

More love should be displayed by God's people.

If we would love one another more, say some, we would not have the desire nor the time to criticize one another; we would not shut out from our fellowship people who may not agree with us on every point. Unfortunately, the great attribute of love is often employed as an excuse for all kinds of compromise and disobedience. True godly love, however, is not characterized by indifference to truth. God's attributes of love and truth are not contradictory but complimentary. We must always remember the statement of Christ, "If ye love me, keep my commandments" (John 14:15). True love issues in obedience to Christ's commands (cf. John 14:21, 23; 15:9, 10). That which claims to be love and deliberately disobeys God's Word is deficient indeed.

Some people have the notion that it is very unloving to present an issue so clearly as to force someone to admit they are wrong. The great defender of the faith, J. Gresham Machen, warned about this when he wrote:

> Presenting an issue sharply is indeed by no means a popular business at the present time; there are many who prefer to fight their intellectual battles in what Dr. Francis Patton has aptly called a "condition of low visibility." Clear-cut definition of terms in religious matter, bold facing of the logical implications of religious views, is by many persons regarded as an impious proceeding. . . . Light may at times be an impertinent intruder, but it is always beneficial in the end. The type of religion which rejoices in the pious sounds of traditional phrases, regardless of their meanings, or shrinks from "controversial" matters, will never stand amid the shocks of life.[3]

If truly born-again believers are filled with love, they will exercise that love in discernment. Shakespeare declared through one of his characters, "Love is blind, and lovers cannot see the pretty follies that themselves commit." While this may be true of some human love, it is never true of divine love. Love is to "abound yet more and more in knowledge and in all discernment" (Phil. 1:9). The word *discernment* includes the thought of making sound judgments. These sound judgments are to be made in love according to this passage. It is not a mark of divine love to ignore that which is wrong or contrary to God's Book.

Some say an evangelist is not to warn about unbelief in churches. He is to preach the gospel, and the Holy Spirit will correctly guide the converts. One thing needs to be understood clearly. The Holy Spirit does not guide believers in a vacuum nor solely through His individual ministry to them as they study the Word. *The Holy Spirit guides believers through pastors and other ministers of the Lord as they correctly teach and apply the Scriptures.* To say that a preacher of God's Word has no responsibility to instruct people concerning false teaching or false churches is totally contradicted by the New Testament. The evangelist is to "perfect the saints" (that is, build them up, make them strong in the faith, Eph. 4:12). He cannot do that if he is silent about the terrible apostasy and the deceitful ministries of the Devil's preachers. An evangelist is to warn his converts about the false "winds of doctrine" (Eph. 4:14). Thus it will not do to respond as did Billy Graham to his critics:

An evangelist is not to warn about unbelief.

> We have been challenged on what happens to converts when the crusade is over. Apparently these brethren have no faith in the Holy Spirit. . . . The work of regeneration is the work of the Holy Spirit. The work of follow-up is the work of the Holy Spirit.[4]

Yes, both things are true, but it is what is left out that is false. The work of regeneration is accomplished as the gospel is preached *through a man.* The work of establishing the saints (follow-up) is accomplished as the Bible is taught *through a man.* Both of these divine works are conducted through human ministry. The Holy Spirit instructs believers about their Christian duties through the ministry of men.

Years ago the popular eastern preacher, Percy

Crawford, undertook to explain Graham's practice of sending the names of the converts in his campaigns to liberal churches. How pathetic and heartrending to read his statement! He speaks of Billy Graham's well-publicized Los Angeles crusade which started him on the road to fame.

> Then came the big break in California. News of the blessing of God on his message spread like wild fire. Then came a difficult choice—was he to work with the National Council of Churches and other modernistic-controlled groups or work independently? This was his big decision: was he to say to converts—"join the church of your choice" or "join a good fundamental church that preaches the Word of God, the blood, and a literal hell!" The latter is what I say. That's why I preach to twenty-five compared with Billy Graham's twenty-five thousand.[5]

The question to ask is obvious: Must we invite converts to Christ-denying churches so as to gain the support of their pastors? May God forgive us for even entertaining the thought!

If liberals want to come, why should we object?

No one is objecting to liberals hearing the gospel. This is not the issue. The issue is simply this: Should we invite liberals to hold places on evangelistic crusade committees, pray at the services and present and honor them in public as though they were true servants of Christ? Billy Graham for years has honored Bible-denying liberal preachers on his platforms. He not only fails to repudiate them and their teachings, but he hails them before his vast audiences as great spiritual leaders. This is wrong. It is completely contrary to the practice of our Savior, to the example of the apostles and to the direct commands of Scripture.

The Tragic Results of Ecumenical Evangelism

What difference does it make whether or not Graham or others engage in ecumenical evangelism? Is it really serious enough to warrant public discussion? Yes, we believe it is. The aftermath of such crusades is devastating indeed.

The Billy Graham crusades have been part of a large, well-supported effort to destroy the barriers that were erected between fundamentalists and liberals during the controversies in the earlier part of the century. This is a major thrust of the new evangelicalism. Let us woo the liberal by being kind and generous, by talking with him and by cooperating with him in common causes. The well-known modernist, E. Stanley Jones, had a most interesting observation concerning Billy Graham back in the days when he was first beginning to practice ecumenical evangelism. It is contained in a letter which he wrote to a liberal periodical.

A deliberate attempt to break down barriers between fundamentalism and liberalism.

> Sirs: If there be truth to Hegel's dictum, and I believe there is, . . . then it seems to be applicable to the controversy regarding the Graham crusade going on in your pages. Hegel said that thesis produces its opposite antithesis and then out of a struggle of opposites a third something is born in which the truth in thesis and the truth in antithesis are gathered up into something larger than each, a synthesis.
>
> The thesis in this controversy in the larger aspects is conservatism, and it has produced its opposite, liberalism. . . . Out of this struggle of thesis and antithesis is emerging a something which seems to be gathering up the truth in each in a higher synthesis.
>
> The Graham crusade is a symbol of that emerging synthesis. Both groups want to share Christ in differing terminology and in differing methods, but both want to share Christ. The synthesis is emerging at a very important place—at the place of evangelism.
>
> After talking with Billy Graham I am persuaded that he is more or less consciously one of the meeting places of the movement toward synthesis.[6]

While this was only an expression of personal opinion at the time, we believe the events of the intervening years have shown much of it to be true. Billy Graham has tried to span the gulf between the historic Christian faith as represented in fundamentalism and the departure from that faith as represented in modern religious liberalism.

A direct attack upon the doctrine of separation.

If the doctrine of separation be a scriptural one, and if believers are not to support nor have fellowship with those who deny the faith, then Graham's philosophy of conducting crusades which incorporate both kinds of people is manifestly wrong. If his modus operandi is proper, then thousands of pastors and churches who embrace separatist views are in error and should seek to become more inclusivistic. Groups of separatist churches such as the General Association of Regular Baptist Churches, the Baptist Bible Fellowship, Bible Presbyterians and many others are occupying the wrong position if Graham is right. Either the Scriptures teach what Billy Graham practices—inclusivism—or they don't. If they do teach it, then separatist bodies are in disobedience to God. If they don't teach it, Billy Graham is in the place of disobedience.

A source of trouble to local pastors.

As we illustrated at the beginning of this chapter, pastors are put in a very difficult position by the methods of Graham and others who imitate him. Crusade leaders are very aggressive in seeking support for the meetings. They want laymen who will give money, help with set-up work, make calls and counsel converts. In some cases, pastors, striving to be true to Biblical principles, seek to hold the line by refusing to cooperate with the crusades; but they are pressured by well-meaning but ill-taught laymen in their churches who are enthusiastic for the campaign. Not a few local congregations have had serious difficulties over the Graham crusades.

Building churches that deny the Word of God.

Graham's operating principle is this: Let converts indicate the church of their choice, send the cards to the pastor of the church, and let the pastor seek to recruit the convert for his church. By following this policy, the Graham crusades send many of the newborn lambs right into the den of the wolf, the apostate minister. Part of the responsibility of any evangelist is to guide his converts into churches that are going to teach them the Scriptures and the way of the Lord. To send them to churches where the gospel is not proclaimed and the whole counsel of God taught is a serious offense.

Sometimes people ask the question, If liberal

ministers do not agree with Graham's theology, why do they support his meetings? The new evangelical periodical, *Christianity Today*, on one occasion sought to answer that question. It stated in part:

> . . . Approval of Graham's ministry is wider than sympathy for his theology. While some Protestant leaders attach little significance to doctrine of any kind, they interpret mass evangelism as a legitimate phase of a wider "return to religion" in contemporary American life. Others, widely apprehensive of Graham's theology, nonetheless welcome his impact on the masses for its inevitable spur to church attendance, and even reinforcement of membership with new recruits at a time of financially burdensome physical expansion. Still others, while in theological disagreement with Graham, feel that his evangelical supporters could greatly enrich the ecumenical movement no less than liberal, neoorthodox, and conservative forces already within its framework have done. To some, Graham holds a strategic key to the ecumenical movement. To others, whatever theological difficulties may be involved for contemporary Protestantism, Graham's ministry demonstrates the *pragmatic* success of his evangelistic message.[7]

Inclusivism is the concept that persons of contrary theological viewpoints can and should cooperate in the work of the Lord. This was the very concept that prevailed (and still does) within the old Northern Baptist Convention (now American Baptist Churches) and resulted in the defection of hundreds of churches who did not accept it as a scriptural principle. The concept was finally (though too late) repudiated by Billy Graham's mentor—W. B. Riley. At the very close of his ministry, he resigned by letter from the Northern Baptist Convention, citing the fact that he was ashamed to remain any longer within a mixed body of believers and unbelievers. Was Riley correct in denouncing the principle of inclusivism, or is Billy Graham right in promoting it? Both positions cannot be correct. The Bible, the final authority in such questions, plainly is on the side of Riley. To obey God one must leave the fellowship of the ungodly.

The spread of the philosophy of inclusivism.

Largely as a result of Billy Graham's whole-hearted endorsement of this principle, it is now embraced by many Christian leaders and professedly evangelical organizations. Other evangelists have followed the example of Graham in conducting mixed campaigns. The towering figure of Graham has made a great impact upon the Christian world. While we thank God for those who have been genuinely born again through his ministry, we grieve over the sad, serious and long-lasting side effects which his crusades have had. Someone has said that it is wonderful to gather the fruit, but if one must wreck the orchard to do so, it is too high a price to pay.

Ecumenical Evangelism:
A Violation of Scriptural Principles

The next chapter gives a more detailed look at the scriptural passages supporting the doctrine of separation. We summarize here reasons why many have not been able to support evangelistic crusades and other endeavors operating on the principles practiced by Billy Graham.

(1) We are to separate from those who are not sound in the faith (2 Tim. 3:5).

(2) We are not to assist the cause of the ungodly (2 Chron. 19:2).

(3) We are not to give honor to one who denies the faith (Gal. 1:6-9).

(4) We are to examine a person's theological position and find it acceptable before cooperating with him in spiritual efforts (1 John 4:1).

(5) We are commanded not to join forces with unbelievers in the Lord's work (2 Cor. 6:14).

(6) We are not to emphasize unity at the expense of doctrinal purity (Jude 3).

(7) We are not to encourage or cooperate with persons of unsound doctrine (2 John 10, 11).

With great grief of heart many separatists have had to refuse to cooperate with Billy Graham. We love him despite our disagreements with him. We pray that God might somehow cause him to return to the "old paths" where is the "good way."

Notes:

1. Robert Shuler (ed.), *The Methodist Challenge* (October 1957).

2. Billy Graham, personal interview, *U. S. News and World Report* (September 1957), p. 72.

3. J. Gresham Machen, *Christianity and Liberalism* (Grand Rapids: Wm. B. Eerdmans Publishing Co., 1974), p. 1.

4. Message delivered April 3, 1957.

5. Percy Crawford (ed.), *Youth on the Move News* (May 1957).

6. E. Stanley Jones, letter published in *Christian Century* (August 14, 1957).

7. Editorial on Graham's ministry, *Christianity Today* (September 6, 1957), p. 4.

Notes

The Scriptural Basis of Ecclesiastical Separation

10

WHAT IS IT that demands separation? Why would the subject even be pertinent to believers? It is the failure of the professing church to maintain a clear witness to the truth which has caused those who love the truth, in whatever age they have lived, to seek to perpetuate such a witness outside of the religious establishment. Repudiation of divine truth within an organized body of professing Christians demands reaffirmation of truth in a newly established body.

As we have already seen, the doctrine of the fall of the church has been reiterated by various separatist groups through the centuries. Many have taught that the corruption of the visible church began with Constantine and the marriage of the church to the state. Regardless of where one might place the origin of departure from apostolic truth, it has been a constantly recurring tendency for the visible church to drift from sound doctrine to false doctrine. Apostasy insidiously works its way until those who long for a pure church are motivated to begin anew. This is one of the laments made by anti-separatists—that the doctrine of separation, premised as it is upon the ideal of a pure church, lends itself to repeated separations. This is true in a sense because every generation must fight its own battles, and the war is never won. The culprit, however, is not the prickly fundamentalist who cannot live at peace with his brethren, but rather the never ending maliciousness of Satan.

Apostasy and Its Implications

To understand the Biblical doctrine of separation, it is necessary to see it against the backdrop of

The nature of apostasy.

scriptural teaching on apostasy. Apostasy requires separation.

The noun *apostasy* is used only twice in the Greek New Testament (Acts 21:21; 2 Thess. 2:3). The concept, however, is much more prevalent. The word is found several times in the Septuagint (e.g., Josh. 22:22; 2 Chron. 29:19). The word was used often in classical Greek in a political sense, the noun referring to a defection or revolt. Apostasy, however, as spoken of in the New Testament, refers to religious defection. It denotes the removal from or forsaking of a person or a system of thought (as in Acts 21:21). Apostasy was epitomized in Satan who revolted against His Creator and deliberately turned his back upon the truth to which he had been exposed (Ezek. 28:11-19). Apostasy is a direct repudiation of divine truth to which one has been clearly exposed and which one has professed. The departure is willful as the very word implies and as the actions of the apostates display (e.g., 1 Tim. 4:1-3). In its verb form, the word *apostasy* is used in the New Testament of personal withdrawal and of withdrawal from the faith as a revealed system of truth (Luke 8:13; 1 Tim. 4:1; Heb. 3:12). Unger more specifically defines apostasy as "the act of a professed Christian, who knowingly and deliberately rejects revealed truth regarding the deity of Christ (I John 4:1-3) and redemption through his atoning sacrifice (Phil. 3:18; II Pet. 2:1). . . .[1]

It should be carefully noted that heresy (using the term in the strict sense in which it is used in the New Testament) is not apostasy. The word *heresy* is used only in Titus 3:10 and refers to a selfish choice which results in party divisions within the church. It emphasizes carnal troublemaking, not theological error.

Apostasy is also to be distinguished from ignorance. Acts 19:1-9 gives an illustration of persons who were inadequately instructed in divine truth, but they were not deliberate rejectors thereof.

The characteristics of apostates.

Various characteristics of apostates are given in the New Testament. Some of them are as follows:

(1) They repudiate the organized system of revealed truth—the faith (2 Tim. 3:5).

(2) They are motivated by demons (1 Tim. 4:1).

(3) They are not truthful (1 Tim. 4:2).

(4) They are deceptive (2 Pet. 2:13).

(5) They oppose divine authority (Jude 8).

(6) They are spiritually dead (Jude 12).

(7) They have a form of religion without power (2 Tim. 3:5).

Satan's doctrines are spread by Satan's "ministers" (2 Cor. 11:13-15). Unsaved people who have no spiritual discernment hail these men as great religious leaders, while the preachers of the truth, God's ministers, are despised as uncooperative, divisive and unloving. The Devil's preachers accommodate themselves to the tastes of their unregenerate hearers and are thus much more popular.

Can the course of apostasy be checked once it has become firmly entrenched in a body? Is it possible, through diligent Bible teaching and evangelism, to oust from a religious denomination those who are teaching error and to bring that body back to the truth? It is at this very point that conflict develops between nonseparatists and separatists. In all centuries nonseparatists have ever nourished the hope that the situation, dark as it might seem, was not completely hopeless; God might intervene, bring revival and a return to scriptural principles. Certain basic facts about apostasy as they appear in a study of the New Testament, however, seem to militate against such optimism. **The progression of apostasy.**

Apostasy is very serious. The entirety of revelation on the subject would indicate that God's anger burns against those who depart from the faith.

Apostasy is definable and discoverable. We need not appear baffled by what constitutes apostasy. It is plainly outlined for us. Those who promulgate it can be readily identified.

Apostasy is pervasive and progressive. False teaching is likened to leaven by the Lord Jesus in His teaching to the disciples (Matt. 16:12). He specifically states that the leaven pictures the "doctrine of the Pharisees and Sadducees." The "leaven of the

Pharisees" is religious externalism (Matt. 16:6; 23:14, 16, 28). The "leaven of the Sadduccees" is skepticism toward the supernatural (Matt. 22:23, 29). The "leaven of the Herodians" is the spirit of worldly compromise (Matt. 22:16-21). All three of these characteristics are seen in modern religious liberalism which has gripped the leading denominations of the world for many years. Certainly they are amply demonstrated in such worldly yet professedly religious groups as the National and World Councils of Churches.

Leaven pictures false doctrine in that it works its way quickly through the mass "till the whole [is] leavened" (Matt. 13:33). It is quite common for interpreters to admit the fact that leaven in Matthew 16 is false doctrine because Christ plainly says so, but they abandon that meaning when interpreting the parable of the leaven in Matthew 13:33. There they see the gospel permeating the world, or some other good influence gradually winning its way. However, Unger is more accurate when he takes Matthew 13:33 as referring to the gradual progress of evil within Christendom, which interpretation "is in agreement with the unvarying Scriptural meaning of leaven."[2]

False teaching is also likened to gangrene. It spreads. The bacteria enters the wound and eats away the flesh (2 Tim. 2:17).

Apostasy is irremediable and awaits judgment (2 Pet. 2:17, 21; Jude 11-15). In none of these passages is any hope given that apostasy will be checked and that truth will triumph. Apostates will not be converted, repent of their errors and return to the fold. For them the "mist of darkness is reserved for ever" (2 Pet. 2:17). They are spiritually lifeless, wandering in their darkness, and doomed for judgment (Jude 12, 13).

Church history yields no example of a group or denomination that, having been captured by apostates, has been rescued and restored to a Biblical witness. No Biblical evidence, to this author's knowledge, supports the concept that the professing church as a whole will return to its pristine and apostolic faith prior to Christ's return. While

separatists are often lampooned as hopeless pes-
simists, their pessimism concerning the future—
both of the world and the professing church—rests
not upon some morose nature but upon specific declarations of Scripture. As the age moves on to its
conclusion, apostasy will deepen, "perilous times
shall come" (2 Tim. 3:1), and "evil men and seducers
shall grow worse and worse" (2 Tim. 3:13).

*Apostasy will come to full fruition during the
time of the tribulation in the mother of harlots, Babylon the Great (Rev. 17).* We will not review all the
various interpretations of this passage. It seems obvious by her name and the context that the harlot is a
false religious system. Unfaithfulness to divine truth
was pictured as harlotry in the Old Testament (cf.,
Isa. 1:21; Jer. 2:20). "She is a harlot. . . . This obviously means she is unfaithful. She professes to be a
system of religious truth and in reality is one of
falsehood. This is confirmed by the name she
assumes—'Mystery Babylon.' "[3] She is ecumenical
(worldwide, Rev. 17:1, 15). She has progeny since
she is a mother. The apostasy of the various Protestant and Catholic bodies (and perhaps other religious
groups) will find its final fulfillment in this religious
abomination which will be judged by God (Rev.
17:14-17).
    What should the child of God do in the face of
the wicked enormities of Babylon?

> And I heard another voice from heaven,
> saying, Come out of her, my people, that ye
> be not partakers of her sins, and that ye re-
> ceive not of her plagues.
> For her sins have reached unto heaven,
> and God hath remembered her iniquities
> (Rev. 18:4, 5).

If the Babylon of Revelation 17 and 18 be symbolic of
the corrupt civilization of this world in its spiritual,
commercial and moral aspects, then it is evident
what God expects His people to do. The Children of
Israel were oft warned to flee out of Babylon since all
that it stood for was opposed to God (Jer. 50:4-9;
51:6).
    The principle that continued fellowship with
apostates contaminates God's children was empha-

sized by ancient separatists such as the Waldensians and the Anabaptists. It is something to be genuinely feared since we can be partakers of other men's sins by disobediently retaining alliances with them. While the specific interpretation of these words refers to a future time, the *principle* of separation from that which is false nevertheless is seen clearly. It makes no difference when or how such wickedness appears. It should be shunned by those who love the Lord.

Practical considerations. When is a body apostate? Disagreement over this has continued for centuries, but it has been especially pronounced in the last half century or so as a result of the fundamentalist-modernist controversy. Edward Carnell declared that a body was apostate: (1) when they removed the gospel from their official creed or confession, and (2) when the believer within the group no longer had the freedom to preach the gospel.[4] Are these correct criteria for determining apostasy? They are not. Apostates care little about creeds or confessions. The Scripture declares that part of the very nature of apostasy is its deceit. Apostates are liars. They operate with "feigned words" (2 Pet. 2:3). They can make something mean whatever they wish. Since they are the instruments of "deceitful spirits," the written confession of a body means nothing to them except as a convenient cover under which to hide their nefarious activities. The communists have been signing declarations and agreements for years and breaking them before the ink was dry. Written documents and position statements mean nothing to lying apostates.

If a group allows a person to preach the gospel, does this mean it is not yet apostate? No! Apostasy must be defined in terms *of what apostates believe and do, not in terms of what they allow others to do.* Leading passages on apostasy emphasize the error in doctrine and practice which characterize them. Nothing is said relative to their generosity in permitting others their views. This is not related to the nature of apostasy. They may be permissive with true ministers of God and still be apostates.

A body is apostate when:

(1) Men and women in its leadership deny the

verities of the Christian faith. If such are welcomed into places of leadership, the body has departed, though individuals within it may yet be sound.

(2) Official periodicals and media presentations promote views contrary to the orthodox Christian faith.

(3) Official schools of the body employ faculty members and/or utilize visiting speakers who teach views that are at variance with essential Christian doctrines.

(4) No effort is made by the leadership of the group or the majority of its constituency to expunge the offending parties.

Sometimes objection is raised that to ascertain what constitutes essential doctrine and to determine when a group is actually apostate requires the making of a judgment. Yes, it is true. Judgments are to be made here as in many other areas of the Christian walk. But this does not invalidate the principle of separation. Because the act of separation requires a judgment does not imply that the judgment is wrong or that the action is wrong. God has given ample spiritual guidelines to help the Spirit-taught believer make those judgments.

Having examined the apostasy which contaminates the professing church, we need to ask, What is the scriptural support for separation? If the separatist position rests merely upon the whims of cantankerous fundamentalists who cannot get along with anyone, that is one thing. If the separatist position rests upon great principles of Scripture, that is quite another. Critics often state or infer that the separatist position is derived solely from a questionable exegesis of 2 Corinthians 6:14-18. Is this true? Certainly one Scripture text is sufficient to declare a truth, but we believe the doctrine of separation is far more pervasive in Scripture than this one example.

The Holiness of God—
the Ground of Biblical Separation

Separation, both personal and ecclesiastical, is grounded in the nature of God. God is the great Separatist. He is absolutely separated from all evil and error. Do His people err in emulating Him?

The character of God's holiness.

The divine abhorrence of sin is without question. All who accept the Bible as authoritative would agree on this point. "Thou lovest righteousness, and hatest wickedness: therefore God, thy God, hath anointed thee with the oil of gladness above thy fellows" (Ps. 45:7). As well as any text in the Bible, this tells us that God is not neutral when it comes to evil. In this day of anemic concepts of deity, the statement would be viewed as an embarrassment by many. That God would hate is repugnant to some. But a God who cannot hate cannot love. A God who does not hate iniquity cannot love righteousness. *Hate* is not a weak word. It describes "an intense aversion or active hostility that is expressed in settled opposition to a person or thing."[5] God is against wickedness with every part of His holy being. If false doctrine is evil, then He is surely opposed to it.

God cannot commit sin.

This, of course, would flow from the fact that He is absolutely holy, but the truth is specifically stated more than once in the Word. ". . . Far be it from God, that he should do wickedness; and from the Almighty, that he should commit iniquity" (Job 34:10). Paul blanches at the very thought that God would be accused of doing something wrong (Rom. 9:14). God is eternally and unchangeably holy.

God has no propensity to sin. He is unable to sin. He is not only holy externally—that is, in what He does—but He is also holy intrinsically—that is, in what He is. He is a "God of truth and without iniquity, just and right is he" (Deut. 32:4). The Lord is "upright" and "there is no unrighteousness in him" (Ps. 92:15).

A holy God can do no less than demand holiness in all moral beings. "Thou art of purer eyes than to behold evil, and canst not look [with favor] on iniquity. . ." (Hab. 1:13). In other words, God cannot overlook, wink at, condone or minimize sin. He cannot tolerate the sins of men without the just reaction of His holiness. Sin must be punished.

The consequences of God's holiness.

At the very center of the necessity for divine redemption is the fact of sin. "For all have sinned, and come short of the glory of God" (Rom. 3:23). It is the divine standard of perfection against which men are measured. They have fallen short. They have missed the mark. They are woefully lacking.

For His own people, however, the standard is no different. It is a lofty one: "Be ye holy; for I am holy" (1 Pet. 1:16). Salvation by grace in no way removes the responsibility for holy living. The wonderful security that the believer enjoys in His Savior does not lessen the force of the divine command, "My little children, these things write I unto you, that ye sin not. . ." (1 John 2:1). No sinning! This is God's standard. Believers are not to be satisfied with fleshly living. They are to press on to be like the Lord—holy—while realizing their weakness and the continued presence of the sin nature.

Not only this, but the Almighty desires His people to be actively opposed to unholiness. Too many, we fear, are ecstatic in pursuing the deeper life, ostensibly a life of holiness, but they want no part of the conflict, bloody and bitter as it is sometimes, between holiness and unholiness. They do not wish to be embroiled in conflicts. They run from theological arguments (as they call them), and wish to be excused from the fray. But to be holy involves a continual controversy with error. James M. Gray, a past president of Moody Bible Institute, wrote, "God Himself was the first to create controversy; to His eternal glory be it said."[6] "Hate the evil, and love the good, and establish judgment in the gate" (Amos 5:15)—these were the words to ancient Israel. False teachers are to be sharply rebuked (Titus 1:13). Contending for the faith involves more than just a few innocuous remarks with no particular point to them. It involves a hearty repudiation of error and a definite, clear enunciation of the truth.

The holiness of God is that attribute which governs the exercise of all His other attributes. God cannot do anything that would sully His holy character. It is extremely important to recognize the preeminence of God's holiness. "Holiness occupies the first rank among the attributes of God."[7] Bancroft declares, "God's holiness is His most exalted and emphasized attribute, expressing the majesty of His moral nature and character."[8]

Many tend to emphasize the love of God in pref-

The relationship between God's holiness and Biblical separation.

erence to His holiness. While they may accept the fact of His holiness, they see Him as exercising His holiness in love rather than His love in holiness. This is a tendency not only among liberals but among evangelicals as well. They see God as soft-hearted and accommodating. The relationship between God's holiness and His love must ever be kept in proper perspective. A. H. Strong clarifies this point:

> That which lays down the norm or standard for love must be the superior of love. When we forget that "righteousness and justice are the foundation of His throne" (Ps. 97:2), we lose one of the chief landmarks of Christian doctrine and involve ourselves in a mist of error.[9]

The question bears upon the subject at hand in this fashion. In the controversy between apostates and fundamentalists within a denomination, which should be the guiding principle of action—holiness or love? Should the emphasis be upon maintaining unity within the body (a so-called demonstration of love) or should it be upon either purifying the body from within or establishing a pure testimony by going without (a concern for holiness)? This is a watershed between inclusivists and separatists. Inclusivists tend to *emphasize* love (we speak now of *emphasis*); separatists tend to *emphasize* purity or holiness. Why? Because separatists believe that the governing attribute of God is His holiness. While not speaking as a separatist, Strong well states that "holy love is a love controlled by holiness. . . . Love cannot direct itself; it is under bonds to holiness."[10]

Yes, God's holiness is His fundamental attribute.

It is emphasized in angelic worship (Isa. 6:3). Charnock writes, "If any, this attribute has an excellency above his other perfections. . . . Where do you find any other attribute trebled in the praises of it, as this?"[11]

It is the quality which man is most particularly commanded to possess (Lev. 19:2; 1 Pet. 1:14-16). God's holiness is the ground of man's moral obligation.

It is the attribute by which God swears (Ps. 89:35). God has no greater attribute by which to pledge His absolute faithfulness and utter fidelity.

It is the attribute basic to man's redemption (Rom. 3:25). God's righteousness, an outward manifestation of His holy character, demanded a perfect substitutionary sacrifice for sin if believers were to be saved from the power of that sin. God's holiness demanded Calvary.

In the light of these considerations, we believe God has paramount interest in the maintenance of His holiness. We agree with Charnock, the great Puritan writer: "Holiness is a glorious perfection belonging to the nature of God. . . . This is His greatest title of honor. . . . This attribute hath an excellency above all His other perfections."[12]

God's demands upon His people are based upon His own standards. Truth and holiness are inseparable companions. If God is separate from evil, He expects His people to be so. Arguments that we can only experience relative and imperfect states of purity here on earth and therefore should accept the status quo of a "mixed multitude" hardly seem to be compatible with the character of God. The entire thrust of the Old and New Testaments supports the assertion that God wants His people to be holy. If true, how does this principle apply to the conflict with apostasy?

God's holiness demands not only holy individuals but also holy congregations. This is the very point that was at issue in the Donatist controversy and the truth emphasized by the Anabaptists. Certainly we cannot achieve the purity that God alone possesses, nor can we even achieve perfect purity on a relative human scale; nevertheless, our goal and objective is purity. The seven letters to the Asian churches (Rev. 2—3) indicate God's concern for church purity. He walks among His churches with eyes as "a flame of fire" (Rev. 1:14). He searches out evil and demands purity.

Congregations are defiled by false teaching and false teachers. To allow them to continue on the plea (popularly used) that the official confessional statement of the denomination is evangelical in nature is whistling in the dark. Hymenaeus and Alexander "made shipwreck" of the faith, and the apostle "delivered [them] to Satan, that they may learn not to blaspheme" (1 Tim. 1:19, 20). Why was Paul concerned? Because such men, spreading their false teachings, defile the house of God and injure the occupants thereof. This is the effect of any denominational fellowship.

Thus the principle goes beyond even the local congregation to fellowship between congregations. How can a congregation, continually existing in cooperative, interdependent association with other congregations, many of whom are led by false teachers, hope to be pleasing to God and to maintain a witness of holiness? Our holiness is defiled by unholy associations of the type required in denominational frameworks. Paul warned that "evil communications corrupt good manners" (1 Cor. 15:33); or we could render it, "Bad company corrupts good morals." Certainly fraternization within a denomination that permits unbelievers to hold and spread their views is bad company. It could not be honestly classified as good company. If, then, either an individual or a congregation persists in running with such bad company, their holy position will be weakened and eventually lost. The principle could be amply illustrated in hundreds of churches across our land who at one time were centers of the true faith and are now rotting hulks, spiritual derelicts.

In the context of the above passage, Paul had been discussing the danger of being deceived by those who deny important doctrines (in this case, the doctrine of the resurrection). Charles Hodge, in commenting on 1 Corinthians 15:33, observed:

> . . .The Corinthians should not be deceived by the plausible arguments or specious conduct of the errorists among them. They should avoid them, under the conviction that all evil is contagious. Evil *communications*. The word properly means *a being together, companionship*. It is contact, association with evil, that is declared to be corrupting.[13]

Nor is it just the idea of daily contact with evil as one would experience in a work situation for example. It is "a being together," a definite association, a commitment to one another, particularly within a spiritual context. This is wrong. It is corrupting. Christians should shun it.

These things being true, it is mandatory for a congregation to maintain a separation from other congregations that deny the faith. It is simply the expected response of a holy people to their holy God.

The Principle of Separation as Seen in the Old Testament

Some balk at even the mention of the doctrine of separation as seen in the Old Testament, believing that any Scriptures cited should be New Testament Scriptures which would apply specifically to church situations. However, it is necessary to realize that a *principle* which transcends the dispensations flows out of the character of God. It is the principle of holiness—repudiation of evil required by a holy God. The principle must be applied in various circumstances and at various times, but it is a valid principle continually. God does not want His people to attempt spiritual fellowship with those who are His enemies. As Eichrodt notes, God's holiness is strongly emphasized in the Old Testament.

> Of all the qualities attributed to the divine nature there is one which, in virtue of the frequency and the emphasis with which it is used, occupies a position of unique importance—namely, that of holiness. Some indication of the significance of this term as a definition of God's nature is given by the fact that it has been found possible to characterize the whole religion of the Old Testament as a "religion of holiness" (Hanel).[14]

The uniqueness of Israel's way of life was stressed when God reminded them of their miraculous deliverance from Egypt. "For I am the LORD that bringeth you up out of the land of Egypt, to be your God: ye shall therefore be holy. . ." (Lev. 11:45). As a matter of fact, the entire Book of Leviticus has special emphasis upon the holiness of the Israelites. For instance, Leviticus 20:22-26 emphasizes purity and holiness. Note particularly verse 26: "And ye shall be holy unto me: for I the LORD am holy, and have separated you from other people, that ye should be mine."

Inclusivism is strongly repudiated in Numbers

In the Mosaic Law.

25:1-3. Balaam, the hireling prophet, was not able to pronounce destruction upon Israel as their enemies had hoped. The Devil, however, had a far subtler plan which Balaam put into operation. The people of God began to commit whoredom with the heathen. This was done through friendly associations, followed by marriages, and resulting in false worship. Such was done "through the counsel of Balaam" (Num. 31:16). It was an effort to corrupt true worship, to intermingle the true with the false. Three times in the New Testament Balaam's ministry is condemned (2 Pet. 2:15, 16; Jude 11; Rev. 2:14). In the latter passage particularly the sin of the prophet is seen to be counseling with the enemies of Israel and promoting the drawing of Israel into forbidden alliances. It is the same subtle strategy often promoted by well-meaning people today. The awful divine judgment is described in Numbers 25. God condemns the mixture of false religion with true.

In Joshua and Judges. One of the strongest chapters in the Bible on the subject of separation from apostasy is Joshua 23. Joshua was about to die and thus to relinquish the leadership of the people of God. He was gravely concerned about what would happen to them after his death, and particularly over the danger of their departure into false worship. The key to his address is found in verse 7, "that ye come not among these nations." Bush comments on this verse:

> That ye have no familiar intercourse, nor form intimate connections with them; which could not be done without contracting some measure of the defilement which their idolatries and iniquities had brought upon them.[15]

They were not to seek to placate the heathen nations by discussing with them the fine points of their beliefs. They were to "cleave unto the LORD" (Josh. 23:8) and refuse to cooperate in any way with the religious practices of the godless.

The Book of Judges contains warnings which reiterate those given by Joshua before his departure. The entire second chapter is devoted to recounting the cycles which Israel followed from obedience, to apostasy, to chastisement and to repentance. What was their sin? They "followed other gods, of the gods of the people that were round about them" (Judg. 2:12). Again in chapter 3 is the lament that Israel "did evil in the sight of the LORD" and "served Baalim" (v. 7). While it is difficult for some of God's people today to see the application, it is very plain indeed. To worship with persons who deny the deity of Christ, His virgin birth, His vicarious death—to covenant with them in a religious association which exists to form a cohesive religious testimony—is to engage in false worship and to help promote false gods.

First Kings 11:1-11 is a heart-searching tale. **In the** Here is described Solomon, the great son of David, **times of** the great man of wisdom, whose heart turned "after **the kings.** other gods" (v. 4). How could it be? What was the cause of the dreadful drift of this leader of God's people? *He fellowshiped with the wrong crowd.* He loved (and took to himself) many foreign women who were of other religions. He was with them continually. He spoke with them, dined with them and learned from them. What things he learned! His wives turned his heart away from the true God. Yes, "bad company corrupts good morals." It is a law that cannot be defied successfully. Solomon, practicing inclusivism instead of separation, was ruined.

A later king of Israel tried the "ecumenical" approach (2 Chron. 18). Invited by the apostate Ahab to engage in a war alliance with him, Jehoshaphat, despite divine warning, went ahead. The lonely and hated separatist, Micaiah, spoke the truth, but no one heeded. Upon the return of Jehoshaphat from the debacle on the battlefield, the prophet Jehu asked him a piercing question. Is it not a timely one for this hour when some of the Lord's people are enlisted on the side of the enemies of God? Jehu inquired, "Shouldest thou help the ungodly, and love them that hate the LORD? (2 Chron. 19:2).

I sat some years ago in the study of a prominent pastor in the Southern Baptist Convention, the leader of one of the largest churches in the world. We discussed the Cooperative Program of the Southern Baptist Convention. Churches put money "into the pot" to be divided among schools and agencies, many of which, either totally or in part, deny the great essentials of the faith. The great pastor wept as we spoke of the terrible apostasy at his alma mater, a Southern Baptist seminary. But after all the tears were gone (and no doubt they were genuine), his church continues to pour money into the support of that over which he weeps. Should we help the ungodly? Should we love (in the sense of giving cooperation to) those who hate the Lord?

In the times of Ezra, Nehemiah and Esther.

As the Israelites began returning from captivity to their ancient land, the question of separation became a key one. Many of them intermarried with peoples of other nations (and religions). Ezra was much disturbed when the report was given:

> ... The people of Israel, and the priests, and the Levites, have not separated themselves from the people of the lands, doing according to their abominations.... ... So that the holy seed have mingled themselves with the people of those lands ... (Ezra 9:1, 2).

Ezra cried to God, as the following verses indicate, and repented of what he saw to be a grievous sin against the Lord.

A similar situation was confronted by Nehemiah when intermarriages with the heathen contaminated the people under his leadership (Neh. 13:23-29). Nehemiah did not take it lightly. He "contended with them" (13:25) and was exceedingly vocal, demanding a renewal of separation before God.

In the messages of the Old Testament prophets.

The prophets of God to Israel were strong in their call for purity of life and witness. Jeremiah stated that the evils which had come upon the nation were because they had walked after other gods and served them (Jer. 16:10-13). Amos 5:21-27 contains a denunciation of the false worship of Moloch in which the Israelites had participated. They had "borne the tabernacle of Moloch" (evidently a little portable tent of some kind; Amos 5:26).

The Old Testament is uncompromisingly against inclusivism, mixed worship and efforts to combine the religious practices of Israel with those of other nations.

Because we have cited Old Testament passages, mention should be made of an objection sometimes raised against the separatist principle. Some argue that, while the Old Testament prophets decried apostasy within Israel, *they did not separate from Israel* but rather remained as continuing witnesses to the truth within Israel. This is true. It proves nothing, however, with regard to the validity of Biblical separation. The prophets were members of a theocracy, a state governed by God. In such an entity the political and the religious were bound together. Today, however, there is no comparable body (though from time to time men have proposed church-state arrangements, as we have already seen). The New Testament church is a free society, composed of those who voluntarily unite with it in response to God's saving grace and to His instruction through His Word. No New Testament mandate binds bodies of believers to one another in a visible organization. There is only the "rope of sand," the common bond of mutually shared convictions.

The Teaching of the New Testament on Separation

God is a separatist. He is separated from all that is evil. Holiness is a principle of His nature. It is consistent, therefore, to expect that bodies which He would establish upon this earth to represent Him would be required to be holy (separated) as well. They would be expected to mirror His character.

Lest one might say that the standards of holiness set forth in the Old Testament are not applicable to the church since it is a New Testament entity, it should be noted that the same standards held up in the Old Testament are maintained in the New as well. Peter declares that the church is a "holy nation" (1 Pet. 2:9), which phrase is also used in Exodus 19:6. While Israel is not the church nor the church Israel, both are challenged with God's perfect standard. When Peter in another passage declares, "Be ye holy; for I am holy" (1 Pet. 1:16), he is merely reiterating in the age of grace what had already been stated in the age of law (cf., Lev. 11:44; 19:2; 20:7). The standard of holiness transcends dispensations.

The standard in both Testaments.

The nature and example of New Testament churches.

No church founded by the apostles and mentioned in the New Testament remained for long in a working relationship with another congregation that had apostasized. The entire tenor of the New Testament teaching would be opposed to this. Part of the reason that many men have opposed the separatist principle is rooted in their concept of the nature of the church. Many of them have held "connectional" views of the church. By this we mean that they do not view each congregation as completely independent, but responsible in some way to another body or to an individual (such as a bishop) or individuals (such as a presbytery or synod). Such brethren (representing various approaches to ecclesiastical organization) believe that in some fashion a local church is responsible to someone on this earth as well as to the Lord. The various separatist groups through the ages were, for the most part, strongly congregational in their polity and emphasized the fact that the local church had no visible head on earth, but was accountable to its risen Head in the glory, the Lord Jesus Christ (Rev. 1—3). In other words, churches in New Testament times (and those patterning themselves after them today) were autonomous bodies. As such they were gathered away from both the synagogues (Jewish worship) and the pagan temples (heathen worship) and were entities to themselves—separated.

One of the requirements for fellowship in the apostolic churches was the acceptance of apostolic doctrine (Acts 2:42; 2 Thess. 2:14, 15). Persons teaching doctrine contrary to that taught by the apostles were "delivered unto Satan" (1 Tim. 1:20), that is, disciplined and refused fellowship in the local congregation. The Anabaptists called the same thing "the ban." We find no record of New Testament churches fellowshiping with apostasy with apostolic or divine blessing. The seven Asian churches are sometimes cited as evidence that allowance should be made for the presence of apostasy in churches today because it was present in some of the churches then (e.g., Rev. 2:14). Yes, apostasy was present, and the direction of the inspired apostle was clear and forthright—get rid of it ("repent," Rev. 2:16). There was to be no equivocation with it and no years of "patient teaching" pursued in order to oust it. It was to be done away with and now! But, says one, this is the very point. We defend the principle that we should stay in and get rid of the corruption. Yes, but note carefully that this principle is not supported by these letters to the seven churches. Swift, positive action against false teaching is demanded by the Head of the church. He declared that if the churches did nothing, He would do something, and that quickly (Rev. 2:16). These passages give no ground for long years of losing combat within an apostate denomination while spiritual deterioration grows worse and those who struggle lose their sharp edge of conviction.

What can be determined from a study of key passages in the epistles that might guide us? Paul wrote:

The testimony of the epistles.

> Now I beseech you, brethren, mark them which cause divisions and offences contrary to the doctrine which ye have learned; and avoid them.
> For they that are such serve not our Lord Jesus Christ, but their own belly; and by good words and fair speeches deceive the hearts of the simple (Rom. 16:17, 18).

Paul warned against those who bring false teaching into the churches. It is not only their lives which are corrupt, but their words. These men "by their smooth and flattering speech" deceive the "hearts of the unsuspecting." The things which they teach are pervasive. What should be done? True believers should "avoid them" (turn away from them). Hodge is correct when he comments, "Those who caused these dissensions, Paul commands, Christians first, *to mark* . . . i.e., to notice carefully, and not allow them to pursue their corrupting course unheeded; and, secondly, *to avoid*, i.e., to break off connection with them."[16] That it is definitely false teaching that was Paul's concern is maintained by Murray, who says that the stumbling "is that caused by false doctrine," and that therefore the believers are "to 'mark' the proponents so as to avoid them and they are to 'turn away from them.' "[17] To remain, therefore, in whatever kind of a religious organization with such persons seems in direct contradiction to the command of the apostle.

The most discussed Scripture passage is 2 Corinthians 6:14-18. The attitude of J. Elwin Wright, an early leader of the National Association of Evangelicals, is typical of the attitude of nonseparatists:

> In a recent editorial I referred to the fact that some believe faithfulness to Christ demands separation from all churches infected with modernism, on the ground that it is required by the command, "Come out from among them and be ye separate." If this scripture (II Cor. 6:17) does, in fact, command withdrawal from a backslidden or unfaithful church, then the premise of those insisting on the formation of schismatic bodies is correct. If, on the other hand, as seems evident from a reading of the two epistles to the Corinthians, it was a command to separate from involvment [sic] in idol worship and heathen practices it does not necessarily have anything to do with the issue of modernism and fundamentalism. There is abundant proof that we should separate from idolatry in every form, but there is no implied or expressed command in the Scripture that we should abandon the field to the forces of evil when they invade the house of God.[18]

Are the remarks of Wright accurate? In applying this passage to mean that Christians should leave apostate groups are we really misapplying it? In examining the statement of Wright, we believe, first of all, that it does not do justice to the context. The immediate context does not deal with the question of idolatry (except as idols are mentioned in one of the contrasts Paul gives). Certainly idolatry alone was not the main burden of Paul's remarks here. Actually, the emphasis is upon the phrase "unequally yoked." The topic sentence is, "Be not unequally yoked." The other statements qualify that imperative. The word *idols*, therefore, is a part of one of those qualifying statements, but is not the main thrust of the passage.

To say that a condemnation of idolatry is all that is in view is to ignore the larger context of the entire epistle of 2 Corinthians, which happens to be an epistle with repeated warnings against false teachers and their teaching. A number of verses in the epistle speak along this line (2:17; 4:2; 6:8; 7:2; 11:4, 13). He does this in connection with one of his purposes in the epistle—to speak of the validity of his own apostleship. As a true "sent one" from God, he is rebuking the false "sent ones" of Satan. Howard Ervin declares, "We . . . conclude that the 'yoke with unbelievers' is . . . a 'yoke' with false teachers and their heretical doctrines [italics not in original]."[19]

The meaning of the term yoked must also be considered. It is a compound of a word used about nine times in the New Testament. In most cases it is used in a spiritual sense. In Luke 14:19 it is used in a literal sense. The word yoke as used in other passages certainly speaks of cooperative service. Christ commands disciples, "Take my yoke upon you" (Matt. 11:29). We are yoked with the Lord, and, in a practical sense, with whomever of His people we work. In such passages as Galatians 5:1 and Acts 15:10, the yoke speaks of intolerable and unnecessary legal regulations. In Philippians 4:3 it certainly emphasizes spiritual cooperation (even if it be a proper name there).

Five contrasts are drawn by the apostle. These contrasts help to answer the question, From what should we "come out?" We should "come out" from: (1) fellowship with unrighteousness; (2) communion with darkness; (3) concord with Belial; (4) part with an infidel; (5) agreement with the temple of idols.

Runia remonstrates with separatists because he says the passage only appeals for separation from the heathen. He then cites Charles Hodge in defense of his position (but fails to cite Hodge's remarks completely, which we will do in a moment). In response to Runia, may it be said that separatists contend that the heathen are not confined to persons in far-off lands who worship sticks and stones. Men and women who deny the living God and the finality of His revelation in His Word and in His Son are heathen, a worse variety than the ones just described. Here lies the root of much of the problem between separatists and nonseparatists. Some nonseparatists do not take as strong a view of the seriousness of false doctrine as is warranted by Scripture. A review of attitudes of "stay-iners" through the ages has already revealed this to some extent.

The "stay-iners" are always more hopeful, more optimistic, more accepting and more tolerant. They do not wish to be too strong in denouncing their "brethren." False doctrine, however, is a very serious matter.

Back in 1956 when the compromising movement we now call the new evangelicalism began to become public, Alva McClain, one of the founders and president of Grace Theological Seminary, responded in the following fashion to one of the new evangelical writers who suggested that profit could come from discussions (dialogues) with the liberals. In his remarks McClain demonstrated the strong feelings that separatists have about false doctrine and the proper response to it. We are afraid that, while many modern evangelicals would claim to have orthodox views, they do not have the strong aversion to false doctrine and its propagators that McClain revealed. It is a difference between "stay-iners" and "come-outers," and it is an important difference.

> Does anyone really think we might "profitably engage in an exchange of ideas" with blasphemers who suggest that our only Lord and Master was begotten in the womb of a fallen mother by a German mercenary and that the God of the Old Testament is a dirty bully? We must never for one instant forget that they are deadly enemies with whom there can be neither truce nor compromise.[20]

Is it proper to apply 2 Corinthians 6 to the modern day issues of apostasy? We believe that it is. The passage means to tell us that we are not to yoke ourselves as believers with anything or anyone that is not in obedience to God's Word. (Note that the word *separate* here is the same word employed in Acts 19:9 where Paul *separated* the disciples from those who "spake evil of that way.") We observed earlier that Runia quoted Charles Hodge, but we cite Hodge's further remarks which we believe are in line with what has just been said.

> It is no doubt true that by unbelievers Paul means the heathen (see I Corinthians 6:6). But it does not follow from this that intimate association with the heathen is all that is forbidden. The principle applies to all the enemies of God and the children of darkness.[21]

We concur with this assessment. The passage warns against unholy alliances wherever they may be found. As such it rebukes those who would remain in league with nonorthodox persons. Paul is simply, yet profoundly, pleading for a complete break with every form of unhealthy compromise.

In another portion of his writings, Paul gives these instructions: "And have no fellowship with the unfruitful works of darkness, but rather reprove them" (Eph. 5:11). The context is contrasting light and darkness and the children of each. This verse is sometimes dismissed as irrelevant to the present discussion because the context is emphasizing *practice*, not *belief*. No doubt the primary thrust of the passage is on *deeds*. Deeds, however, are the products of beliefs. "The result of false teaching is the growth of ungodliness. Creed and conduct are inseparable. Ungodly conduct is advanced by an ungodly creed."[22] Do the "works of darkness" include false teaching as well as false deeds? Unquestionably.

Notice also that clear rebuke was to be part of the believer's responsibility. The longer the believer remains within the fellowship where false doctrine and practice are condoned, the more difficult it becomes to rebuke consistently. The spirit of tolerance grows the longer one refuses to take a clear-cut stand.

In yet another pertinent passage (2 Tim. 2:15) the believer is exhorted to utilize properly the "word of truth." Immediately following that is an extended portion dealing with the believer's attitude toward false doctrine and those who proclaim it (2 Tim. 2:15-21). That doctrinal deviation is the subject is plain in verse 18—"who concerning the truth have erred"—and the specific area of error is mentioned. The continuous spread of evil doctrine is here established. It eats like gangrene. Once introduced into a body, it makes its way slowly but steadily. John Calvin has a most helpful note.

> We have now explained the etymology; but all physicians pronounce the nature of the disease to be such, that, if it be not very speedily counteracted, it spreads to the adjoining parts, and penetrates even to the bones, and does not cease to consume, till it

has killed the man. Since, therefore, "gangrene" is immediately followed by ... mortification, which rapidly infects the rest of the members till it ends in the universal destruction of the body; to the moral contagion Paul elegantly compares false doctrines; for, if you once give entrance to them, they spread till they have completed the destruction of the Church. The contagion being so destructive, we must meet it early, and not wait until it has gathered strength by progress; for there will then be no time for rendering assistance.[23]

This is one of the very concerns of those who are separatists. The gangrene of false doctrine spreads. The only remedy is to separate from that body into which it has been introduced and where it is protected and encouraged. While sincere brethren have been trying (some of them for years) to excise the tumor in their respective denominations, they have yet to produce an illustration of a denomination into whose bosom apostasy has been introduced that was later restored to a state of spiritual good health. We do not know of such an illustration. God's formula is the only successful one—"shun profane and vain babblings."

In the opening section of 2 Timothy 3, Paul describes the awful degradation that will characterize the last days. He concludes by predicting that men will possess "a form of godliness" but will "deny the power thereof" (2 Tim. 3:5). The last days, therefore, will not be totally irreligious, but will feature a religion that is humanistic and lacks divine authority or power. It would seem to be an apt description of that creeping blight called liberalism which has afflicted the churches of the world for many years now. It is a form. It has no spiritual power because it does not accept the great truths which give a message power. It is empty and cold. Lest we are befuddled concerning the exact nature of the apostle's remarks, more concrete statements are made in 2 Timothy 3:7-9. The Egyptian magicians withstood the truth of God as represented in Moses. Contemporary emissaries of Satan reject the truth as well. They are "reprobate concerning the faith" (3:8).

What should be the response of the believer to

such? Should we seek to hold conferences with them? Should we sit on boards of religious agencies with them? Should we conduct evangelistic campaigns with them? The answer is plain: "from such turn away." "It was then the duty, when such persons appeared, to have nothing to do with them; now that the evil is incomparably more developed, that duty is still more imperious."[24] Separation is a matter of plain obedience to a command. It is not a matter for debate and the gathering of this opinion and that. It is a matter for action—now!

The great apostle of love was also a strong advocate of truth and righteousness. We speak of the beloved disciple, John. In his first epistle he emphasizes the nature of and requirements for Christian fellowship. Certainly he shares the fact that fellowship is not merely "gushy-wushy" sentimentalism, nor is it based merely upon mutual love; but fellowship is based upon "light" (1 John 1:5, 6) and "truth" (1 John 1:6 and 2 John 1-4). True Christian love functions within the bounds of truth (cf. 3 John 1—"whom I love in the truth"). How can we happily fellowship with those who deny the truth, the verities of divine revelation which constitute the heart of our Christian faith?

Specific instruction concerning separation is given by the apostle. He writes:

> If there come any unto you, and bring not this doctrine, receive him not into your house, neither bid him God speed:
> For he that biddeth him God speed is partaker of his evil deeds (2 John 10, 11).

John, of course, was writing of those who teach false doctrine. Westcott notes this when he writes, "By 'cometh' is to be understood an official 'coming.' St. John is not dealing with the casual visit of a stranger but with that of a teacher who claims authority."[25] The verse forbids the continual fellowshiping of those who are in doctrinal error. By retaining associations with such within a denominational or other organizational framework, we disobey this command of Scripture. Lenski, in perhaps a somewhat stronger outburst than would normally characterize his writing, comments:

The state locks up murderers, thieves, criminals, as a matter of protection. Is the church to aid and abet spiritual murderers and thieves? Not for one moment, all maudlin sentiment in the state and in the church to the contrary notwithstanding.[26]

The Apostolic Emphasis upon Sound Doctrine

What is the basis of true Christian fellowship? Various answers would be given to that question today. Many would answer that the ground of our fellowship is the Person of Christ. This sounds good at first but must be analyzed closely. Whose Christ forms the basis of fellowship? The Christ of the liberal? The Christ of the neoorthodox? Who is Christ? Is He truly God? Do we mean the Christ Who clearly identified the written Scriptures as infallible, or do we mean some other Christ?

Some, on the other hand, find the basis of Christian fellowship in a shared experience. All who have been born again should have fellowship one with the other. However, questions would remain about this. What do you mean by being born again? (It has become a popularly used expression with varying interpretations.) How many times must I be born again? Am I born again through baptism or a sacrament or by faith alone?

We submit for consideration the fact that there is a doctrinal basis for Christian fellowship. We agree completely with Martyn Lloyd-Jones, who wrote:

> My contention is that the teaching of the New Testament is quite clear about this, that there is an absolute foundation, an irreducible minimum, without which the term "Christian" is meaningless, and without subscribing to which a man is not a Christian. That is "the foundation of the apostles and prophets"—the doctrine concerning "Jesus Christ and him crucified," and "justification by faith only." . . . Apart from that there is no such thing as fellowship, no basis of unity at all.[27]

In the old Life and Work movement, one of the branches that finally helped form the World Council of Churches, they had a slogan: "Doctrine divides;

service unites." This is still a very appealing concept, even to some evangelicals. It is not that they reject doctrine completely, but they minimize it and accommodate it so greatly in the interests of love and Christian fellowship that its importance is largely diminished. Many evangelicals can state clearly their own convictions regarding a doctrinal matter, but they are so accepting, flexible and non-judgmental that they do not become greatly disturbed if other evangelicals hold differing views—*even in critical areas like those of creationism or Biblical inspiration*. We are constrained to refer again to Lloyd-Jones's incisive criticism which is so needed in our day:

> I find it amusing to notice in the reviews of books that a point which is almost always emphasized is whether the writer has been entirely positive or not. We must never be negative; we must never be critical of other views. That is regarded as "sub-Christian." It is the spirit that matters. So we must never criticize, still less must we denounce anything. Views which are totally divergent are to be regarded as valuable "insights" which point in the direction of truth.[28]

Separatists through the ages have ever had a strong commitment to doctrine. If they have had to make a choice between loyalty to God's truth in His Word and the continuance of personal fellowship with friends and cohorts, they have opted for truth and broken fellowship. This is why separatists are frequently criticized. But should they be? Doctrine is important.

The New Testament emphasized that doctrine has been revealed by God. It is not merely the invention of men. Doctrine is truth about God and His works. Paul in 1 Corinthians 2:9-12 defends the divine source of his doctrine. Sound doctrine produces healthy Christians (1 Tim. 6:3; 2 Tim. 1:13—"wholesome, sound, healthy words"). Solid doctrine makes well-rounded, stable believers (2 Tim. 3:16, 17—"that the man of God may be perfect"). Accurate doctrine will produce godly living (Titus 1:1). Jude made a pregnant statement about doctrine in Jude 3. He declares that doctrine is: (1) cohesive ("the faith," interrelated, systematic truth); (2) exclusive (not "a faith" but "the faith"); (3) authoritative ("delivered to the saints" — revealed from Heaven).

Notice especially Ephesians 4:1-16. The theme of the section is that of harmony in the Body of Christ. Chapters 1—3 of the epistle are primarily doctrinal in nature. The practical exhortation to unity (4:1-3) flows out of the doctrinal portion. Note the two phrases which do not contradict but rather complement one another: "the unity of the Spirit" (4:3) and "the unity of the faith" (4:13). The Holy Spirit teaches us through God-appointed pastors and brings us to the unity of the faith which, of course, is doctrinal in nature. "The faith" involves doctrine. It is an entire system of divinely revealed truth. We are to heartily reject false doctrine (4:14), gratefully embrace sound doctrine (4:11-13), and thus enjoy the blessings of fellowship within the Body (4:15, 16). This is certainly contrary to the notion that doctrine should be minimized in order to promote fellowship, a concept not uncommon among those who oppose separation on doctrinal grounds, thinking they are promoting Christian unity. Several years ago the editor of *Eternity* magazine offered twenty-five dollars to anyone who would produce a Scripture verse that stated we should separate from another Christian because of doctrine.[29] The same gentleman strongly spoke against ministers who would refuse to fellowship in a ministerial organization because modernists were in it also. He called such an attitude "divisive."[30] What a tragedy that this man with his brilliance should fail to see the importance of building fellowship around doctrine!

What should be the attitude of true believers toward the presence of false teachers within the professing church? George Eldon Ladd, in an article concerning "doctrinal purity" and "visible unity," cites 2 Timothy 2:16-21 as one of the most significant passages in seeking to determine what to do with false teachers. He argues from this passage that Hymenaeus and Philetus were teaching false doctrine; that disciplinary action had already been taken against Hymenaeus (1 Tim. 1:19); that this earlier disciplinary action had been ineffective; that we must expect and accept the fact that the church ("great house," v. 20) will contain various persons of mixed doctrinal viewpoints; that we must be kindly toward those in the church who teach false doctrine (v. 24); and finally, that we must have as our chief aim not separation, but reclamation of these false teachers.[31]

What is the heart of his argument? It is simply this: that the presence of false teachers does not render a church apostate nor require separation from it. According to Ladd, God is teaching us that false teachers will always be in the church, and that this fact should not require us to leave a given body. Is this a valid argument? Does 2 Timothy 2:16-21 support these conclusions? We do not believe this is what the passage teaches at all. Why?

In 2 Timothy 2:15 Paul declares that teachers should be "rightly dividing" (handling accurately) "the word of truth." He then warns against those who do not expound it accurately (vv. 16-18). He warns that their false teaching: (1) will provoke further examples of ungodliness (v. 16); (2) will spread like a terribly infectious gangrene (v. 17); and (3) will upset the faith of some (v. 18). Did Paul then, as Ladd contends, argue that despite these dire consequences we should allow the false teachers to continue to propagate their doctrine with no attempt to separate from them?

Paul went on to contrast the true church with the false. The true church is constituted by the eternal choice of God: "The Lord knew [aorist] them that are his" (2 Tim. 2:19). That is, He knew in eternity past those that were His, and they are sealed and kept for Him. Those thus chosen display the fact that they belong to God by their living. They "depart from iniquity" (abstain from wickedness, 2 Tim. 2:19).

In what specific ways does a true believer abstain from wickedness and depart from iniquity? He must "purge himself from these" (v. 21). To what does the word these refer? It refers to the dishonorable vessels, the false teachers, just mentioned in verse 20. Fairbairn rightly says, after speaking of the class of vessels which are "unto dishonor": "There follows, therefore, a virtual exhortation to separate oneself from this class. . . ."[32] Interestingly, Ellicott calls attention to the "great practical principle involved in this verse" which he says is that there should be "no communion with impugners of fundamentals."[33] Another commentator brings insight to the meaning with these remarks:

> Likewise, the contamination which clings to the dishonored vessels must not be allowed to infect the honored ones. Therefore, the true servant of God must purge himself from the company of the valueless ones. By doing so, he will have become separated from evil . . . and thus be of use to the Master of the household.[34]

In other words, Paul is *not* teaching that we should accept with some resignation the fact that the church will constantly be plagued with false teachers, and that, since this is God's will, we should not seek to separate ourselves from an associational relationship with them, but rather seek to love them and win them back. He is saying that we should exercise discernment, should locate the false teachers, and should cleanse ourselves from them and their pernicious doctrines by whatever means is appropriate in each given case. True saints are to be active and aggressive in "purging themselves," and not wait for some action to be initiated by the false teachers.

God is not pleased with the promiscuous and unchallenged presence of evil doctrine among His people. When vital doctrines of the Christian faith are rejected and heterodox views are either embraced or tolerated within a fellowship that purports to be Christian, the obedient believer must leave. He must follow His Lord "without the camp, bearing his reproach" (Heb. 13:13).

One of the most moving accounts of how a prominent Christian wrestled with the question of his personal response to the presence of liberalism in his denomination is given in Richard Ellsworth Day's biography of Henry Parsons Crowell, the founder and leader of the Quaker Oats Company. He had been a lifelong Presbyterian and for long years a member and elder of the Fourth Presbyterian Church in Chicago. Crowell was also an active board member of the Moody Bible Institute and a large financial supporter of that institution. In May 1943 when Crowell picked up a Chicago newspaper, he read that the notorious liberal and president of Union Theological Seminary in New York, Henry Sloane Coffin, had been elected moderator of the Northern Presbyterian Church. Under the faithful Bible teaching of William R. Newell years before, Crowell had learned about the nature of apostasy and about the believer's responsibility to separate from it. To make matters worse, Crowell's own pastor had seconded the motion to nominate the liberal Coffin to this high office. Crowell, then a very elderly man, set aside an extended period of time to pray and seek God's face as to what he should do. His biographer tells of his agony of soul.

> . . .What was the will of God for him?
> Perhaps he ought to advise with friends. He quickly decided against that. He knew that many who affirmed loyalty themselves would beg the question with a plea for "denominational loyalty," or a bromide of "it will come out all right. Be patient."[35]

He examined afresh the evidences that Dr. Coffin was a liberal, and the evidences were clear from his own statements. On June 25, 1943 Mr. Crowell dictated a letter to his pastor, Dr. Anderson. It read in part:

> The conclusion that I have finally reached is not in harmony and sympathy with the decision of the Assembly in electing Dr. Henry Sloane Coffin, the President of Union Theological Seminary of New York City, as Moderator of the Assembly. In arriving at this decision, I believe the delegates have made a serious error and one difficult to understand. . . . How could a majority of them cast their ballot for a man known to be an outstanding modernist for many years, as well as the President of the Union Theological Seminary of New York City ever since 1926? . . .
> I have protested against Modernism before and have done many things that I have hoped might check it, but the present issue and its apparent popularity indicate that the trend is now stronger than ever before.
> There is one further protest that I can make and as I have been led to it through prayer, communion, and fellowship with the Lord Jesus Christ, I make it known to you. I desire to sever all relationship that I may have with

the Presbyterian denomination. I hereby resign from membership in the Fourth Presbyterian Church of Chicago and retire from the office of Elder in said church, which service of love I have prized for many years. . . .

Something should be done at once to stop this drift toward Modernism and I have thought of nothing better than for me to withdraw from the church as a definite forceful protest against changing standards and the weakening of the church's loyalty and devotion to Jesus Christ. . . .[36]

Notes:

1. Merrill F. Unger, "Apostasy," *Unger's Bible Dictionary* (Chicago: Moody Press, 1966), p. 72.

2. Merrill F. Unger, "Leaven," *Unger's Bible Dictionary*, p. 652.

3. Charles Ryrie, "Apostasy in the Church," *Bibliotheca Sacra* (January—March 1964), p. 50.

4. Carnell, *The Case for Orthodox Theology*, p. 137.

5. H. L. Drumright, "Hate, Hatred," *Zondervan Pictorial Encyclopedia of the Bible*, III, 46.

6. Editorial, *Moody Monthly* (October 1929).

7. H. C. Thiessen, *Introductory Lectures in Systematic Theology* (Grand Rapids: Wm. B. Eerdmans Publishing Co., 1949), p. 129.

8. Emery Bancroft, *Elemental Theology*, ed. Ronald Mayers (Grand Rapids: Zondervan Publishing House, 1977), p. 89.

9. Augustus Hopkins Strong, *Systematic Theology* (New York: Fleming Revell, 1907), p. 272.

10. Ibid.

11. Stephen Charnock, *The Existence and Attributes of God* (Grand Rapids: Kregel Publications, 1958), p. 449.

12. Ibid., p. 448.

13. Charles Hodge, *An Exposition of the First Epistle to the Corinthians* (Grand Rapids: Wm. B. Eerdmans Publishing Co., 1950), p. 340.

14. Walter Eichrodt, *Theology of the Old Testament*, trans. J. A. Baker (Philadelphia: The Westminster Press, 1961), I, 270.

15. George Bush, *Notes on Joshua* (Minneapolis: James and Klock, 1976), p. 203.

16. Charles Hodge, *A Commentary on the Epistle to the Romans* (Philadelphia: Grigg and Elliott, 1835), pp. 581, 582.

17. John Murray, *The Epistle to the Romans* (Grand Rapids: Wm. B. Eerdmans Publishing Co., 1968), p. 236.

18. J. Elwin Wright, "The Issue of Separation," *United Evangelical Action*, IV (August 15, 1945), 12.

19. Howard M. Ervin, "A Reexamination of 2 Corinthians 6:14—7:1," *Baptist Bulletin*, XV (April 1950), 21.

20. Alva McClain, "Is Evangelical Christianity Changing?" *King's Business* (January 1957).

21. Hodge, *An Exposition of the First Epistle to the Corinthians*, p. 166.

22. Homer Kent, *The Pastoral Epistles* (Chicago: Moody Press, 1958), p. 275.

23. John Calvin, *Commentaries on the Epistles to Timothy, Titus and Philemon* (Grand Rapids: Wm. B. Eerdmans Publishing Co., 1948), p. 224.

24. William Kelly, *An Exposition of the Two Epistles to Timothy* (London: C. A. Hammond, 1948), p. 274.

25. Brooke F. Westcott, *The Epistles of St. John* (London: Macmillan, 1883), p. 220.

26. R. C. H. Lenski, *The Interpretation of the Epistles of St. Peter, St. John, and St. Jude* (Minneapolis: Augsburg Publishing House, 1945), p. 571.

27. D. Martyn Lloyd-Jones, *The Basis of Christian Unity* (Grand Rapids: Wm. B. Eerdmans Publishing Co., 1962), p. 45.

28. Ibid., p. 53.

29. Donald Grey Barnhouse, "One Church," *Eternity* (July 1958), p. 20.

30. Donald Grey Barnhouse, "We Are One Body in Christ," *Eternity* (March 1957), p. 42.

31. George Eldon Ladd, "The Evangelical's Dilemma: Doctrinal Purity vs. Visible Unity," *Eternity* (June 1962), pp. 8, 9.

32. Patrick Fairbairn, *Commentary on the Pastoral Epistles* (Grand Rapids: Zondervan Publishing House, 1956), p. 354.

33. C. J. Ellicott, *A Critical and Grammatical Commentary on the Pastoral Epistles* (London: John U. Parker, 1856), p. 128.

34. Kent, *The Pastoral Epistles*, pp. 277, 278.

35. Richard Ellsworth Day, *A Christian in Big Business* (Chicago: Moody Press, 1946), p. 280.

36. Ibid., pp. 283-285.

Arguments for the Anti-Separatist Position Analyzed

11

AS HAS BEEN seen, separatist and anti-separatist groups have existed through the centuries of church history. As one reads about the struggles in earlier times between these groups, one is struck with the similarity of the arguments propounded regardless of the century in which they are offered. Some of the arguments Augustine of Hippo used against the Donatists are still used today by new evangelicals and others who oppose a separatist church concept. These arguments fall generally into two categories—those based upon supposed scriptural or theological grounds, and those of a more practical nature. Many in the latter category center around deficiencies or objectionable features, real or imagined, in the attitude and approach of separatists.

The Scriptural and Theological Arguments Advanced

Upon what grounds would persons refuse to separate from that which was tainted by apostasy? Various reasons supporting their attitudes and actions have been advanced. We examine some of the representative ones.

This argument was mentioned in chapter 10. The prophets were members of a theocracy, an entirely different entity from a local church or even from a modern-day denomination. Israel was a theocratic state. A person was born into the state and also into the religious body. He could not separate himself from that of which he was a part by divine decree, by birth. It should be noted, however, that when apostasy overtook the Northern Kingdom (af-

The prophets, though decrying apostasy, remained within Israel.

191

ter the division of Israel), thousands of godly Jews relocated from the north to the south in order to separate themselves from the contamination of apostasy and to remain true to the worship of Jehovah alone.

A born-again believer today cannot separate himself from the Body of Christ, the universal church, because he is inseparably joined to that body. He can and should, however, separate himself from churches or other groups that have departed from the faith or are dangerously compromising it. Believers today enjoy liberty of conscience and the right and responsibility of dissent against those things which seem contrary to God's holy commands in His Word.

Separation is incongruous with a proper doctrine of the church.

Most persons advancing this argument are of a Reformed persuasion with regard to the nature of the church; that is, they see the church as a continuation of Israel, the "spiritual Israel" of New Testament times. Edward Carnell took to task J. Gresham Machen for failing to appreciate the Reformed doctrine of the church in adopting his separatist position. Carnell wrote:

> Ideological thinking prevented Machen from seeing that the issue under trial was *the nature of the church*, not the doctrinal incompatibility of orthodoxy and modernism. Does the church become apostate when it has modernists in its agencies and among its officially supported missionaries? The older Presbyterians knew enough about Reformed ecclesiology to answer this in the negative. Unfaithful ministers do *not* render the church apostate.[1]

Carnell then invoked John Calvin to prove his point. The Reformer, Carnell argued, held that while there existed apostasy and corruption in Israel, the prophets desired to preserve "the unity of the church" and therefore refused to forsake it. Here Calvin, of course, confounded Israel and the church. He strongly denounced the "Cathari and the Donatists" who "imagine the Church already perfectly holy and immaculate" and who "must allow no infirmity in the Church."[2]

While some separatists follow Calvin in his view of the church as a spiritual Israel, this would not be the view accepted by the larger proportion of separatists. Certainly it is not taught in the Scriptures. The church is a special creation of God, unique to this age and composed of those who have been placed into it by the baptism of the Holy Spirit. The Church is distinct from the *churches*. Local churches are composed of true believers who have banded themselves together for worship, fellowship and the propagation of the gospel.

Anti-separatists are often guilty of too closely identifying denominational alignments with the Body of Christ. That is, they tend to emphasize that visible unity should be displayed to the world, and that this unity is at least partly seen in denominational alignments or ecclesiastical groupings whose solidarity should be protected so as to render a good testimony before the world. The New Testament nowhere, however, identifies modern denominational arrangements with the Body of Christ. The whole denominational concept is a fairly recent phenomenon in church history. If the public display of Christian unity is dependent upon a perpetuation of such, how was Christian unity displayed prior to the inception of denominational bodies?

While not all anti-separatists employ the argument, Berkhouwer points out that a popular view is to distinguish between the church and her members.[3] This was essentially the point of Augustine. He said the church *per se* was holy, but distinguished the church from her members, many of whom were unholy. In this view the church is an organic reality apart from her members. This, of course, has become a prominent argument used by traditional Roman Catholic theologians, but aspects of it are embraced by others as well. The Donatists contended that the *people* within the church were required by Scripture to be holy, and that no refuge for unholiness could be taken in the fact that the invisible church as an entity was holy. This is the reason one noted young evangelical leader, Tom Howard, in discussing his view of the church as "one, holy, catholic, and apostolic," writes:

> As touching the second word, "holy," I have come to an Augustinian view as opposed to a Donatist view. That is, the holi-

ness of the church is not restricted to the few who exhibit manifest godliness in their lives. To believe otherwise leads to the interminable proliferation of schism. . . . Hence the church needs something more than earnest individuals with their New Testaments in hand. . . . The church is founded by Christ on the foundation of the apostles. Into their hands he gave the teaching authority, and they passed this on to their successors, to the apostles.[4]

Eenigenburg, writing an article entitled "Separatism Is Not Scriptural," is confused about the distinction between the Church and the churches. He writes:

Separatists often speak of the church as if it were a voluntary society or association. . . . The logic seems to be: My membership in the church is voluntary. . . . I have come by my own decision, what is to restrain me from voluntarily forsaking it. The right to leave is an implication of my right to join.

But the church is not a voluntary association at all. It is not formed by our decision, but Christ's. "I will build my church," He says (Matt. 16:18). . . . He has given us place in His church. . . .[5]

This is the very point. The issue of separation does not involve our relationship in an invisible church. It involves our relationship to *visible* churches. *The local visible church is a voluntary society*. It is joined freely by those who feel convicted so to do. While membership in the *Body of Christ*, the so-called universal church, is by the sovereign disposition of the Spirit, membership in a local congregation is by the free choice of a believer as he responds to what the Scriptures teach. Freedom of association is at the very root of separatist practice and teaching.

Despite problems, the Corinthians did not separate from their church.

In discussing the church at Corinth, one defender of staying in declares, "At no point does the apostle Paul suggest that sincere Christians should abandon the church because of the presence of problems."[6] Separatists have never contended that churches should be abandoned on account of the kinds of problems manifested in the Corinthian church. These problems were almost altogether interpersonal and moral in nature. While serious to the internal peace of a congregation, they did not involve apostasy from the revealed faith. Separatists believe that when the faith revealed by God has been repudiated, it is time to withdraw fellowship. Such was not the case at Corinth.

Separation rends Christ's Body and is a sin against its unity.

This is one of the most frequently used arguments, particularly by contemporary evangelicals who oppose the separatist principle. No doubt the ecumenical spirit of the day has enhanced its importance for some.

The statement has been made that, for separatists, separation is "the normal course of action whenever a petty disagreement arises. There is no sorrow over the division in the Body of Christ."[7] Is this true? We would have to say that it has *sometimes* been true of *some* separatists. Fundamentalists have been divided over petty issues. This is lamentable, and many fundamentalist leaders do sorrow over it. It is no doubt also true that *some* view separation from almost anything and anyone with a bit of glee and perhaps with gloating, thinking they have demonstrated their loyalty to the faith and their ruggedness of conviction. However, we do not think it is justifiable to employ this as an argument against the Biblical principle of separation. We believe that many sound, sane separatists desire to demonstrate what measure of outward Christian unity they can, but they feel they must do so without compromise of vital Biblical principles. While they do not talk as much (in public at least) about the "sin of division" as do some new evangelicals and others, they nevertheless possess a concern over the many unnecessary rifts that exist between brethren who agree on so many things.

Goen makes the judgment, "All separatism is perforce based on a sectarian doctrine of the church which exalts local independency and autonomy at the expense of acknowledging the larger fellowship of catholic Christianity."[8] However, in contrast to this, it should be stated that separatists have a concern for the entire testimony of Christ in His Church, but that concern is of a different nature than that emphasized by nonseparatists. Separatists first of all are concerned that a pure testimony be maintained. No doubt some separatists have lacked sufficient concern about the concerted witness and testimony of the church as a whole. On the other hand, some nonseparatists have shown relatively little concern for the growing, blatant and poisonous blasphemy of those who profess to be leaders of Christ's Church.

If the Biblical view of Christ's Body is perceived, it will be apparent that His Body cannot be divided. It is a spiritual entity. This is evident from an examination of such passages as 1 Corinthians 12:13; Ephesians 1:18-23; 4:11-16 and Colossians 1:18. It is a divine creation, formed by the work of the Spirit, and is incapable of being sundered by human effort. Its earthly and outward expression is found primarily through the interpersonal fellowship of individual believers and the congregational fellowship within local churches. An inter-congregational fellowship is exhibited in the New Testament as well, but not in the sense of most modern denominations. True spiritual unity, however, must be seen within a doctrinal context. The very passage where such unity is stressed also warns against false doctrine (Eph. 4:14), magnifies the work of teachers of doctrine (Eph. 4:11, 12), and envisions spiritual growth through the study of doctrine (Eph. 4:12, 13, 15).

We believe the above consideration militates against the view expressed by one of the modern spokesmen for an evangelical ecumenism, Lesslie Newbigin, who argues:

> But of course the unity of believers with Christ and with one another in Him is of a far deeper nature than intellectual agreement. It is not in its essential nature an intellectual agreement at all. . . . In its essential nature it is a work of the Holy Spirit binding us to one another in the love wherewith Christ loved us. . . . The true character of this union of believers with one another is disastrously distorted when it is conceived of essentially in terms of doctrinal agreement. The effect of such distortion is to break the Christian fellowship into rival parties, each based upon some one-sided doctrinal formulation, and eventually into completely separated bodies. . . .[9]

Newbigin is upholding the position that Christian fellowship is primarily based on a shared experience or a mutual relationship to Christ, not on doctrinal agreement. Yet this seems directly contradictory to the statement of Acts 2:42 where the "apostle's doctrine" (teaching) is mentioned first as the ground for the "fellowship" which follows. While it is appealing to many moderns to fancy Christian fellowship without the bother and strain of difficult doctrinal questions, such a dream is neither scriptural nor practical.

Newbigin argues also that persons who are incorporated into Christ's Body by the sacrament of baptism are participants in the "continuing life of Christ among men."[10] He sees a continuity of sacramental grace which is disrupted by the act of separation from the "mother" church. This, of course, has been and is a problem to those who have a connectional or sacramental view of the church. They perceive its unity as connected with the holy sacraments by which recipients receive divine grace. The large majority of separatists of the past and present would not hold this view of the church. They believe that the ordinances (not sacraments) bestow no saving or sanctifying grace, but are only symbols of spiritual truth and divine activity.

Many sincere believers feel that any repudiation of another believer or any refusal to fellowship with him is unloving and unworthy of Christ. But is this true?

The act of separation is incompatible with Christian love.

We admit that some separatists need more love in their hearts for their fellowmen. We do not believe, however, that this is a shortcoming confined to separatists. Part of the collective fruit of the Spirit is love (Gal. 5:22). We are commanded to "love one another with a pure heart fervently" (1 Pet. 1:22). All who are Christ's are obligated to obey.

If I, on the basis of personal conviction wrought by Biblical instruction, sever organizational fellowship with my fellow believer, have I ceased to love him? This is at the heart of the question. The answer is, "Not necessarily." It may be that in so separating my heart may grow cold and bitter attitudes may develop. This is a possibility and should be guarded against by all separatists. However, sundered organizational fellowship does not in and of itself mean discontinued love. It is possible to love those with whom I cannot have practical fellowship because of a disagreement over doctrine or practice. The Lord Jesus strongly denounced the scribes and Pharisees of His day, yet one would hesitate to state that our Lord did not love them. Love has muscle. Love expresses itself in loyalty to God and His Word. God is love, but He is also a "consuming fire" (Heb. 12:29). He has both aspects to His character, and they are held in perfect balance.

Edward Carnell, former professor at Fuller Seminary, informs us, "While we must be solicitous about *doctrine*, Scripture says that our primary business is *love*."[11] He fails, however, to reveal the scriptural source of such a statement, which we do not believe is true. It is not a mark of Christian love to wink at that which is contrary to God's Word. Love is not wishy-washy in its views of divine truth.

> In our own day there is danger of mistaking lazy or weak indifferentism for Christian charity. It is convenient doctrine that the beliefs of our fellow Christians are no concern of ours, even when they try to propagate what contradicts the creed. . . . To plead for tenderness, where severity is needed, is not charity, but Laodicean lukewarmness; and mistaken tenderness may easily end up in making us "partakers in evil works."[12]

The tares are to remain with the wheat.

This argument, first employed by Augustine against the Donatists, is based upon the parable of our Lord. Upon discovery of the "false wheat" (tares) among the true, the command was given, "Let both grow together until the harvest. . ." (Matt. 13:30). The application of anti-separatists is this: The professing church has good and bad elements. We are not to seek to root out all the bad elements, but live with them until God, Who alone knows all of them, will remove them at the last judgment. Eenigenburg is representative of many others when he comments:

> Without question "weeds" (Matt. 13:24 ff. RSV) are continually found in the "field" of the Kingdom or church, but the Lord has commanded to let weeds and wheat grow to-

gether until the harvest (v. 30). In God's harvest-time his appointed reapers will do the work of separating the one from the other.[13]

What of this argument? Actually, the field is neither the kingdom nor the church, as the writer erroneously indicates. We are specifically told that "the field is the world" (Matt. 13:38). The passage does not deal with unsaved persons who are in the church, but with the presence of evil persons in the world. Nor does the passage prohibit all segregation of the unsaved from the saved. If that were prohib-ited, then to insist upon a regenerate church mem-bership would be in violation of the passage since, in receiving only saved persons, a church would be at-tempting to divide the wheat from the tares.

This argument has no bearing on the question of whether or not the purity of the churches should be maintained.

Years ago when I was a seminary student, the noted Bible teacher and author Donald Grey Barn-house visited our institution. After speaking in chapel, he was a guest lecturer in one of the classes. A question and answer session was held, during which the following question was asked: "Dr. Barn-house, how do you justify your continued presence within the Presbyterian denomination in light of the apostasy into which it has fallen?" Many of us waited with bated breath to hear the reply, since we anticipated some learned, cogent and Biblical de-fense of the position. What should come forth but this: "I remain in the Presbyterian Church on the basis of Revelation 3:2 where we are instructed to 'be watchful, and strengthen the things which remain, that are ready to die.' Next question, please." We could hardly believe our ears, yet it was true. This, from a master of the Scriptures, was the sum and substance of scriptural defense for the position of "staying in." Nor was this a chance occasion or a misinterpreted utterance because, in response to an individual's inquiry about the same matter, Barn-house replied:

> Thank you for your letter which I read with great interest. Concerning my affilia-

Believers (specifically pastors) are to "strengthen the things that remain."

200 • BIBLICAL SEPARATION

tion with the Presbyterian Church, I take the
position that "come out from among them
and be ye separate . . ." does not refer to the
denomination, but rather to the pagan temples. My basis for staying in is in Revelation
3 where we are told to strengthen the things
that remain that are ready to die. The Lord
told me to feed His lambs and His sheep and
I am not given the right to make speci-
fications about the fold in which the sheep
are to be found. For better or for worse, more
than 90% of the Lord's sheep are in the denominations. I, as a Bible teacher, must stay
in and feed them.[14]

We would ask one question: Is it not a
shepherd's responsibility to guide the sheep into the
proper pastures and to direct them into the proper
folds? The shepherd is not to follow the sheep into
the places where they wish to go. He is to guide them
into the places where he (the shepherd) knows they
should go. Such is clearly the teaching of John
10:4—the shepherd "goeth before them, and the
sheep follow him." The Bible does make speci-
fications as to the fold in which the sheep are to be
found. Definite requirements are set forth in Scripture governing the establishment of a local church
(fold) and the nature of its membership.

Do the instructions to the church at Sardis
which Barnhouse cites really teach us that we are to
remain within apostate denominations in order to
serve the Lord and to help His people? We believe
that they do not for the following reasons:

(1) The continued presence of believers within
an apostate denomination dominated by leaders who
do not believe the truth militates against the spiritual
watchfulness commanded ("be watchful," "wake
up," Rev. 3:2). Believers are lulled to sleep by the
continued fellowship of their church with apostasy.
They soon begin to rationalize their presence and to
minimize the extent of the false teaching (as Barnhouse himself did in his later years).

(2) The term the things is neuter, which means
that to strengthen "things" involves more than just
ministering to people (or feeding the sheep). The call
is for the strengthening of principles, institutions,
activities. If these cannot be strengthened, the command cannot be carried out successfully. Barnhouse

and others like him tried for years (some are still trying) to strengthen the Presbyterian Church. Their efforts have failed, and the church is no closer today to solid orthodoxy than it was when Machen and others left it years ago.

(3) The church at Sardis was not an apostate church. It had not repudiated the truth, but was holding the truth in an academic, uncommitted fashion. It was incomplete in fulfilling God's will. It was "dead" (3:1) with the exception of a few who evidenced spiritual vitality (3:4). Today we face the spectacle of entire denominations whose leaders have publicly and clearly renounced the faith. It is not a question of a cold but orthodox heart. It is a question of the repudiation of the faith and the embracing of error.

(4) The words of the Lord do not imply a long period of condescension toward their sin during which their current state would continue. Rather, He speaks strongly of pending judgment if repentance is not forthcoming (3:3).

> The argument is put by one advocate as follows:
>
> In 2 Corinthians 6:17 Paul does advise the Corinthian Christians to "come out from among them, and be separate from them." This is at the command of the Lord himself. Separatists have liked to quote this verse in justification of their deed. But Paul here is *not* calling upon one group of professing Christians to separate themselves from another band of professing Christians. The "them" refers clearly to unbelievers (v. 14). Separatists have tended to say, "Well, they are unbelievers, even if their names are on the church rolls. They are the apostate church." But nowhere in the New Testament are some Christians given the privilege of declaring other professing Christians "unbelievers."[15]

We have no right to pass judgment upon the salvation of others.

Is this an accurate statement? Are we required by virtue of "Christian generosity" to accept all "professing Christians" as genuine without further inquiry, and to fellowship with them as though they were genuine with no questions asked?

The New Testament very definitely demands an inquiry into the spiritual state of persons claiming to be Christians. "Beloved, believe not every spirit, but try the spirits whether they are of God. . ." (1 John 4:1). This does not refer to an examination of disembodied ghosts, but rather a close scrutiny of human beings through whom false spirits work and spread their errors. We are to "mark" them which oppose apostolic doctrine (Rom. 16:17). They do not belong to Christ and are to be avoided. The word mark is rather pointed in its thrust, meaning "to fix attention upon, to keep your eyes on, observe closely." We are by no means to take everyone at his word who claims to be a Christian. Many profess to know the Lord, but their works evidence the fact that they do not (Titus 1:16). Are we to ignore the testimony of their deeds in favor of the testimony of their mouths? Were the principles stated above (refusing to declare professing Christians as unbelievers) followed by local churches, they would be forced to receive every applicant for membership on the strength of his verbal profession with no weight being placed upon his observed conduct.

While it is certainly true that only the Lord knows infallibly "them that are his" (2 Tim. 2:19), believers have the responsibility to exercise discernment with regard to those who claim to be followers of the Lord but are in reality not (cf. Matt. 7:15-23). We are certainly to be "fruit inspectors," and if the fruit of the tree is rotten, we have reason to suspect that the tree is not healthy.

Christ's prayer for unity needs visible expression.

Much has been made in recent years (especially since the rise of ecumenism) of the Lord's great prayer recorded in John 17:21: "That they all may be one; as thou, Father, art in me, and I in thee, that they also may be one in us: that the world may believe that thou hast sent me." Representatives of the National and World Councils of Churches have often used this as scriptural support for their ecumenical activities. They seem to have little concern for Scripture except where they feel they can locate a text that might justify their disobedience. Evangelicals have also invoked this verse in inveighing against the "scandalous divisions" of the visible church. How does this prayer of our Lord's relate to the controversy over the matter of separation?

To put it bluntly, the matter would be described by anti-separatists in this fashion: "Our Lord prays that His people might be united. You separatists are dividing them. You, therefore, are sinning against the Lord, Who desires the unity which you are destroying." This is a rather serious charge. Are separatists fighting against the will of God in their practice of separation from apostasy? If so, they should indeed repent and seek to make amends. Let us examine John 17 more closely.

The prayer of the Lord obviously has to do with the unity of believers. He prays for "the men which thou gavest me" (v. 6); for those who "have believed" (v. 8); and for those who are "not of the world" (v. 14). Separation, therefore, at least from unbelievers, would not dishonor in any way the heart cry of the Lord. He is not pleading here for continued unity between unbelieving apostates and true believers. He is speaking of unity between those who are genuinely saved.

Note also that He mentions several times in His prayer God's Word and God's truth (vv. 6, 14, 17, 19). This is not a prayer to ignore truth in favor of unity. It is a prayer reflecting unity in truth.

> Moreover the semblance of love which does not maintain the truth, but accommodates itself to that which is not the truth, is not love according to God. ... In the last days the test of true love is maintenance of truth. God would have us love one another; but the Holy Ghost ... who pours the love of God into our hearts is the Spirit of truth. ...[16]

The Lord's prayer is *not for something we should do*, but expresses *something He has done*. He is not asking the disciples to maintain unity. He is addressing the Father and requesting Him to keep His people within that unity He has created (vv. 11, 21, 23). The impression is often given that if we do not do our part and maintain the visible unity of believers, we are somehow dishonoring the prayer of the Lord. His prayer, however, was not addressed to us and did not give us instructions as to what we should do.

The unity which Christ asks the Father to maintain is a spiritual unity. It is the unity such as the

Holy Trinity sustains (v. 21). It is not an organizational unity. While some evangelicals grant that, they go on to state that the Lord prayed here for some kind of *visible* unity such as the world can observe so that they will be convinced of the truth of Christ's claims. This is the argument of Colquhoun.[17] There is a flaw in the thinking of many who use this argument, however. They are thinking of some sort of denominational or interdenominational structure, some organized body through which this unity is to be expressed. Thus, when separatists sunder any organized structure, anti-separatists castigate them for violating the principle of unity and giving the world cause to mock the Christian faith because it does not visibly evidence oneness in Christ. This, we believe, is a misunderstanding of the visible expression of Christian unity called for in the New Testament. The New Testament knows no denominational structure and gives no pattern for one. New Testament churches fellowshiped together, but they were not under any denominational compulsion. Unity and love in Christ can be expressed without any structure.

The apostate should be purged, and the orthodox should remain.

Several opponents of the separatist position have noted that in the New Testament it was the heretics who left the church, not the orthodox. ". . .The Church did not separate itself from the false teachers; the false teachers separated of their own accord from the Church."[18] Another defends the same concept when he writes, "In the New Testament itself, this rupture means the expulsion of the heretics. The New Testament does not know the situation of a church in which error has obtained an official place."[19]

Certainly separatists have no objection to the dismissal of heretics from churches. Time was when there was a rumpus over the presence of false teachers within the visible churches. In 1893 the General Assembly of the Presbyterian Church suspended C. A. Briggs from the ministry for heretical views. Any effort to do that today within the same body would end in a miserable failure since the vast majority of men not only embrace the heresies of Briggs but go much farther than did he.

That apostates should be put out of the church is absolutely correct. Such a statement, however, assumes that the orthodox within the church have sufficient numbers to control its actions and thus to purge out the offender. Any person familiar with the ecclesiastical situation today knows full well that this situation does not obtain in the major denominations. It raises an interesting question. Why does an apostate who knows he is not in the traditional doctrinal heritage of his church remain in it? Why does he not voluntarily leave? One liberal who was dismissed by a Baptist college but remained within the denomination which supported the college gave some reasons why people like himself remain in.

> The heretic nearly always elects to stay in. Loyalty to his denomination; the sense of obligation because of having been a beneficiary; the desire to work with crowds and to represent an impressive organization; the missionary motive, leading him to share with those of his own group the knowledge he has gained; economic pressure; the example of older and prominent leaders who have stayed in successfully though they were heretics; fears, as of loss of friends; group approval or family peace, are some of the controlling considerations that hold the heretic within his orthodox connections.[20]

What of the argument that the heretic should be purged? Runia defends it and cites several Scriptures in an effort to prove the point (Gal. 1:8, 9; 2 Tim. 3:5; Titus 3:10, 11; 1 John 4:1 ff.; 2 John 7-11; Rev. 2:14).[21] An examination of these passages proves nothing with regard to *the manner* in which the apostate is to be disfellowshiped. Terms are used such as "turn away" (2 Tim. 3:5), "reject" (Titus 3:10), "receive him not" (2 John 10). Since the New Testament had no counterpart to the modern denomination, no specific instruction is given as to the organizational details involved in separation. It is very clear, however, that apostates are to be disfellowshiped. When they take control of ecclesiastical bodies, it is evident that the command to disfellowship them requires separation from the body. *The major thrust of the New Testament commands is that of refusal of fellowship*. The manner in which this is to be done may vary depending upon the circumstances. Separation from an existing denomination is certainly not tantamount to separation from the true church. It is simply an effort to manifest the purity of the invisible church in the visible.

The commands to purge unbelievers and false teachers from the church as found in the New Testament presuppose: (1) a believer's church; that is, a church composed of the regenerate; (2) the possession of spiritual discernment on the part of the church's membership so as to recognize false teaching and teachers; and (3) the commitment of the church to obey God's commands. Most of the contemporary denominations would be incapable of purging out error and her advocates because their constituencies are composed largely of unregenerate persons and their leaders themselves are teachers of error. In light of this, the argument that false teachers should be separated or removed from the church rather than true believers separating from the church is not really valid. A church must be a true, Christ-honoring church to be able to perform this duty. Large numbers of churches are not.

The New Testament emphasis is on unity, not purity.

We noted earlier that a major distinction between separatists and nonseparatists is found in their emphasis. Separatists emphasize the church's purity; nonseparatists its unity. Ockenga indicated this when he wrote:

> The cause of the fundamentalist defeat on the ecclesiastical scene lay partially in fundamentalism's erroneous doctrine of the Church which identified the Church with believers who were orthodox in doctrine and separatist in ethics. Purity of the Church was emphasized above the peace of the Church.[22]

Our comments on the priority of holiness (chapter 10) are an adequate reply to this observation by Ockenga.

Klaas Runia, in his articles entitled "When Is Separation a Christian Duty?" called the separatist position the "surgical" approach to reformation.

> Usually this whole position is marred by two defects. First, no serious attempt is made to reform the "fallen" church. It is simply abandoned. And second, behind it all is an

unscriptural perfectionism that looks for the "pure" church. This type of separatism is a dead end. It is not only unscriptural; it is also impractical for there is no end to separation.[23]

But is the search for a "pure" church impractical "perfectionism"? Separatists make a distinction between a "pure" church and a "perfect" church. The former embodies the thought of doctrinal fidelity and scriptural practice though held by imperfect humans (saved by grace), while the latter implies the type of fellowship that would be impossible to attain this side of glory. The claim that separatists have made no serious attempt to purge existing bodies is not true uniformly throughout church history. For instance, in modern times orthodox men in the Presbyterian Church as well as the Northern Baptist Convention made titanic efforts to cleanse those bodies. Unbelief is like leaven, however, and it works its insidious way throughout the mass.

The Practical Objections to Separation

One of the critics of separatism, J. Marcellus Kik, suggests that separatists evidence a "spirit of belligerency." He describes further what, in his opinion, are their characteristics:

Separatists are extremists and have an overly critical spirit.

> There are many sores—grievous sores—on the body ecclesia. They attract a certain type of evangelical as physical sores attract flies. They buzz and molest but make no real attempt to apply the balm of Gilead. . . . They gloat over sores and shed no tears. They cater to the appetite of sensationalism. They even castigate fellow evangelicals for not following in their ways and using their methods.[24]

Regrettably, this is probably a just criticism of *some* separatists. Some separatists are an embarrassment to the entire cause due to their cantankerousness. This fact, however, does not justify men's refusal to occupy a scriptural position—outside the camp of unbelief. Paul was concerned that the truth be preached despite the fact that some who preached it manifested a poor spirit in so doing (Phil. 1:12-17).

God's truth must take precedence over human attitudes. We decry the spirit of some soldiers; but the battle is the Lord's, and we must fight it.

Schism is a grievous sin.

What is the distinction, if any, between schism and separation? The answer given usually depends upon the viewpoint of the one discussing the question. Grounds tried to distinguish the schismatic from the separatist in three ways: (1) a schismatic is unconcerned about church disunity; (2) a schismatic sees every doctrine as equally important; (3) a schismatic believes his church alone is the true church.[25]

The word *schism* comes from a Greek word meaning "to cleave or cut." It has historically referred to a division in the visible church. It has a bad connotation, is a scare word and is generally used by opponents of the separatist position for this reason. I question whether or not it is beneficial to try to distinguish between schism and Biblical separation. Generally speaking, in common ecclesiastical parlance, schism would be thought of as a division generated by party strife, personal jealousies or power struggles—a disruption arising out of petty differences and without true scriptural justification. If this be the definition placed upon schism, then separatists would deny being schismatics. The doctrine of separation, rightly understood, is grounded in theological and Biblical considerations.

Vested denominational interests should be retained.

When the struggle between the fundamentalists and the liberals was at its height in the Northern Baptist Convention, R. S. Beal, leader of the Fundamentalist Fellowship at the time and well-known Arizona pastor, described the conservatives within the Convention:

> Ours is not a separatist movement. Why should we surrender to liberalism the great institutions built up by orthodoxy for the perpetuation of the faith of our fathers? Modernism does not build churches; it steals them. It does not build missions; it steals them too.[26]

One can understand how pastors with large churches and many investments in denominational work would be reluctant to leave all of it behind. Better to leave it, however, than to become contaminated by the unbelief and compromise of the apostasy while trying to save it. The honor of Christ and the purity of His churches must be our primary consideration. Our treasures ought not to be here on earth, but laid up "where neither moth nor rust doth corrupt, and where thieves do not break through nor steal" (Matt. 6:20).

One of the most difficult arguments to refute successfully (to its proponent) is this one: "I have prayed about it, and God has led me to remain in my denomination." What can be said? Simply this. God does not lead people contrary to His revealed will in His Word. If the case for separation is solidly based upon scriptural teaching (and we believe it is), then the author of holy Scripture, the Spirit of God, would not lead some believer to reject that teaching and pursue a different course. Always the believer's prayer should be, "Order my steps in thy word: and let not any iniquity have dominion over me" (Ps. 119:133). It is the Word of God that gives us our direction. Believers must walk in truth (2 John 4). "Thy word is truth" (John 17:17). Any appeal to prayer or other source of spiritual illumination which leads us to act contrary to the Word is spurious.

The leading of God must be followed.

I recall a brilliant lady who advanced that argument many years ago. She attended the independent church occasionally, but she retained her membership in a church affiliated with an apostate group. She had a large, ladies' Bible class there, and she maintained that the Lord was using her. Gradually she came to see the error of that position, and she removed her membership from the apostate group. In the years that followed, God opened to her a Bible class ministry in homes around the city where her ministry far surpassed anything she had ever had in the apostate denomination. She obeyed God, and He honored her for it.

A fruitful ministry is possible in apostate denominations.

We must never disobey God in order to seek to honor God. We must ask, "What are the scriptural principles which I must obey?" and then we must obey them. God will take care of our ministries and see that we accomplish what is His will for us.

Separatists are judgmental.

We should hesitate, says one, to pass judgment on the poor performance of others. Paul exhibited Christlike love, even for erring brethren, and we ought to do the same.[27]

Is it always wrong to pass judgment? We think not on the basis of Scripture. Paul, while loving the erring brethren, also called upon a local church to excommunicate one (1 Cor. 5:13). In doing so, he was commanding the church to pass judgment on him as unworthy of their fellowship. Paul named and denounced Hymenaeus and Alexander as false teachers, thus passing judgment on their teaching (2 Tim. 2:16-18). In choosing candidates for church offices—pastors and deacons—qualifications are given which require a judgment—does a person meet them or not (1 Tim. 3:1-13)? The proper kind of judgment is equated with sagacity, discernment and discrimination. To be sure, some judgments made by separatists may be mistaken, but the same could be said of their opponents.

Separatists engender controversy within the church.

Actually, separatists often are blamed for the "dirty work" performed by apostates and compromisers. These persons undertake their nefarious activities, and Bible-believing Christians blow the whistle on them. For so doing, the separatists are deemed troublemakers and disturbers of the peace. Some separatists, by virtue of their own personalities and contentious spirits, cause *unnecessary* trouble in some places. Such persons can be found in all walks of life and various theological positions. But legitimate *necessary* trouble needs to be caused. With what audacity did Ahab, the apostate, ask Elijah, the prophet of righteousness, "Art thou he that troubleth Israel?" (1 Kings 18:17). Troubler of Israel, indeed! It was that foul apostate Ahab that squatted upon the throne of Israel like an ugly toad and caused the poison of apostasy to be spread abroad. So it is with present-day apostates. Separatists recognize they are not perfect and that their courses of action may not always be the best. But they stand for the right, for the Bible and for the truth. May God increase their number!

But, says one, I do not stoop to controversy. Listen to the pungent comments of Vance Havner, old-time warrior of the faith:

Some Christians who once championed sound doctrine beat a retreat once in a while and from stratospheric heights announce that they do not "stoop to controversy." When a man contends for the faith in New Testament style he does not stoop! Contending for the faith is not easy. It is not pleasant business. It has many perils. It is a thankless job. And it is highly unpopular in this age of moral fogs and spiritual twilights. It is a day of diplomats, not prophets. It is nicer to be an appeaser than an opposer. It is the day of Erasmus, not Luther; of Gamaliel, not Paul.[28]

Some have taken the various Biblical passages on separation and endeavored to refute them. Some, like Colquhoun, conclude that many of the passages on separation are stressing separation on moral rather than theological grounds. He does admit that in certain extreme cases separation on theological grounds might be justified.[29]

The separation practiced by separatists is un-Biblical.

What would anti-separatists view as proper grounds for separation? Runia wrestled with this question and concluded that separation is justified when:

(1) The church itself in its *official doctrinal statements* may oppose the Gospel and refuse to repeal its errors.
(2) The church may *compel* the believer to believe or do things that are clearly contrary to the Word of God.
(3) The church may *no longer* give freedom to believe or to do what is clearly commanded by the Word of God.
(4) The church in its official capacity . . . may *refuse to deal with notorious heretics*, in spite of protests or charges.[30]

He made this observation, however:

I have the impression that the first three of these do not often occur in today's Protestant churches. Most denominations, officially, still have their original creeds and confessions, and even the more recent statements of faith are fairly pure in their positive affirmations—the real harm is usually in the omissions. There is also generally a considerable amount of liberty in the churches both for the liberal and for the evangelical. The real issue of our day is found in the fourth situation, the case in which a church refuses to deal with heresy. At this point, however, evangelicals disagree among themselves about which course of action to take.[31]

He concluded: "Only those who have seriously tried to bring the church to reformation and have found that the church not only refuses to reform, but continues to protect error and heresy in fundamental areas of the Christian faith—only those persons have the right and the duty to separate."[32]

Edward Carnell held a similar position. He sought to clarify the "legitimate conditions of separation" and came up with three.

First: All other things being equal, a Christian should remain in the fellowship that gave him spiritual birth. A filial obligation requires this. . . .
Secondly: A Christian should judge the claims of a church by its official creed or confession, not by the lives of its members. . . .
Thirdly: Separation from an existing denomination is justifiable on only two criteria.
    a. Eviction. . . .
    b. Apostasy. If a denomination removes the gospel from its creed or confession, or if it leaves the gospel but removes the believer's right to preach it, the believer may justly conclude that the denomination is apostate.[33]

One's heart aches as he reads such words. How unspeakably sad that intelligent men, whom we assume love our Lord, would base their course of action upon such flimsy, unscriptural and illogical principles! Yes, separatists do weep. They weep when they ponder such reasoning. They pray earnestly that somehow God might bring brethren who espouse it to their senses. What good, pray tell, is a confession or creed whose content and meaning are blissfully and openly ignored by most of the clergy whose position it is supposed to represent? And to think of comforting oneself with the thought that, while the liberal has freedom to spread his heresy, evangelicals, too, have freedom to preach the gospel of Christ. Furthermore, how can we legitimately restrict our judgment of religious groups to their official statements only, ignoring the true state of things as revealed in the lives of their leaders and members? Our Lord judges His churches, not by what they have in print, but by what they display in life. Christ could care less about what the churches claim to be. He is interested in what they actually are as is incontrovertibly seen in the seven letters to the Asian churches (Rev. 2—3). To each of them He said, "I know thy works. . . ." The Scripture rightly declares, "Man looketh on the outward appearance, but the LORD looketh on the heart" (1 Sam. 16:7).

L. Nelson Bell, Billy Graham's father-in-law, a Presbyterian, argues that the doctrine of separation "can lead people to abandon the opportunity for witness where it is most greatly needed." And where, one would naturally ask, is this great mission field which will be cut off by Biblical separation? Bell answers, "It is highly distressing that perhaps the greatest field for Christian witnessing today is *within* the Church. . . . "[34] It would seem, on evidence of the New Testament, that if one belonged to a church group that was so filled with unsaved persons as to constitute a mission field, he had better be looking for a different church. The churches of Christ are to be gathering places of the redeemed. Bell, however, looks at it differently.

Separation hinders witnessing opportunities.

> I happen to belong to a denomination in which many positions that I have felt to be right have been overruled and defeated again and again. This makes some of my friends very unhappy, and some have looked for another church in which their views might predominate. I too would enjoy such a fellowship, but, win or lose, I feel it my duty to stand by . . . hoping and praying that my own witness . . . will by God's grace, be effective in the hearts of some.[35]

Not a line of New Testament instruction, to my knowledge, encourages true believers to view the church as a mission field in which we must faithfully remain regardless of the sin and blasphemy of its members. A New Testament church is a body of those who have received God's Word into their hearts (Acts 2:41), of blood-washed saints whose faith is in the Savior (Phil. 1:1). One of the main purposes for a church is to prepare believers for the work of ministry (Eph. 4:11-13). This being so, a regenerate church membership is demanded, not a church in which are found many numbers who are candidates for evangelism.

No doubt many anti-separatists are truly children of God. No doubt they hold their position in sincerity, believing it to be scriptural and honoring to God. However, how a true Biblical defense of such a position can be made, we do not see. The holy character of God demands a much more decisive approach to the prevailing apostasy than that set forth by these brethren.

Notes:

1. Carnell, *The Case for Orthodox Theology*, p. 115.

2. John Calvin, *Institutes of the Christian Religion*, trans. John Allen (Philadelphia: Presbyterian Board of Christian Education, 1936), Book IV, Chap. VIII, p. 428.

3. G. C. Berkhouwer, *The Church* (Grand Rapids: Wm. B. Eerdmans Publishing Co., 1976), p. 340.

4. Tom Howard, "Steeplechase: How I Changed Churches," *Eternity* (February 1977), pp. 15, 16, 23.

5. Elton M. Eenigenburg, "Separatism Is Not Scriptural," *Eternity* (August 1963), p. 19.

6. Ibid., p. 20.

7. "Pro and Con on Separatism" editorial, *Eternity* (August 1963), p. 6.

8. Goen, *Revival and Separatism in New England: 1740-1800*, p. 288.

9. Lesslie Newbigin, *The Household of God* (London: SCM Press, 1953), p. 54.

10. Ibid., p. 77.

11. Carnell, *The Case for Orthodox Theology*, p. 121.

12. Alfred Plummer, "The Pastoral Epistles," *The Expositor's Bible*, ed. W. Robertson Nicoll (New York: A. C. Armstrong, 1905), XXIII, 305.

13. Eenigenburg, "Separatism Is Not Scriptural," p. 20.

14. Donald G. Barnhouse, personal letter (September 28, 1953).

15. Eenigenburg, "Separatism Is Not Scriptural," p. 20.

16. J. N. Darby, *Synopsis of the Books of the Bible* (London: Stow Hill Bible and Tract Depot, 1948), V, 357, 358.

17. Frank Colquhoun, *The Fellowship of the Gospel* (Grand Rapids: Zondervan Publishing House, 1957), p. 20.

18. Ibid., p. 44.

19. Klaas Runia, "When Is Separation a Christian Duty?" Part 2, *Christianity Today* (July 7, 1967).

20. Donald George Tinder, "Fundamentalist Baptists in the Northern and Western United States: 1920-1950" (doctoral dissertation, Yale University, 1969) citing *Watchman-Examiner* (May 24, 1923), p. 649.

21. Klaas Runia, "When Is Separation a Christian Duty?" Part 1, *Christianity Today* (June 23, 1967), p. 4.

22. Ockenga, "Resurgent Evangelical Leadership," p. 12.

23. Runia, "When Is Separation a Christian Duty?" Part 2, p. 7.

24. J. Marcellus Kik, *Ecumenism and the Evangelical* (Philadelphia: Presbyterian and Reformed, 1958), p. 134.

25. Vernon Grounds, "Schismatic or Separatist," *The Dynamics of Christian Unity*, ed. W. Stanley Monneyham (Grand Rapids: Zondervan Publishing House, 1936), pp. 35-39.

26. R. S. Beal, from a sermon, *Rivers in the Desert* (Tuscon: First Baptist Church, n.d.), IV, 21.

27. Eeigenburg, "Separatism Is Not Scriptural," p. 20.

28. Vance Havner, "The Forgotten Anathema," *Sword of the Lord* (January 7, 1955).

29. Colquhoun, *The Fellowship of the Gospel*, pp. 37-45.

30. Runia, "When Is Separation a Christian Duty?" Part 2, p. 8.

31. Ibid.

32. Ibid.

33. Carnell, *The Case for Orthodox Theology*, pp. 133-137.

34. Bell, "On Separation," p. 26.

35. Ibid., p. 27.

Implementing
Separatist Convictions

12

IT IS ONE thing to embrace Biblical truth concerning separatism. It is quite another to implement it in day-to-day relationships. While one may possess good convictions, he will likely be confronted with problems and situations in which his course of action may not be as clearly discernible as he would wish. The separatist faces many questions as he seeks to obey His Lord. Separatists are not always agreed among themselves as to the proper response to a given problem. Attention needs to be given to the implementation of that which we believe.

The Problem of
Secondary Separation

Perhaps nothing has stirred discussion and disagreement among separatists any more than the question of so-called "secondary separation." In recent years (since the fundamentalist-modernist controversy) the term "secondary separation" has been coined. A secondary separatist would be one who will not cooperate with (1) apostates; or (2) evangelical believers who aid and abet the apostates by their continued organizational or cooperative alignment with them; or, as employed by some (3) fundamentalists who fellowship with those in the previous category.[1]

To even suggest that one born-again believer should not fellowship with another born-again believer is anathema to many. Yet, as we have already seen, at times fellowship cannot be maintained. How may we determine with whom we should fellowship? This is not a simple question.

Various levels of Christian fellowship.

The problems posed for fellowship may vary at different levels. We suggest at least four such levels: (1) personal Christian fellowship between individual believers; (2) local church fellowship; (3) inter-church fellowship; and (4) interdenominational fellowship. The first two seem self-explanatory. The third is associational or denominational fellowship between churches of similar convictions. The fourth is fellowship in an interdenominational group to which an individual, a church or a group of churches might belong.

Pondering these levels, we realize that we might be able to have personal Christian fellowship with persons who are genuinely born again, but with whom we could not enjoy local church fellowship. Why? Because the moment you establish a local church fellowship, you establish doctrinal criteria beyond those required for individual fellowship. You might enjoy personal fellowship with a friend who is a Presbyterian. However, you cannot have fellowship with him within the membership of a local church because he does not feel obliged to be immersed, and you believe that immersion is a pre-requisite for church membership. You can enjoy the personal fellowship; you cannot enjoy church fellowship.

The same is true if one contrasts local church fellowship and interchurch fellowship. Hypothetically, let us consider an Assemblies of God church that applies for membership in a Baptist association. The association refuses the Assemblies church fellowship. Why? The Baptist association believes in the eternal security of the believer and also rejects the doctrine of tongues held by the Assemblies of God congregation. The association would be justified in refusing fellowship because it would violate their standards.

It is impossible to have harmonious, working fellowship with all believers at all of these levels. Doctrinal considerations govern certain types of fellowship. Some Baptist pastor may enjoy visiting on a personal level with a born-again pastor who differs with him on the necessity of immersion. Some spiritual benefit may be derived from such interpersonal acquaintance. However, the Baptist pastor would never nominate his pastor-friend as a trustee of the Baptist college nearby. Why? Because the college is committed to a particular doctrinal stance which the pastor-friend would not occupy. Personal fellowship does not lead to organizational fellowship in every case.

What specific circumstances prevent our cooperative fellowship with other truly saved believers?

What prevents our fellowship with other believers?

If the believer teaches false doctrine and refuses to be corrected. While some hold the position that one believer should never separate from another believer on doctrinal grounds, we believe this position is incorrect. If a professing believer is teaching error and he cannot be persuaded to the truth, he must be excluded from fellowship. An example of this principle is found in 1 Timothy 1:18-20. Hymenaeus and Alexander had departed from sound doctrine. Paul said they were "delivered unto Satan" (v. 20); that is, they were excommunicated from fellowship (cf. 1 Cor. 5:5, 13). Paul evidently entertained the hope that the two were genuine believers, and trusted that, if they were, the action would result in repentance. The principle applies whether the professing believer is in our own local church or in some other kind of connectional relationship to us, such as a denominational affiliation.

If the professing believer is walking in immorality. A believer in the church of Corinth was involved in moral sin. Paul wrote to the church and demanded his dismissal (1 Cor. 5:1, 13). Unity and fellowship cannot be maintained when there is unconfessed sin in the camp. The pure witness of the church is sullied thereby, and separation from such a person is the only course of action.

If, by cooperating with a Christian leader who is walking contrary to Scripture in some vital area, we would become partakers of his wrongdoing. It is possible to become a "partaker of other men's sins" (1 Tim. 5:22). The context of this verse deals with the matter of public ordination to the ministry. This, we believe, is the reference, despite the attempts of some modern expositors to make it refer to the restoration of erring elders. Paul is speaking about elders (pastors), their qualifications, their ministry and their responsibilities (cf. vv. 17-21). Then he says (v. 22), "Do not too hastily put your stamp of approval upon a candidate for eldership lest you be reproached for having approved his sins." The plea is for careful scrutiny of church leaders. Paul is concerned about purity—"keep thyself pure" (v. 22). The emphasis is upon *thyself*. Regardless of what others do, *you* maintain purity.

Here again is a *principle* which flows out of specific instruction. A servant of God may contaminate his own testimony by giving public recognition or endorsement to another who, though a brother in Christ (the verse does not speak of apostates), nevertheless is not maintaining a walk that is pleasing to God. The word translated "partaker" is the word *koinonia*, which is rendered often by the word "fellowship" in the New Testament. It is possible to have fellowship with a man's sins if we publicly endorse an unscriptural position which he has taken. The laying on of hands was a symbolic commendation of and identification with a minister of the Word in the act of ordination. If it is wrong to approve his sin in the act of ordination, it can hardly be right to approve it afterward.

If the professing believer is walking in a disrupting manner. In 2 Thessalonians 3:6-15 Paul deals with a problem faced by the church. Note several points in his argument. The entire passage gives the clear impression that apostolic teaching was to be regarded as authoritative for individuals and churches (vv. 6, 14). Paul's "word by this epistle" (v. 14) was not merely his opinion, but was something to be obeyed as having come from the Lord.

Some believers were disregarding the apostolic instructions. They are referred to as "disorderly" (vv. 6, 7, 11). The word is a military one and was used of soldiers who marched out of step or who broke rank. It referred to those who failed to follow the prescribed rules and to maintain the required standards. Specifically, Paul says they were "not busyworkers, but busybodies" (a play on words in the original language, v. 11). Apparently these people were so enthusiastic over the possibility of Christ's return that they were failing to continue the normal pursuits of life. They were refusing to work and were pestering their Christian brethren and causing problems. Their improper actions were caused by their incorrect grasp of doctrine.

How were believers to respond to those who were not walking in accordance with divine instructions? "Withdraw yourselves" (v. 6) and "have no company with" (v. 14). The American Standard Version renders the first expression "keep aloof." It means, "to abstain from familiar intercourse, to remove or withdraw oneself" (force of middle voice which is used here). The second expression (v. 14) means "do not get mixed up together." Paul is also deeply concerned about the *attitude of heart* with which such separation is enforced. The man is not to be hated, but to be admonished as a brother (v. 15). We are to be careful lest with nasty and vicious language (either oral or written) we violate the exhortation here given.

The main question among separatists is this: Does this portion of Scripture apply only and exclusively to people who leave their work, sponge off other believers and live lives of idleness which contribute to spiritual confusion? Certainly this is the context of the passage as it is written. Is it not true, however, that the *principle* clearly seen here applies to other situations? The *principle* is this: When our brethren do things which are wrong—caused by an incomplete knowledge of or deliberate disobedience to some teaching of Scripture—we should not merely continue to fellowship with them as those who have done nothing wrong, but we should warn them, remonstrate with them and seek to recover them to a Biblical position. It is the *principle* of maintaining a pure walk that should be stressed. This *principle* should not be overlooked by an overemphasis on the particular situation in this church to which the principle was applied.

If one should ask, Does 2 Thessalonians 3 teach secondary separation?—then the response would have to be given, It depends on what you mean by secondary separation. Does it specifically state that a separatist church or school should not use a certain noted preacher because he is in the Southern Baptist Convention, which has liberals within its rank? It does not *specifically* state that. It does, however, present an important *principle* which God's people by the direction of His Spirit must seek to apply in various situations (including the one just mentioned). It is the principle of refusing to condone, honor or utilize persons who continually and knowingly are following a course of action which is harmful to other believers and to the welfare of the churches. The psalmist in a beautiful expression states, "I am a companion of all them that fear thee, and of them that keep thy precepts" (Ps. 119:63). He says we should be in happy companionship *with those who are keeping God's Word.* Paul says we should not have happy companionship ("have no company," 2 Thess. 3:14) with those who do not keep the Word.

Separatists have a problem here, however. It is no doubt at the root of some of the debate over the question of so-called secondary separatism. To what extent must a person be keeping God's precepts? What are the doctrinal limitations beyond which one cannot go in fellowship? Do any scriptural guidelines aid us in determining to what extent we should fellowship with other believers?

First of all, it is clear that no *direct* scriptural teaching will cover every problem we face. As in so many areas of Christian thought and life, we must determine our practice by the application of doctrines, principles and emphases that are found in the Bible. The exercise of personal judgment, in the light of known divine truths, is required. It is this element of separatism which nonseparatists often attack. They decry separatists as too individualistic and their position too dependent upon individual judgment. This criticism, however, can be brought against almost any position. It has been one of the chief arguments used by the Roman Church against Protestantism. But God has charged the individual believer with the responsibility of studying the Scriptures, praying, walking in the Spirit and thus determining the will of God for himself. Yes, it is dangerous in the sense that not all will come up with the right answers and make the right judgments. Some will also go to extremes. Nevertheless, it is a privilege given by God to each believer—the right of private judgment and soul liberty in things divine.

A few questions are suggested by Scripture that will aid the sincere believer in determining the boundaries of fellowship.

Am I honoring God by my fellowship? "Whether therefore ye eat, or drink, or whatsoever ye do, do all to the glory of God" (1 Cor. 10:31). If a believer remains in an apostate denomination, supporting by his money and presence enemies of the Lord, does he thus honor the Lord? In all that we do we must earnestly seek to honor God.

Am I aiding or encouraging someone to continue a walk of disobedience? The Bible clearly teaches that believers are to separate from apostasy. If some great preacher continues to remain within a group largely influenced by apostates, and he is used as a speaker in a separatist church, is this helping or hindering others? After Paul was converted, he went to Jerusalem where he received the "right hand of fellowship" from James, Peter and John (Gal. 2:9). Later, however, when Peter came to Antioch, Paul says he "withstood him to the face, because he was to be blamed" (Gal. 2:11). Peter had not clearly enunciated by lip and life the fact that believers were delivered from the Mosaic Law; so Paul undertook to correct his Christian brother. In this case, Peter repented of his error, and the purity of the faith was preserved. True fellowship demands confrontation when problems arise.

In the name of brotherly love, we can employ men who are yet in the apostasy as our Bible conference speakers or as writers in our papers, but in so doing we are really telling them that what they are doing is not so bad after all. This does not seem to be the way to assist them from the path of disobedience.

Will my cooperation with a person or organization give the impression that I condone a lackadaisi-

Guidelines for determining the extent of cooperative fellowship with other believers.

cal attitude toward apostasy and compromise? Did not the writer of Proverbs say, "The fear of the LORD is to hate evil . . . " (Prov. 8:13)? Is the support of apostasy, its publications, schools, spokesmen and missions evil? If it is, do I as God's child truly hate it? Or do I have softer feelings toward it? Believers cannot afford to have lackadaisical attitudes toward false religious systems which the Lord hates. Yet if they continually fellowship with people who remain in these and support them, what are they saying by such actions?

Will others under my leadership or influence be tempted to further compromise or be confused or weakened in their testimony because of my actions? Leaders are to be examples to other believers (1 Tim. 4:12). We must always ask the question, "What is my responsibility to others?" We cannot live to ourselves. We are responsible for our brethren as well.

What long-range effects will cooperation have? Bob Jones, Sr., often repeated the adage, "Never sacrifice the permanent on the altar of the immediate." It is a principle worth pondering and applying. We must consider what effects, good or bad, will accrue from a certain course of action.

Henry Parsons Crowell, the great Christian businessman referred to earlier (pp. 186-188), pondered much the reason for the success of the apostasy within his own denomination and others. His biographer (who, incidentally, spent many weeks in personal conference with Mr. Crowell) gives this analysis of Mr. Crowell's conclusions regarding the limits of cooperative fellowship:

> Mr. Crowell finally realized that all attacks on faith were essentially the same; the discrediting of the Bible as the inerrant and perfect revelation of Truth and the Will of God. That was the Leaven of the Sadducees, whether it was the innuendoes of a maturing mind, or the broadside blasts of an endowed professor.
>
> The integrity of the Bible, he felt, was the issue to be maintained no matter where it led! You can see in his own life just where it led him!

He began his Christian life by holding the Bible as true and authentic history.

Then, he began to feel that his belief was a necessary qualification for every gospel worker.

Then he realized the case could be lost if it were not implemented at this point. No general worker should be kept on church pay rolls who did not accept the Bible as true and authentic history. Moreover, no one should be tolerated in *high authority* who did not accept the Bible as true and authentic history.

To his amazement, he saw that even with these precautions, Faith was still losing the battle!

He realized that not only must Faith be careful to select workers and leaders who are Bible believers; but *these workers and leaders themselves must be intolerant of unbelievers in office!* If they were tolerant it could bring defeat just as effectively as if they themselves were infidels. Therefore,

FAITH MUST NOT SUPPORT MEN IN AUTHORITY WHO, THOUGH THEY ARE THEMSELVES BIBLE BELIEVERS, ARE TOLERANT OF OTHERS IN POSITIONS OF TRUST AND AUTHORITY WHO DO NOT SO BELIEVE....

Mr. Crowell saw that the battle against the Leaven of the Sadducees was being lost in Christendom today by reason of—*Tolerance toward believers who were tolerant toward unbelievers.*[2]

Some General Considerations for Separatists

Separatists need to remember certain axioms as they wend their way through the maze of varied situations which they constantly face.

Fundamentalists and separatists are accustomed to seeing things in blacks and whites. For them (theoretically at least) there are no grays. From God's viewpoint that is true. Our problem is, we cannot always tell immediately what is the right or wrong course of action in a given situation. Not everything is always crystal clear. Some separatists, quick on the draw and perhaps blessed with more discernment or faster spiritual reflexes than others, come immediately

Some issues are complex.

to what they consider the heart of a problem, draw the lines and expect everyone immediately to step over them. Many factors, however, must be considered in approaching a problem. Some may still be weighing those factors and trying to determine the mind of God while some of their brethren have already "passed over Jordan." Sometimes we give the impression that there are pat and easily accessible answers for every decision we must make regarding separation. That is not always true. Life is complex and we must face that fact.

Personalities differ.

Some people are by nature scrappers. They are not afraid to confront a situation immediately and take a strong and open stand. Some are by nature pugnacious and rather enjoy a good fight. Others, who may possess separatist convictions, are more reticent by nature to become involved in open controversy. They will follow separatist convictions when driven to a decision, but they will tend to avoid a confrontation if possible. Many of these differences are reflections of varying personalities. Separatists are people too! There are different kinds of them. In fairness we must recognize and accept that and be careful lest we, too, carelessly mark as a compromiser someone who may not approach a problem in the same manner as do we.

Contexts differ.

One may see an issue a bit differently than another because of the context in which he is operating. We all tend to be influenced by our background and experiences, and we all have different points of reference. A separatist must try to see his brother's point of view before acting too hastily to turn his back on him. This is especially true if a brother has maintained a consistent separatist testimony through the years, but may differ with someone else on some isolated question of implementation. We must be careful not to compromise vital convictions, but at the same time we must be big enough to allow another person to differ with us without rejecting him.

The Practical Implementation of Separatist Convictions

Separatists may have personal friendships which are broader than their official ties. Personal Christian fellowship is grounded primarily in a mutual knowledge of Christ as Savior. Personal interaction with other Christians is not wrong if it is not found in contexts where compromise and disobedience are involved.

Personal relationships.

Most pastors face the question at one time or another of what other churches in the community should be included in fellowship with their church. Here are some questions which should be asked about any church whose fellowship you are contemplating:

Cooperation with other churches.

(1) Is the church happily cooperating with apostasy? If it is in an apostate group, and contentedly so, proper fellowship would be impossible.

(2) Is the church moving toward separation from an apostate group? If God is working in a church and dissatisfaction with their present apostate affiliation has been evidenced, such a church should be encouraged. The fellowship of separatists could be such an encouragement.

(3) Is a godly pastor seeking to strengthen the stand of the church which has had new evangelical tendencies? If so, a helping hand may be timely.

(4) Does the church have a good reputation in the community?

(5) Are the doctrines of the church compatible with those of your church? This would not imply (in my opinion) 100 percent agreement, but it would demand a considerable agreement. Here again, prayerful judgment must be exercised.

(6) How do your members feel about such cooperation? Will it cause a problem in your church?

(7) Will such cooperation damage the clear witness your church has maintained (assuming it has maintained such)?

This can be a sticky problem for pastors since members of separatist churches often have direct or indirect connections with some interdenominational

Cooperation with inter-denominational groups.

bodies. Some of the problems that separatists face with interdenominational groups are as follows:

(1) Their doctrinal positon is usually rather general and broad.

(2) Comparatively few interdenominational groups take a strong separatist position because to do so would be to offend much of their constituency.

(3) They may tend to cultivate people's loyalties and wean them away from, or at least weaken, their participation in the local church.

(4) If their stand on separation is weak and they have an influence within your church through some of its members, confusion and conflict can result.

Many separatist pastors have had many heartaches as a result of interdenominational influence in their churches. The spirit of interdenominationalism is broad, and it is difficult to coordinate it with a separatist testimony. Some interdenominational organizations, however, have sought to be faithful to Biblical separation.

Invitations to speak.

Not all separatists face a problem in this area to the same extent, but it can be a very real one for separatist leaders who may receive many requests for their ministry. A speaker may not have a personal knowledge of the pastor or church who extends the invitation, yet care must be exercised because damage can be done if a separatist leader seems to condone someone who is not standing where he should. How does one evaluate requests to speak?

(1) What is the doctrinal position of the church or group? This can be ascertained either from those familiar with it or from a printed statement.

(2) Does this organization cooperate with the apostasy in any way? If it does, and a separatist speaks there, it will be interpreted as approval.

(3) Will your participation create a problem for local pastors in the area? Sometimes faithful separatist pastors discover that one of their leaders is a featured speaker in some church or group which has opposed the testimony of the local separatist churches for years. It can be extremely embarrassing for local pastors if their people say, "You have told us for years that so-and-so is not taking a firm stand, but here is Dr. What's-His-Name, a leading

separatist, speaking at his church next Sunday. Why is this?"

(4) Do you run the risk of damaging the overall separatist testimony by your appearance? If so, is a one-time exposure really worth that?

Some leaders operate on the principle that they will use speakers who are well-known—even though they may be shaky in their convictions in some areas—because they have specialities that are helpful and thus can be a blessing to their congregations. The wisdom, however, of following this course of action is very doubtful. For instance, the president of a separatist school may be asked to consider using some outstanding Bible preacher in his chapel or Bible conference. The man may have expertise in the Scriptures, be fundamental in doctrine and possess a tremendous gift of communication. He may also be one who goes everywhere, evidencing little discernment in the choice of places where he ministers, speaking one week at the separatist college and perhaps the next at a Bible conference controlled by new evangelicals or their sympathizers. Some see no harm in using such a man. They look only at the messages he delivers from the platform which, in themselves, may be without fault.

Whom to invite to your platform.

But a man is more than his pulpit messages. He brings to the pulpit a lifetime of associations, actions and perhaps writings. He comes as a total person. Is he in his total ministry the type of person you would want the young people at the separatist college to emulate? Perhaps you, as an adult, mature believer, could make the necessary adjustments in thinking and divorce what he is from what he says. Most of the youth would not be capable of doing that. The same would be true of most church members. They would be influenced by the man's example as well as by his preaching. If he is a compromiser, his example would be harmful, and the college president would be at fault for setting him up as such. The separatist cause is not advanced by featuring nonseparatists.

Missions is a romantic and sacred word to a large number of fundamentalists. If it is *missions*, it must be good, they reason. Unfortunately, this is not

Missionary and educational support.

true. Compromise with unbelief has infiltrated many mission agencies, and careful screening should be done to see where they stand on the vital question of separation, as well as other doctrinal matters. It is sometimes difficult to obtain clear information on this topic from certain agencies. They want to put nothing in writing that will jeopardize their support from any portion of their rather widely varied constituency; so they will make generalizations but avoid specifics. One should be interested not only in the published or official statement on separation (if there is such), but also in ascertaining what is the actual practice on the field. Often there are considerable discrepancies.

Certainly a separatist pastor should be discerning as to schools which he recommends to his young people. More than one youth from a separatist congregation has been sent off to a supposedly fundamental school only to come back a full-blown new evangelical or, at best, a watered-down separatist. Does the school contemplated take a public and consistent stand on the question of Biblical separation? How do you know? The separatist position will be perpetuated as we have leaders who are well trained in the Scriptures and have internalized separatist convictions rather than merely adopting those of someone else. Normally such leaders will be produced in institutions that possess such convictions themselves.

The Pitfalls of Separatists

Separatists are human. They have sins. They are not perfect. While the matters about to be discussed are not problems exclusively for separatists, separatists are especially vulnerable to them by virtue of the uniqueness of their position.

An improper spirit. It is possible to believe the right things, but to hold them and present them in the wrong way. Paul tells us this when he speaks of those in Philippi who preached Christ "of envy and strife" and "of contention" (Phil. 1:15, 16). He was saying that he was happy for their message—Christ—but saddened by their spirit. Because separatists are in almost constant conflict in order to maintain their position against the tremendous attacks mounted against them, they can develop a spirit of bitterness and acrimony. They are under the gun most of the time, and this can take its toll. It is very important to be "speaking the truth in love" (Eph. 4:15). Some separatists on occasion may be long on truth and short on love.

The issues are matters related to the apostasy and the response of separation. Some preachers become specialists in exposing the apostasy. They become consumed with the negative. They fail to feed upon the Word themselves, and they fail, therefore, to feed their people. The pastor is to declare "all the counsel of God" (Acts 20:27). This means he must not major on any one theme, but seek for a full orchestration of Biblical truth. In some separatist congregations, people starve for lack of wholesome food while their pastor rants about the issues.

Over-occupation with the issues.

Some separatists see a new evangelical under every bush and a compromiser in every other pulpit. They are constantly "uncovering the dirt" about other brethren. They have just heard this, or they have just heard that. They see sinister meaning in perfectly innocent actions. It is this characteristic, probably more than any other, that is sometimes referred to by nonseparatists as part of the "separatist mentality." We would not hesitate to confess that this could be said of *some* separatists. On the other hand, we believe that it is not of the essence of separatism, and it would be most heartily repudiated by most separatist leaders.

Uncontrolled suspicion.

Certainly separatists should immerse themselves in 1 Corinthians 13. Paul makes an interesting statement: "Love . . . believeth all things" (1 Cor. 13:7). Does this mean we should gullibly accept whatever we are told? Does this support the idea that we should accept everyone's Christian profession with no questions asked? No. We believe Lenski has a helpful observation when he says that love "refuses to yield to suspicions of doubt. The flesh is ready to believe all things about a brother and a fellow man in an evil sense. Love does the opposite. . . . "[3]

**A desire
to dominate.**

Separatists tend to produce some strong-willed leaders. In the conflicts of separatism, this can be an asset; but it can also be a drawback. In the process of arriving at their positions of leadership, separatist leaders must guard against an insatiable desire to dominate everyone and everything and to build empires. If someone disagrees with us on some minor issue, we should resist the temptation to make a major issue of it, brand the offender as a new evangelical, and ostracize him from our fellowship. Separatists must ask God for humility. We do not know everything. We can yet learn from others. Our Lord was "meek and lowly in heart" (Matt. 11:29). We ought to emulate Him.

**Failure
to see
the larger
picture.**

Sometimes the action of a certain separatist may be interpreted by his brethren as compromise. He may have someone in his pulpit who, in the judgment of other separatists, is not taking a proper stand. However, he may be ignorant of all the facts and thus have invited a particular man. Separatists need to learn to distinguish between occasional lapses or misjudgments, which are part of the frailty of human nature, and patterns of consistent compromise. The former must be looked upon with some charity, while the latter is more serious and demands a stronger stance. We ought not to make a man "an offender for a word."

**Caustic
language.**

Some separatists have evidently tried to imitate Martin Luther and other controversialists of his age (and other ages) in employing rather strong, colorful and pungent language about their evangelical brethren. It is true that some rather strong language is used in the New Testament of apostates. However, caution and restraint need to be employed when speaking of those who are our brethren but with whom we may disagree. Tongues and pens need to be controlled by the Spirit. A young lady in tears approached me a few years ago. She had written a separatist leader, expressing disagreement with him on a minor point. She received a three-page diatribe in reply (which she shared) in which the man called her names and used very strong language, professing horror that anyone would dare to disagree with him.

I was extremely embarrassed, since the writer of the letter was a well-known figure. "My brethren, these things ought not so to be" (James 3:10).

At times matters of serious import must be discussed in public and proponents of erroneous views must be exposed in public. On the other hand, some times public discussion is most certainly not in order. Some separatists take to the printed page with barbs, innuendoes and castigations of their brethren without ever checking privately and carefully to see if they have the facts straight. If it is a personal grievance or a compromise (real or imagined), they make no effort to correct it privately, but simply blast away in some public organ. Broadside attacks and startling revelations about the supposed shortcomings of other brethren may make readable copy (depending upon one's tastes), but such an approach may not be the finest and most productive method of dealing with problems. This is especially true when one is dealing with other brethren who take the same general position as do they.

> **Public instead of private rebuke.**

The matters here discussed should not in any way become a cause for the repudiation of the doctrine of separation. It rests upon a solid foundation—the Word of God. No Biblical doctrine should ever be rejected because of the faults and foibles of its advocates. Certainly its advocates, however, should humbly seek the face of God and inquire as to how they might improve their testimony before other believers and before the world. I certainly do not agree with everything that John Smyth, the early Baptist leader, wrote; but I think all separatists could profit by reading his last book, written in the closing days of his life. In it he confessed the bad spirit which characterized some of his earlier debates, and, while still maintaining what he viewed as truth and defending his right to argue for it, he pled for a proper spirit in so doing.[4]

Some Closing Thoughts for Separatists

I have been involved in the separatist movement for many years. No finer group of men and women could be found anywhere, and the fellowship with them has been life-enriching and challenging. Most separatists, we believe, have a desire to do God's will, to honor God's Son and to "adorn the doctrine of God" by a Spirit-filled life (Titus 2:10). How may this be accomplished?

We must base our position upon Scripture, not personal opinion.

Some separatists find it difficult to separate the two. We must avoid the danger of elevating our own personal tastes or opinions to the level of divine revelation. People with strong convictions (and most separatists are such) have difficulty distinguishing between their opinions and scriptural principles. In an effort to avoid appearing wishy-washy or uncertain in areas of doctrine, some separatists go to an extreme and take hard, irrevocable stands on every minor issue as though it were a major item of the faith. Often they become quite emotional when confronted with the unreasonableness of their position or their attitude.

We must seek to be consistent.

It is hard for anyone to be completely consistent. We are human. Our humanness shows in our inconsistencies. Yet, we need to seek, to the best of our ability as God directs us, to implement our separatist convictions consistently.

We must allow for inconsistency.

While this may seem contradictory to the previous point, it is really complementary to it. We must realize that separatists are imperfect. They will sometimes say and do things with which other of their brethren will not completely agree. This does not call for immediate excommunication and isolation. It calls for conference, for prayer and for efforts to come to an understanding.

We must allow for honest differences.

Some separatists give the impression that everyone must hold the same positions and interpretations as do they in order to be a "true blue" separatist. Artificial tests of fellowship are created. If someone uses a different translation or approves a pantsuit or holds a different view on the question of divorce, some separatists make an international issue over it and brand the brother who differs as a compromiser. We need to be able to distinguish minor points from major issues. We must be free to discuss subordinate theological issues on which we may disagree without making them a test of fellowship. Many separatists can do this. Regrettably, some cannot.

Vicious statements have sometimes been made about separatist and nonseparatist brethren which have no basis in fact. Our God "desirest truth in the inward parts" (Ps. 51:6). He also commands that we "speak every man truth with his neighbour" (Eph. 4:25). In heart and lip we must be truthful. Righteous causes are not forwarded by lies. They are forwarded by truth.

We must be factual and truthful.

Conclusion

Our blessed Lord is our example. He was the great Separatist. His character is described as "full of grace and truth" (John 1:14). He was perfectly balanced. He spoke gracious words and performed gracious deeds. He also spoke burning words and performed purifying deeds. He exemplified that which every separatist and every believer in Christ needs—*balance*. Our tendency is to become imbalanced. In the words of an old writer, whose identity has been lost but whose advice is cherished, our way as separatists is charted:

> The grand difficulty is to combine a spirit of intense separation with a spirit of grace, gentleness, and forbearance; or, as another has said, "to maintain a narrow circle with a wide heart." This is really a difficulty. As the strict and uncompromised maintenance of truth tends to narrow the circle around us, we shall need the expansive power of grace to keep the heart wide and the affections warm. If we contend for truth otherwise than in grace, we shall only yield a one-sided and most unattractive testimony. And, on the other hand, if we try to exhibit grace at the expense of truth, it will prove, in the end, to be only the manifestation of a popular liberality at God's expense—a most worthless thing!

Notes:

1. In opposition to secondary separation, see John R. Rice, *Come Out— Or Stay In?* (New York: Thomas Nelson, Inc., 1974) and various articles in his paper, *The Sword of the Lord.* In favor of secondary separation, see Charles Woodbridge, *Bible Separation* (Halifax, Canada: The People's Gospel Hour Press, 1971). In favor of the concept of secondary separation but disliking the term, see Bob Jones, Jr., "Scriptural Separation: First and Second Degree" (Greenville, SC: Bob Jones University Press, 1971).

2. Day, *A Christian in Big Business,* pp. 268, 269.

3. R. C. H. Lenski, *The Interpretation of St. Paul's First and Second Epistles to the Corinthians* (Minneapolis: Augsburg Publishing House, 1961), p. 560.

4. John Smyth, *The Last Book of John Smyth Called the Retraction of His Errours, and the Confirmation of the Truth.*

Bibliography

Books

Allix, Peter. *The Ecclesiastical History of the Ancient Churches of the Albigenses*. London: no publisher given, 1692.

Allix, Peter, and Maitland, Samuel R. (trans.). *Facts and Documents Illustrative of the History, Doctrine, and Rites of the Ancient Albigenses and Waldenses*. London: Rivington, 1832.

Armitage, Thomas. *A History of the Baptists*. New York: Bryon, Taylor, and Co., 1893.

Augustine. "Letters" in *The Fathers of the Church*. 66 vols. Edited by Joseph Deferrari. New York: Fathers of the Church, Inc., 1953.

Bainton, Ronald. *Here I Stand: A Life of Martin Luther*. Nashville: Abingdon Press, 1950.

Baker, Derek (ed.). *Schism, Heresy, and Religious Protest*. Cambridge: University Press, 1972.

Bancroft, Emery. *Elemental Theology*. Edited by Ronald Mayers. Grand Rapids: Zondervan Publishing House, 1977.

Barclay, Robert. *The Inner Life of the Religious Societies of the Commonwealth*. London: Hodder and Stoughton, 1876.

Bartlett, Billy Vick. *A History of Baptist Separatism*. Springfield, MO: Baptist Bible Fellowship Publications, 1972.

_____. *The Beginnings: A Pictorial History of the Baptist Bible Fellowship*. Springfield, MO: Baptist Bible College, 1975.

Beach, Bert B. *Ecumenism: Boon or Bane?* Washington, D.C.: Review and Herald Publishing Association, 1972.

Bender, Harold S., et. al. (eds.). *Studies in Anabaptist and Mennonite History*. Goshen, IN: The Mennonite Historical Society, 1953.

————. *Conrad Grebel*. Scottdale, PA: Herald Press, 1971.

Benedict, David. *History of the Donatists*. Providence: Nickerson, Sibley, and Co., 1975.

Berkhof, Louis. *History of Christian Doctrine*. Grand Rapids: Wm. B. Eerdmans Publishing Co., 1959.

Berkhouwer, G. C. *The Church*. Grand Rapids: Wm. B. Eerdmans Publishing Co., 1976.

Bevenot, Maurice (trans.). *St. Cyprian*. London: Longmans, Green, and Co., 1957.

Bogue, David, and Bennett, James. *The History of Dissenters*. 2 vols. London: Frederick Westley and A. H. Davis, 1833.

Bradford, Amory H. *The Pilgrims in Old England*. New York: Fords, Howard and Hubbert, 1893.

Broadbent, E. H. *The Pilgrim Church*. London: Pickering and Inglis, 1931.

Burrage, Champlin (ed.). *An Answer to John Robinson of Leyden*. Cambridge, MA: Harvard University Press, 1920.

————. *The Early English Dissenters*. 2 vols. New York: Russell and Russell, 1912.

Bush, George. *Notes on Joshua*. Minneapolis: James and Klock, 1976.

Calvin, John. *Commentaries on the Epistles to Timothy, Titus and Philemon*. Grand Rapids: Wm. B. Eerdmans Publishing Co., 1948.

————. *Institutes of the Christian Religion*. 2 vols. Translated by John Allen. Philadelphia: Presbyterian Board of Christian Education, 1936.

Campbell, Douglas. *The Puritans in Holland, England, and America*. 2 vols. New York: Harper Brothers, 1892.

Carnell, Edward John. *The Case for Orthodox Theology*. Philadelphia: The Westminster Press, 1959.

Carroll, J. M. *The Trail of Blood*. Lexington, KY: Ashland Ave. Baptist Church, 1931.

Cauthen, Kenneth. *The Impact of American Religious Liberalism*. New York: Harper & Row, 1962.

Charnock, Stephen. *The Existence and Attributes of God*. Grand Rapids: Kregel Publications, 1958.

Clark, Henry. *History of English Nonconformity*. 2 vols. New York: Russell and Russell, 1965.

Clasen, Claus Peter. *Anabaptism: A Social History, 1525-1618*. Ithaca, NY: Cornell University Press, 1972.

Cohen, Gary G. *Biblical Separation Defended*. Philadelphia: Presbyterian and Reformed Publishing Co., 1966.

Cole, Stewart. *The History of Fundamentalism*. Hamden, CT: Archon Books, 1953.

Colquhoun, Frank. *The Fellowship of the Gospel*. Grand Rapids: Zondervan Publishing House, 1957.

Conwell, Russell H. *Life of Charles Haddon Spurgeon*. Philadelphia: Edgewood Publishing Co., 1892.

Cooke, George Willis. *Unitarianism in America*. Boston: American Unitarian Association, 1902.

Darby, J. N. *Synopsis of the Books of the Bible*. 5 vols. London: Stow Hill Bible and Tract Depot, 1948.

_____. *The Collected Writings of J. N. Darby*. 35 vols. Edited by William Kelly. Kingston-on-Thames, England: Stow Hill Bible and Tract Depot, n.d.

D'Aubigne, J. H. Merle. *History of the Reformation of the Sixteenth Century*. 5 vols. New York: American Tract Society, n.d.

Day, Richard Ellsworth. *A Christian in Big Business*. Chicago: Moody Press, 1946.

Delnay, Robert. *A History of the Baptist Bible Union*. Winston-Salem, NC: Piedmont Bible College Press, 1974.

Dexter, Henry Martyn. *The Congregationalism of the Last Three Hundred Years*. 2 vols. New York: Burt Franklin, 1970.

Dollar, George. *A History of Fundamentalism in America*. Greenville, SC: Bob Jones University Press, 1973.

Durnbaugh, Donald F. *The Believers' Church: The History and Character of Radical Protestantism*. London: Macmillan Co., 1968.

Eichrodt, Walter. *Theology of the Old Testament*. 2 vols. Translated by J. A. Baker. Philadelphia: The Westminster Press, 1961.

Eliot, Samuel. *Heralds of a Liberal Faith*. 2 vols. Boston: American Unitarian Association, 1910.

Ellicott, C. J. *A Critical and Grammatical Commentary on the Pastoral Epistles*. London: John U. Parker, 1856.

Erickson, Millard. *The New Evangelical Theology*. Westwood, NJ: Fleming Revell, 1968.

Fairbairn, Patrick. *Commentary on the Pastoral Epistles*. Grand Rapids: Zondervan Publishing House, 1956.

Farrar, Frederic. *Lives of the Fathers*. 2 vols. Edinburgh: Adam & Charles Black, 1889.

Ford, S. J. *The Origin of the Baptists*. Nashville: Southwestern Publishing House, 1860.

Frend, W. H. C. *Martyrdom and Persecution in the Early Church*. New York: New York University Press, 1967.

————. *The Donatist Church*. Oxford: The Clarendon Press, 1952.

Freve, Walter H. *The English Church*. 8 vols. New York: AMS Press, 1970.

Freve, Walter H., and Douglas, Charles (eds.). *Puritan Manifestoes*. London: SPCK, 1954.

Frothingham, Ebenezer. *The Articles of Faith and Practice, with the Covenant, That Is Confessed By the Separate Churches of Christ in General In This Land. With a Discourse, Treating Upon the Great Privileges of the Church of Jesus Christ*. Newport, CT: no publisher given, 1750.

Furniss, Norman J. *The Fundamentalist Controversy: 1918-1931*. Hamden, CT: Archon Books, 1963.

Gaebelein, A. C. *The Annotated Bible*. 9 vols. New York: Our Hope, 1913.

Gasper, Louis. *The Fundamentalist Movement*. Paris: Morton and Co., 1963.

Glover, Willis B. *Evangelical Nonconformists and Higher Criticism in the Nineteenth Century*. London: Independent Press, 1954.

Goen, C. C. *Revivalism and Separatism in New England: 1740-1800*. New Haven, CT: Yale University Press, 1962.

Gordon, Emert. *The Leaven of the Sadduccees*. Chicago: The Bible Institute Colportage Association, 1926.

Gui, Bernard. "The Manual of the Inquisition," *The Development of Civilization*. 2 vols. Edited by Harry Carroll, et. al. Glenview, IL: Scott, Foresman and Co., 1969.

Hall, Edwin. *The Puritans and Their Principles*. New York: Baker and Scribner, 1846.

Haller, William. *The Rise of Puritanism*. New York: Harper and Row, 1938.

Hatfield, Mark. *Conflict and Conscience*. Waco, TX: Word Books, 1971.

Herbert, Gabriel. *Fundamentalism and the Church*. Philadelphia: The Westminster Press, 1957.

Helwys, Thomas. *The Mystery of Iniquity*. London: Kingsgate Press, 1935.

Hershberger, Guy (ed.). *The Recovery of the Anabaptist Vision*. Scottdale, PA: Herald Press, 1957.

Hodge, Charles. *A Commentary on the Epistle to the Romans*. Philadelphia: Grigg and Elliott, 1835.

_____. *An Exposition of the First Epistle to the Corinthians*. Grand Rapids: Wm. B. Eerdmans Publishing Co., 1950.

Hooker, Richard. *Of the Laws of Ecclesiastical Polity*. London: J. M. Dent and Co., n.d.

Horsch, John. *Modern Religious Liberalism*. Scottdale, PA: Fundamental Truth Depot, 1920.

Kelly, William. *An Exposition of the Two Epistles to Timothy*. London: C. A. Hammond, 1948.

Kent, Homer. *The Pastoral Epistles*. Chicago: Moody Press, 1958.

Ketcham, Robert T. *The Answer*. Chicago: General Association of Regular Baptist Churches, 1950.

Kik, J. Marcellus. *Ecumenism and the Evangelical*. Philadelphia: Presbyterian and Reformed, 1958.

Klotsche, E. H. *The History of Christian Doctrine*. Burlington, IA: The Lutheran Literary Board, 1945.

Knox, Ronald A. *Enthusiasm: A Chapter in the History of Religion*. New York: Oxford University Press, 1961.

Kromminga, John. *All One Body We*. Grand Rapids: Wm. B. Eerdmans Publishing Co., 1970.

Latourette, Kenneth Scott. *The History of the Expansion of Christianity*. 7 vols. Grand Rapids: Zondervan Publishing House, 1970.

Lea, Henry Charles. *A History of the Inquisition of the Middle Ages*. 3 vols. New York: Russell and Russell, 1958.

Lechler, Gotthard V. *John Wycliffe and His English Precursors.* London: The Religious Tract Society, 1904.

Lenski, R. C. H. *The Interpretation of the Epistles of St. Peter, St. John, and St. Jude.* Minneapolis: Augsburg Publishing House, 1945.

————. *The Interpretation of St. Paul's First and Second Epistles to the Corinthians.* Minneapolis: Augsburg Publishing House, 1961.

Lewis, John. *The History of the Life and Sufferings of John Wycliffe.* New York: AMS Press, 1973.

Lightner, Robert P. *Neoevangelicalism Today.* Schaumburg, IL: Regular Baptist Press, 1979.

Littell, Franklin H. *The Anabaptist View of the Church.* Boston: Starr King Press, 1958.

————. *The Free Church.* Boston: Starr King Press, 1967.

Lloyd-Jones, D. Martyn. *The Basis of Christian Unity.* Grand Rapids: Wm. B. Eerdmans Publishing Co., 1962.

Loetscher, Lefferts. *The Broadening Church.* Philadelphia: University of Pennsylvania Press, 1954.

Lumpkin, William L. (ed.) *Baptist Confessions of Faith.* Philadelphia: Judson Press, 1959.

Machen, J. Gresham. *Christianity and Liberalism.* Grand Rapids: Wm. B. Eerdmans Publishing Co., 1974.

————. *What Is Christianity?* Edited by Ned Stonehouse. Grand Rapids: Wm. B. Eerdmans Publishing Co., 1951.

Mason, Roy. *The Church That Jesus Built.* Tampa: Central Ave. Baptist Church, n.d.

McCook, John J. *The Appeal in the Briggs Heresy Case.* New York: John C. Rankin, 1893.

McIntire, Carl. *Outside the Gate.* Collingswood, NJ: Christian Beacon Press, 1967.

————. *Servants of Apostasy.* Collingswood, NJ: Christian Beacon Press, 1955.

Meyer, F. B. *Elijah and the Secret of His Power.* London: Morgan and Scott, n.d.

Middlekauff, Robert. *The Mathers.* New York: Oxford University Press, 1971.

Miller, Perry. *Orthodoxy in Massachusetts: 1630-1650*. Gloucester, MA: Peter Smith, 1965.

Moeller, Wilhelm. *History of the Christian Church in the Middle Ages*. Translated by Andrew Rutherford. London: Swan Sonnenschein Co., 1893.

Monneyham, W. Stanley (ed.). *The Dynamics of Christian Unity*. Grand Rapids: Zondervan Publishing House, 1963.

Morland, Samuel. *The History of the Evangelical Churches of the Valleys of Piedmont*. London: Henry Hills, 1658.

Murch, James DeForest. *Cooperation Without Compromise*. Grand Rapids: Wm. B. Eerdmans Publishing Co., 1956.

_____. *The Free Church*. Cincinnati: Restoration Press, 1966.

Murray, Ian. *The Forgotten Spurgeon*. London: The Banner of Truth Trust, 1966.

Murray, John. *The Epistle to the Romans*. Grand Rapids: Wm. B. Eerdmans Publishing Co., 1968.

Neal, Daniel. *The History of the Puritans*. 2 vols. New York: Harper Brothers, 1843.

Neander, Augustus. *General History of the Christian Religion and Church*. 6 vols. Translated by Joseph Torrey. Boston: Houghton, Mifflin and Co., 1871.

Neatby, W. B. *A History of the Plymouth Brethren*. London: no publisher given, 1901.

Newbigin, Lesslie. *The Household of God*. London: SCM Press, 1953.

Newman, Albert Henry. *A Manual of Church History*. 2 vols. Philadelphia: The American Baptist Publication Society, 1948.

Nigg, Walter. *The Heretics*. Translated and edited by Richard and Clara Winston. New York: Alfred A. Knopf, 1962.

Orchard, G. H. *A Concise History of the Baptists*. Lexington, KY: Ashland Ave. Baptist Church, 1956.

Owen, John. *The True Nature of a Gospel Church and Its Government*. Edited by John Huxtable. Greenwood, SC: The Attic Press, 1947.

Parker, G. H. W. *The Morning Star*. Grand Rapids: Wm. B. Eerdmans Publishing Co., 1965.

Payne, Ernest. *The Baptist Union*. London: Carey Kingsgate Press, 1958.

Plummer, Alfred. "The Pastoral Epistles," *The Expositor's Bible*. 25 vols. Edited by W. Robertson Nicoll. New York: A. C. Armstrong, 1905.

Poole-Conner, E. J. *Evangelicalism in England*. London: The Fellowship of Independent Evangelical Churches, 1951.

Quasten, Johannes. *Patrology*. 2 vols. Westminster, MD: The Newman Press, 1964.

Quebedeaux, Richard. *The Worldly Evangelicals*. New York: Harper & Row, Publishers, 1978.

————. *The Young Evangelicals*. New York: Harper & Row, Publishers, 1974.

Rian, Edwin H. *The Presbyterian Conflict*. Grand Rapids: Wm. B. Eerdmans Publishing Co., 1940.

Rice, John R. *Come Out— Or Stay In?* New York: Thomas Nelson, Inc., 1974.

Roberts, Alexander, and Donaldson, James (eds.). *The Anti-Nicene Fathers*. 8 vols. Grand Rapids: Wm. B. Eerdmans Publishing Co., 1951.

Rouse, Ruth; Neill, Stephen Charles; and Jey, Harold (eds.). *A History of the Ecumenical Movement*. 2 vols. Philadelphia: The Westminster Press, 1968.

Rowdon, Harold. *The Origins of the Brethren*. London: Pickering and Inglis, 1967.

Russell, Jeffrey. *Dissent and Reform in the Early Middle Ages*. Los Angeles: University of California Press, 1965.

————. *Religious Dissent in the Middle Ages*. New York: John Wiley and Sons, 1971.

Ruth, John L. *Conrad Grebel: Son of Zurich*. Scottdale, PA: Herald Press, 1975.

Sandeen, Ernest R. *The Roots of Fundamentalism*. Chicago: The University of Chicago Press, 1970.

Schaff, Philip (ed.). *A Select Library of the Nicene and Post-Nicene Fathers*. 8 vols. Grand Rapids: Wm. B. Eerdmans Publishing Co., 1956.

————. *History of the Christian Church*. 8 vols. Grand Rapids: Wm. B. Eerdmans Publishing Co., 1910.

Sheldon, Henry C. *Unbelief in the Nineteenth Century*. New York: Eaton and Manis, 1907.

Shelley, Bruce L. *Conservative Baptists*. Denver: Conservative Baptist Theological Seminary, 1960.

Simons, Menno. *The Complete Writings of Menno Simons*. Translated by Leonard Verduin; edited by John C. Wenger. Scottdale, PA: Herald Press, 1956.

Smith, H. Shelton; Handy, Robert; and Loetscher, Lefferts. *American Christianity*. 2 vols. New York: Charles Scribner's Sons, 1960.

Spinka, Matthew. *John Hus and the Czech Reform*. Hamden, CT: Archon Books, 1966.

————. *The Letters of John Hus*. Manchester, England: Manchester University Press, 1972.

Stealey, Sydnor (ed.). *The Baptist Treasury*. New York: Thomas Crowell Co., 1958.

Stowell, Joseph M. *Background and History of the General Association of Regular Baptist Churches*. Hayward, CA: J. F. May Press, 1949.

Strayer, Joseph R. *The Albigensian Crusades*. New York: The Dial Press, 1971.

Strong, Augustus Hopkins. *Systematic Theology*. New York: Fleming Revell, 1907.

Tatum, E. Ray. *Conquest or Failure? A Biography of J. Frank Norris*. Dallas: Baptist Historical Foundation, 1966.

Thiessen, H. C. *Introductory Lectures in Systematic Theology*. Grand Rapids: Wm. B. Eerdmans Publishing Co., 1949.

Torbet, Robert. *A History of the Baptists*. Valley Forge, PA: Judson Press, 1973.

Townsend, George (ed.). *The Acts and Monuments of John Foxe*. 8 vols. New York: AMS Press, 1965.

Troeltsch, Ernest. *The Social Teaching of the Christian Churches*. 2 vols. New York: Macmillan, 1949.

Tulga, Chester E. *The Doctrine of Separation in These Times*. Chicago: Conservative Baptist Fellowship, 1952.

————. *The Foreign Missions Controversy in the Northern Baptist Convention*. Chicago: Conservative Baptist Fellowship, 1950.

Turberville, Arthur S. *Medieval Heresy and the Inquisition*. London: Archon Books, 1964.

Underwood, A. C. *A History of the English Baptists*. London: Carey Kingsgate Press, 1947.

Van Braght, Thielman J. *The Bloody Theater or Martyrs Mirror*. Translated by Joseph Sohm. Scottdale, PA: Herald Press, 1950.

Vanderlaan, Eldred C. (comp.). *Fundamentalism Versus Modernism*. New York: H. W. Wilson Co., 1925.

Vaughn, Robert. *The Life and Opinions of John de Wycliffe*. 2 vols. New York: AMS Press, 1973.

Vedder, Henry C. *A Short History of the Baptists*. Philadelphia: The American Baptist Publication Society, 1907.

Verduin, Leonard. *The Anatomy of a Hybrid*. Grand Rapids: Wm. B. Eerdmans Publishing Co., 1976.

————. *The Reformers and Their Stepchildren*. Grand Rapids: Wm. B. Eerdmans Publishing Co., 1964.

Von Mosheim, John L. *Institutes of Ecclesiastical History*. 3 vols. Translated by James Murdock. New York: Stanford and Swords, 1854.

Wakefield, Walter. *Heresy, Crusade, and Inquisition in Southern France: 1100-1250*. Los Angeles: University of California Press, 1974.

Wakefield, Walter, and Evans, Austin (trans.). *Heresies of the High Middle Ages*. New York: Columbia University Press, 1969.

Waldenses, The. Philadelphia: Presbyterian Board of Publication, 1853.

Walker, Williston. *A History of the Christian Church*. New York: Scribner's, 1947.

Walton, Robert. *The Gathered Community*. London: Carey Press, 1946.

Warner, H. J. *The Albigensian Heresy*. 2 vols. New York: Russell and Russell, 1922, 1928.

Wenger, John C. (ed.). *Glimpses of Mennonite History and Doctrine*. Scottdale, PA: Herald Press, 1940.

———— (trans.). *Conrad Grebel's Programmatic Letters of 1524*. Scottdale, PA: Herald Press, 1970.

Westcott, Brooke F. *The Epistles of St. John*. London: Macmillan, 1883.

Westin, Gunnar. *The Free Church Through the Ages*. Nashville: Broadman Press, 1958.

White, Barrington R. *The English Separatist Tradition*. London: Oxford University Press, 1971.

Williams, George H. *The Radical Reformation*. Philadelphia: The Westminster Press, 1962.

————— (ed.). *Spiritual and Anabaptists Writers*. Philadelphia: The Westminster Press, 1957.

Williams, Roger. *The Complete Writings of Roger Williams*. 7 vols. New York: Russell and Russell, 1963.

Willis, Geoffrey G. *Saint Augustine and the Donatist Controversy*. London: SPCK, 1950.

Woodbridge, Charles. *Bible Separation*. Halifax, Canada: The People's Gospel Hour Press, 1971.

Wright, Eliphalet. *The Difference Between Those Called Standing Churches and Those Called Strict Congregationalists Illustrated*. Norwich, CT: no publisher given, 1775.

Ziff, Larger (ed.). *John Cotton on the Churches of New England*. Cambridge, MA: Harvard University Press, 1968.

Encyclopedias and Dictionaries

"Albigenses," *Cyclopedia of Biblical, Theological and Ecclesiastical Literature*, I, 133, 134.

Bender, Harold S. "Church," *The Mennonite Encyclopedia*, I, 595.

Clot, Alberto. "Waldenses," *The New Schaff-Herzog Encyclopedia of Religious Knowledge*, XII, 241-255.

Clouse, Robert. "Albigensians," *The New International Dictionary of the Christian Church*, p. 22.

"Donatism," *Westminster Dictionary of Church History*, p. 275.

"Donatists," *Cyclopedia of Biblical, Theological and Ecclesiastical Literature*, II, 863.

Dossat, Y. "Waldenses," *New Catholic Encyclopedia*, XIV, 770, 771.

Drumright, H. L. "Hate; Hatred," *Zondervan Pictorial Encyclopedia of the Bible*, III, 46, 47.

Faul, D. "Donatism," *New Catholic Encyclopedia*, IV, 1001-1003.

Giacumakis, George. "Bogomiles," *The New International Dictionary of the Christian Church*, pp. 139, 140.

McDonald, H. D. "Novatianism," *The New International Dictionary of the Christian Church*, p. 717.

Neff, H. S. B. "Felix Manz," *The Mennonite Encyclopedia*, III, 473.

Newman, Albert Henry. "Donatism," *The New Schaff-Herzog Encyclopedia of Religious Knowledge*, III, 486-488.

_____. "Paulicians," *The New Schaff-Herzog Encyclopedia of Religious Knowledge*, VIII, 417, 418.

Norman, J. G. G. "Paulicians," *The New International Dictionary of the Christian Church*, p. 755.

"Paulicians," *Cyclopedia of Biblical, Theological and Ecclesiastical Literature*, VII, 836.

Reid, W. S. "Calvinism," *The New International Dictionary of the Christian Church*, pp. 179-182.

Scott, C. A. "Donatists," *Encyclopedia of Religion and Ethics*, III, 844, 845.

Toon, Peter, "Puritans; Puritanism," *The New International Dictionary of the Christian Church*, pp. 814, 815.

Unger, Merrill F. "Apostasy," *Unger's Bible Dictionary*. Chicago: Moody Press, 1966, p. 72.

_____. "Leaven," *Unger's Bible Dictionary*. Chicago: Moody Press, 1966, p. 652.

Williams, C. Peter. "Peter de Bruys," *The New International Dictionary of the Christian Church*, pp. 767, 768.

Periodicals

"A Conversation with Young Evangelicals," *Post-American* (January 1975), p. 7.

Barnhouse, Donald Grey. "One Church," *Eternity* (July 1958), pp. 17-23.

_____. "We Are One Body in Christ," *Eternity* (March 1957), pp. 4, 5, 39-42.

Bauman, Clarence. "The Theology of the Two Kingdoms: A Comparison of Luther and the Anabaptists," *The Mennonite Quarterly Review*, XXXVIII (January 1964).

Baxter, David. "Why I Joined the N.A.E.," *United Evangelical Action* (January 1964), pp. 6ff.

Bell, L. Nelson. "On Separation," *Christianity Today* (October 8, 1971), pp. 26, 27.

Blackwood, Glenwood, "Standing for God and Right in a Big City," *United Evangelical Action* (February 1, 1953).

Christianson, Paul. "From Expectation to Militance: Reformers and Babylon in the First Two Years of the Long Parliament," *Journal of Ecclesiastical History* (July 1973), pp. 225-244.

Crawford, Percy (ed.). *Youth on the Move News* (May 1957).

Durnbaugh, Donald. "Theories of Free Church Origins," *The Mennonite Quarterly Review* (April 1968), pp. 83-95.

Editorial, *Moody Monthly* (October 1929).

Editorial on Graham's ministry, *Christianity Today* (September 6, 1957), p. 4.

Editorial, "The Perils of Independency," *Christianity Today* (November 12, 1956), pp. 20-23.

Editorial, "Pro and Con on Separatism," *Eternity* (August 1963), p. 6.

Eenigenburg, Elton M. "Separatism Is Not Scriptural," *Eternity* (August 1963), pp. 16-22.

Ervin, Howard M. "A Reexamination of 2 Corinthians 6:14—7:1," *Baptist Bulletin*, XV (April 1950), 4, 5, 20, 21.

Graham, Billy. Personal interview, *U. S. News and World Report* (September 1957), p. 72.

Grounds, Vernon. "Separatism—Yes, Schism—No," *Eternity* (August 1963), pp. 17-22.

Havner, Vance. "The Forgotten Anathema," *Sword of the Lord* (January 7, 1955).

Henry, Carl F. H. "Conflict Over Biblical Inerrancy," *Christianity Today* (May 7, 1976), pp. 23-25.

Hitt, Russell T. "The Latin American Experiment," *Eternity* (November 1975), pp. 14-17.

Howard, Tom (contributor). "On Not Leaving It to the Liberals," *Eternity* (February 1977), pp. 24, 25.

———. "Steeplechase: How I Changed Churches," *Eternity* (February 1977), pp. 15, 16, 23.

Jewett, Paul King. "Why I Favor the Ordination of Women," *Christianity Today* (June 6, 1975), pp. 7-10.

Jones, E. Stanley. Letter concerning Billy Graham, *Christian Century* (August 14, 1957).

Ketcham, R. T. "*Christianity Today*—An Analysis," *Baptist Bulletin* XXII (March 1957), 8, 9.

Kraus, C. Norman. "Anabaptist Influence on English Separatism as Seen in Robert Browne," *The Mennonite Quarterly Review*, XXXIV (January 1960), 5.

Ladd, George Eldon. "The Evangelical's Dilemma: Doctrinal Purity vs. Visible Unity," *Eternity* (June 1962), pp. 7-9.

McClain, Alva. "Is Evangelical Christianity Changing?" *King's Business* (January 1957).

Millheim, John. "A Consortium of Compromise," *Baptist Bulletin* XXXX (October 1974), 9-11.

Newbigin, Lesslie. "The Scandal of Our Apartness," *Eternity* (February 1961), pp. 13, 14.

Ockenga, Harold J. "Resurgent Evangelical Leadership," *Christianity Today* (October 10, 1960), pp. 14, 15.

Oyer, John. "The Writings of Melancthon Against the Anabaptists," *The Mennonite Quarterly Review*, XXVI (October 1952), 275.

Quebedeaux, Richard. "The Evangelicals: New Trends and Tensions," *Christianity and Crisis* (September 20, 1976), pp. 197-202.

Ramm, Bernard. "Welcome, Green-Grass Evangelicals," *Eternity* (March 1974), p. 13.

Reuther, Rosemary. "The Reformer and the Radical in the Sixteenth Century Reformation," *Journal of Ecumenical Studies*, IX (Spring 1972), 271-284.

Runia, Klaas. "When Is Separation a Christian Duty?" 2 parts, *Christianity Today* (June 23, 1967), p. 4 and (July 7, 1967), pp. 7, 8.

Ryrie, Charles. "Apostasy in the Church," *Bibliotheca Sacra* (January—March 1964), pp. 44-53.

Sandeen, Ernest R. "Toward a Historical Interpretation of the Origins of Fundamentalism," *Church History*, XXXVI (March 1967), 66-83.

Shriver, George. "A Summary of Images of Catharism and the Historian's Task," *Church History*, (March 1971), pp. 48-54.

Shuler, Robert (ed.). *The Methodist Challenge* (October 1957). Published while Mr. Shuler was pastor of Trinity Methodist Church, Los Angeles.

Sprunger, Keith L. "English Puritans and Anabaptists in Early Seventeenth Century Amsterdam," *The Mennonite Quarterly Review* (April 1972), pp. 113-128.

Spurgeon, Charles H. *The Sword and Trowel* (November 1887).

Taylor, G. Aiken, "Is God As Good As His Word?" *Christianity Today* (February 4, 1977), pp. 22-25.

Walther, Daniel. "Were the Albigenses and Waldenses Forerunners of the Reformation?" *Andrews University Seminary Studies* (July 1968), pp. 178-202.

Waltner, Erland. "The Anabaptist Conception of the Church," *The Mennonite Quarterly Review*, XXV (January 1951).

Wright, J. Elwin. "The Issue of Separation," *United Evangelical Action*, IV (August 15, 1945), 12, 13.

Dissertations

Brown, Lawrence Duane. "The New Testament Doctrine of Apostasy." Doctoral dissertation, Bob Jones University, 1965.

Tinder, Donald George. "Fundamentalist Baptists in the Northern and Western United States: 1920-1950." Doctoral dissertation, Yale University, 1969.

Walsh, James Patrick. "The Pure Church in Eighteenth Century Connecticut." Doctoral dissertation, Columbia University, 1967.

Wray, Frank. "History in the Eyes of the Sixteenth Century Anabaptists." Doctoral dissertation, Yale University, 1953.

Miscellaneous Sources

Barnhouse, Donald Grey. Personal letter (September 28, 1953).

Beal, R. S. From a sermon, *Rivers in the Desert*. Tuscon: First Baptist Church, n.d. IV, 21.

Constitution. American Council of Christian Churches.

Graham, Billy. Message delivered October 21, 1973.

————. Message delivered April 3, 1957.

Jones, Bob, Jr. "Scriptural Separation: First and Second Degree." Greenville, SC: Bob Jones University Press, 1971.

LaSor, William. "Life Under Tension," *The Authority of Scripture at Fuller*. Booklet published by Fuller Theological Seminary, n.d.

Subject Index

Scripture Index